Transitioning from Librarian to Middle Manager

Pixey Anne Mosley

UNLIMITED

A Member of the Greenwood Publishing Group

Westport, Connecticut • London

Library of Congress Cataloging-in-Publication Data

Mosley, Pixey Anne.
    Transitioning from librarian to middle manager / Pixey Anne Mosley.
      p.   cm.
    Includes bibliographical references and index.
    ISBN 1-59158-117-6 (pbk. : alk. paper)
      1. Library administrators. 2. Library science—Vocational guidance.
    3. Librarians—Job descriptions. 4. Middle managers. I. Title.
    Z682.4.A34M67   2004
    023'.4—dc22   2004048640

British Library Cataloguing in Publication Data is available.

Library of Congress Catalog Card Number: 2004048640
ISBN: 1-59158-117-6

First published in 2004

Libraries Unlimited, 88 Post Road West, Westport, CT 06881
A Member of the Greenwood Publishing Group, Inc.
www.lu.com

Printed in the United States of America

The paper used in this book complies with the
Permanent Paper Standard issued by the National
Information Standards Organization (Z39.48–1984).

10 9 8 7 6 5 4 3 2 1

Contents

Acknowledgments

Although one name appears on the title page and in the Library of Congress CIP data, there were many who helped to make this book a reality. One very important figure during the entire writing of this book was my husband, Joel Kitchens, a fellow librarian who served as a sounding board for ideas and encouraged me through every single chapter. It is to him that I dedicate this book.

However, I especially want to recognize the long-term support of my parents, Glenda and Jerry Mosley, for the importance they placed on my education and their assistance, support, and encouragement when I redirected my career from aerospace engineering to librarianship. Without their loving guidance, I would never have succeeded so well in life.

Many others helped as well. I would like to express my thanks to Jeanne Harrell for her guidance in how to contact a book publisher with an idea; Charles Gilreath for his suggestions and supervisory support of the project; Bill Chollett for his feedback on Chapter 4; and Wendi Arant Kaspar for her help in proofing early drafts of chapters. Also, I would like to express my appreciation to Martin Dillon for his patience in working with a novice to the book authorship world.

Finally, a word of acknowledgment to the many librarians and staff I have worked with during the past 10 years. Although all of the Mid State Library case studies and other examples are fictitious, some of you may recognize bits and pieces of yourselves in some of the characters. Thanks for the support, insights, and growth opportunities you tendered in helping me to become the library manager I am today.

Pixey Anne Mosley
January 2004

Introduction

Librarianship is a profession where an eventual move into a managerial role is not automatically assumed. There are primarily three career tracks librarians may pursue, with some overlap between them depending on the individual institutional expectations and job descriptions. The first track is the career librarian. These librarians have focused their development on the professional assignment or job description. They build expert knowledge in a manner that focuses on specific resources and operations of an organization in order to address the needs of library users. Many librarians spend their entire careers doing special formats cataloging or honing their skills as reference librarians. The second track is that of the scholar. Usually found at academic, faculty-status institutions, these are librarians who often have advanced subject degrees and spend significant time and effort conducting published research that will benefit both the library profession and the world of their subject knowledge as a whole. They work as peer researchers with faculty and may liaise with a particular academic department or focus on developing collections through acquiring or cataloging a narrow area. The third career track available to librarians, and the focus of this book, is that of library management. Depending on the size and organizational structure of an institution, this is commonly described as any position at the department/branch head or above.

In several ways, the librarian manager track differs from the other career track options. Because an opportunity to become a manager is limited by a particular position becoming available, librarians cannot pursue this career track solely on their own initiative. They have to have some degree of recognition for their potential and support by library administrators. Also, the other paths of career development tend to occur in a continuous, gradual manner, like moving up a ramp. The move into management is more sudden and parallels climbing steps. It is usually associated with assuming a new title and a clearly defined change in organizational responsibilities. Although some larger academic libraries may promote from within, this can be a slow process. Moving up the management chain on a deliberate timetable or within a particular area of operations may require librarians to be willing to change institutions and relocate geographically. Understanding and anticipating the challenges associated with becoming a new manager in the current library environment helps the new manager and upper administration establish realistic expectations, evaluate success, and address personnel development needs more effectively.

The creation of good library managers is not a "wave the magic wand" or "abracadabra" type of process. It involves recognizing potential in entry-level and mid-career librarians and giving them the opportunity to grow and develop skills that are appropriate to managerial responsibilities. Even with natural talent and the base set of skills in place, the act of assuming a managerial position represents a significant change for librarians and requires them to adjust their thinking, actions, and knowledge to the new environment. The first few years will present them with many challenges to preconceived ideas and force new realizations of what being a manager is all about.

By reading this book, librarians considering a management track will get a realistic understanding of what it means to be a manager, and identify relevant skills and knowledge they should work on developing. New managers will gain insight and ideas on how to address some of the challenges they will encounter. Additionally, they will gain a sense of affirmation through the realization that many of the things they are experiencing are part of the normal transition encountered by many managers. This book will help them develop professionally by offering concepts and topics that are appropriate for thoughtful introspection and hypothetical discussions with a mentor or supervisor. Though written primarily for potential and new managers, experienced administrators can also benefit from being reminded how difficult the managerial transition can be in this rapidly changing and litigious world, and by better understanding what issues are most challenging for today's librarians moving into middle management.

The book is composed of two types of chapters. Some sections, such as Chapter 1, "Roles of the Middle Manager," and Chapter 2, "Your

Time Is No Longer Your Own," are meant to encourage readers to adjust their mental models and expectations of life as a manager. Other sections, such as Chapter 5, "Dealing with Budgets," and Chapter 10, "Evaluating Employee Performance," present more specific how-to knowledge and address operational issues that new managers encounter with varying degrees of preparation. Each chapter will include one or more case studies based on the fictitious Mid State Library and a Thought and Discussion Exercises section that prompts the reader to apply the material read in the chapter or identify areas where skills or knowledge need to be expanded. Usually, the exercises do not have simple solutions. Rather they are meant to encourage new managers to think through complicated problems and discuss them with mentors to gain a better understanding of organizational practices.

Finally, there are many good resources on management issues that have been published, both general in nature and specifically directed toward library organizations. The trade literature of the business world and the professional library journals also offer many tips, case studies, best practices ideas, and so forth. Another excellent source of support and information can be found within the various state and national/division level professional associations such as the American Library Association, Public Library Association, and Association of College and Research Libraries. The Association of Research Libraries offers a number of workshops, both on-site and online, to encourage the development of managerial skill sets. Readers wishing to gain more in-depth information can refer to the To Learn More and Notes sections of each chapter or to the annotated bibliography at the end of the book. These selections, primarily books, were chosen based on their readability and relevance to most academic or larger public library environments, and represent the types of books that are available to assist in self-education in managerial skills. Even though these books help one develop a general knowledge base, provide a basic toolset, or serve as excellent reference books, they do not address the cultural adjustment and detailed learning that comes with assuming a management role for the first time. This book attempts to fill in the gap between the theoretical textbook and the specific in-house training that has to occur at any institution. By reading through it, I hope that librarians turned managers will better understand what questions need to be asked as they are introduced to managerial challenges and adjust to their new responsibilities.

CHAPTER 1

Roles of the Middle Manager

The first significant step for most librarians moving into management is the position of middle manager, such as the head of a specific unit operation, department, or branch library. By doing so, your role in the organization undergoes a significant change. In order to be effective in the new position, your thinking, outlook, behavior, and actions must reflect this change. This chapter identifies six typical roles the new manager will encounter quickly: planner, implementer, assessor, leader, mediator/ counselor, and lone ranger. It is important to establish and adjust performance expectations or behaviors to accommodate these new areas of responsibility.

Planner

Instead of being the last to know and simply carrying out the assigned tasks associated with a predefined project, the middle manager is the one that must develop the detailed plan for how the unit conducts its routine business and responds to organizational initiatives. Planning is something everyone does to different degrees of effectiveness and complexity. At an individual level, everyone plans what he will do each day. In planning something within a unit, it is essential to take into consideration the same things you look at for personal planning: Is it affordable, is there time to do it, are external factors a consideration (such as when a store or office is available), and how important is it? Unit planning has similar concerns; they are just more complex and often messier. The new manager may remember what it was like on the front lines and want to immediately give everyone a chance to be a part of the planning process. When feasible, grassroots planning can have a positive effect on employee morale and allow frontline staff to gain an understanding of organizational complexities. Also, it is relatively easy to use this approach for smaller planning projects where the frontline employees recognize the need and there is immediate improvement to their workflow as a result. However, when the plan represents a major philosophical or paradigm shift, has a larger institutional impact, or seems unnecessary on the surface, it is much more difficult for frontline staff to be participatory in the initial planning process. The vagueness of the plan may be alarming as they have difficulty translating exactly how it will impact their daily workflow. This does not mean they should be kept in the dark. At a minimum, staff should be apprised in general terms that an idea is being explored and reassured that their input will be sought at the appropriate time.

The types of authority encountered as a middle manager are discussed later in the book, but generally middle managers will be required to get approval from an upper-level manager/administrator to develop new initiatives or make a significant departure from customary practice. This is especially true during the first few years that one is in a particular managerial role. As a consequence of this checks-and-balances system, it is important to learn how to prepare an accurate plan and effective proposal. In this respect libraries are similar to the corporate environment.

Originally developed in engineering disciplines and adopted into the commercial business world, structured planning is one part of the project management model. Project management is a methodology and toolkit for seeing a project through, from initial concept to successful completion based on resources, timelines, milestones, objectives, and goals. The details of project management as presented in the business literature can be extremely complex. Most library projects carried out by middle managers do not require the sophistication of a project management expert. However, some of the basic techniques can be useful when acting in the planner role. Most introductory resources present similar concepts in developing a plan for a project. The first step is to define the project. This includes identifying the scope and justification for the project. This is also the point at which the planner specifies the goals, objectives, and assumptions associated with it. The next step is to identify the specific tasks that make up the project. Examples of task identification might be hire five new student workers, or buy a computer and then get it configured by the computer support department, or conduct training. Once the tasks necessary to complete the project are identified, the planner must further define the tasks by establishing the amount of time required and resources needed to accomplish the task.

Identifying resource needs, both for initial implementation and ongoing support, is a difficult part of the planning process. Financial resources need to include costs related to staffing, facilities, and supplies. One big issue in financial planning at a departmental level is the concept of one-time versus recurring costs. One-time costs, such as for special supplies or a finite amount of student worker or temporary staff wages, are usually easier to negotiate. Recurring costs that must be absorbed into the organization's base budget and paid out repeatedly are much more difficult to incorporate, especially if the current economic picture is not a positive one. In all likelihood, either case will mean involving senior management and budget/business office staff, and even human resources personnel if staffing changes are involved. Chapter 5 will provide more detail about understanding an organizational budget.

Another significant challenge of the planning process is developing an accurate time estimate. While working on the completion time for each task, it is important to remember that seldom can a department simply stop their normal work in order to participate on a special project. Instead, the new tasks must be integrated into current workflows, which themselves may have to be redesigned. This has a significant effect on how long it takes to accomplish a project and when the most appropriate time for implementation is. For example, in academic environments, one should try to avoid implementing something new during the first two weeks or the last two weeks of a semester or term. Public librarians must take community calendars into consideration and not schedule a major event at a branch library on the outskirts of town the same weekend as a downtown Founders Day Festival. In either case, there are too many other distractions and uncontrollable factors to consider. Similarly, one should always incorporate into the plan the expectation of some kind of problem or delay. No matter how thorough one tries to be, it is impossible to anticipate every possible problem, and crises are inevitable. It is also important to recognize that even though the project may be a high priority to one unit, it will not necessarily get the same status within other library, university, or municipal departments, such as purchasing. It is important to develop the ability to think systemically and understand if there are impact factors or cause/effect variables affecting other areas of the organization that need to be taken into account. Planning specialists have developed techniques for building a realistic timeline for a project and generally recommend doubling or tripling an initial estimate based on the factors presented above. The time spent gaining support must also be factored into the timetable. Most library organizations are rather like very large ships—they do not have a reputation for turning or committing to a new course quickly, even the most dynamic and agile of them.

Once each task is clearly defined with the time and resource characteristics, the next step is to connect them. New managers will find that some tasks, called parallel or concurrent tasks, can be done at the same time, whereas others, called series or sequential tasks, can only be done one after another. By setting up the tasks that must be accomplished sequentially and concurrently, the planner will get a better understanding of the overall timeline and critical points in the process. The next steps are to estimate overhead costs for personnel or equipment needed for the project and develop these needs into a budget or spreadsheet. Depending on the scope and definition of the project, it may be necessary to add in some discreet communication tasks and quality assurance reviews. This may also be the step at which the proposal is developed and administrative approval obtained. Finally, the staff involved in the plan are identified and given preparation for assuming their responsibilities. At the same time, the equipment resources are purchased and prepared. At this point the planning process ends and the full implementation of the plan begins.

Two core documents come out of the planning process. One is the detailed plan that covers all of the material mentioned in earlier paragraphs. The other document is the administrative proposal. Proposals should be short (no more than a page or two) and briefly present the benefits gained from the project, the financial and resource costs, and an overview of the proposed timetable for implementation. It is better to err on the side of clarity with brevity than to go into extensive details. Most administrators will follow-up when they have questions on specific points. The key purpose of the proposal is not to explain the project in depth, but instead to capture the administrator's interest. If there is a legitimate concern that the library administrators will have difficulty understanding the significance of the project, then a foundation for the proposal can be established through a preliminary meeting or by approaching a relevant committee. In this forum, one should focus on discussing the general concept, identifying the need for further investigation, and volunteering to continue the study by preparing a proposal. By gaining early visibility and recognition for the problem, the proposal can focus on the solution.

Implementer

Once an idea or project has been given the go ahead, there are still many details to be worked out. This might appear to be the point to simply turn it over to the frontline staff. This is a positive thing and they should definitely be given the opportunity to participate in task-level workflow design. However, even the most hands-off manager may need to maintain a more hands-on approach if the project is visionary or represents a level of change that the staff are reluctant to embrace or unsure how to accomplish. Communication is critically important if the project will have a secondary or tertiary impact on another unit's operation. For example, it is very bad form to change the hours on a service point without notifying other service points in the same facility that may be making referrals. Similarly, the acquisition of a new collection of books is a good thing. But follow-through implementation should include letting the shelving department know about it so they can create the necessary shelf space in a timely fashion.

Throughout any implementation, it is critical to keep eyes and mind open to the need to make changes to the plan as it is being implemented. New knowledge may come to light that will have an impact on the ability to follow-through on initial expectations. Communicating this back through library administration is very important in order to maintain realistic expectations.

Depending on the historical trends of the organization, implementation of a new service or process change may require firmness and resolution. Some people are simply not comfortable with change and will practice either passive or active resistance against the implementation of new methods or ideas. There are different ways of dealing with this, but avoiding the issue and hoping it will fix itself is not an option. Sometimes, one can engage reluctant individuals through patience and by taking baby steps in implementation and nibbling away at a comfort zone. In other cases, employees respond positively by being given the freedom to have some control and input into the redesign of their workflow. Yet others just want to be told what to do so they do not have to take responsibility when something does not work as planned, as they are sure will be the case. Finally, there may be employees who fight tooth and nail against change with active resistance and borderline or outright insubordination. When running up against this degree of hostility, one must reassess the importance of the implementation and the specific employee's role in the proposed change. In some cases, it might be possible to let the person emulate a rock in the stream. The rest of the implementation can go around the person with little impact on the overall plan. In other cases, the person's role is essential and comparative decisions must be made between the objective of the implementation and the employee's role in the department. When dealing with the seriously recalcitrant cases, it is important for middle managers to communicate with their supervisors (administrators) and utilize the knowledge of human resources experts to develop realistic expectations given the organization's position on evaluations and employee development.

Assessor

The days of libraries being recognized for the public good and given unquestioned budgets no longer exist, if they ever did. One issue every manager, and even some frontline librarians, must expect to address is support for the culture of assessment that is developing in many libraries. This movement employs measurable quantitative and qualitative data to explore whether a unit is operating in an appropriately efficient and effective manner to meet the expectations of users and library administrators. It is important that managers look at their operations to identify how they can provide legitimate statistics and results that indicate where changes may be needed and whether an implemented plan has met the desired goals.

Often library administration will determine what type of assessments are desired and some of the tools that will be used. They will indicate whether the assessment activities should focus on user service tie-ins or benchmarking best practices for efficiency and consistency. One may be asked to assess the time it takes for a book to go from being discharged to being back on the shelf or how long it takes to process a book order. Assessment may also be applied externally to evaluate vendor performance for approval or subscription plans. It is the middle managers' role to take a cue from the library administrators and engage in assessment activities within their operational areas. These assessments should then be used to justify resource needs and operational restructuring.

Leader

Many management texts would have put this role first, saying it is the most important. Leadership is important to an organization, but it is also a role that most newly minted middle managers have only a limited opportunity to explore. As previously discussed, most library organizations are hierarchical and bureaucratic, and both of these characteristics can reduce the opportunity for significant, visionary leadership at the frontline and middle-management ranks. The leadership role usually exercised by a new middle manager in any library has two components: messenger and expert feedback. With time, successful middle managers will have learned more about the library administrative culture and established credibility with administration. While doing so, they will develop additional leadership skills, become more empowered, and have opportunities to initiate broader organizational change.

The first, and most frequent, opportunity for leadership by the newer middle managers is in the role of messenger. This involves passing along communications and decisions made at the library administrative level. As an example, suppose the library director has chosen to move in a new direction. This may be a simple process change or a major reorganization. The middle manager's leadership role is to promote this in the best reasonable light to the employees in the unit, even if it is something that the manager does not agree with on a personal level. This does not mean the manager has to take an openly hypocritical or falsely optimistic approach to everything and be oblivious to unit feedback. Rather it means that one should express concern and acknowledgment that the new initiative might be difficult to accomplish, even as one is emphasizing a commitment to the initiative and communicating the overall importance to the organization that it be accomplished. By becoming a manager, one buys into being a transitional part of the administrative team. The same way an athletic team can become distracted if individual players go to the media with public sniping about a particular player or coach, so will an organization be handicapped by a manager openly criticizing an administrative position or decision to the frontline staff. The latter scenario fosters a negative impact on employee morale and diminishes the pride employees will take in being part of the organizational team.

The expert feedback component of middle-management leadership is exercised with peer managers or administrators. Based on one's background, individual knowledge base, and understanding of one's assigned department staffing and operation, the middle manager helps to contribute to organization-wide dialogue and decision making. This may be in periodic meetings of peer middle managers, on focused teams, or in one-on-one discussions with a particular administrator or coordinator. The advantage that the manager has over the frontline staff is that the manager should be able to better understand the big picture objectives, communicate a balanced perspective accompanied by detailed knowledge, and depersonalize the impact of the decision. For example, suppose a library is looking at implementing a new collection-development service model that has been requested by the teaching faculty. Most frontline staff will be focused on the personal level of how it impacts them and the job tasks they do on a daily basis. A middle manager has to set aside the distraction of implementation details and enter discussions from the unit-wide/customer-focused perspective. An appropriate contribution would be communicating whether or not the unit has the necessary skill set among the current staff, how it will require reassigning broad responsibilities, and whether special computer upgrades would be necessary. It might also be the middle manager who has the knowledge to explain why something is not feasible and put the brakes on the director's "brilliant idea." In this situation, one usually needs to seek a postponement of a final decision while investigating the issue and subsequently producing supporting data/documentation to back one up. "I just don't think it will work" is generally not an acceptable reason. As middle managers gain experience and a positive reputation in this role, they will be given more opportunity to engage in leadership activities.

In an academic library where librarians have faculty status, there may be a separate leadership role that a manager still plays as part of the faculty community. As new initiatives impact the faculty as a whole, the middle manager will need to recognize that an issue that must be supported to subordinate classified (non-MLS) staff and librarians from an operational perspective may be more open for discussion, interpretation, and dialogue in faculty meetings. Academic freedom policies at most institutions will support the right of a faculty member who is also a manager to hold a dissenting opinion on an issue without fear of repercussion so long as a professional demeanor and dialogue is maintained. Leadership roles in this forum are different from the managerial responsibilities and actually allow one to take a position to this all-professional audience that may be less popular administratively. This does assume that there is consistent understanding of the role duality at all levels of administration, from the topmost director to the newest untenured frontline librarian. If this is not the case, the individual may have to make a call on which role, that of faculty member or administrative team player, is more important personally and follow a career path that supports the prioritization. Public library managers may encounter similar issues if they choose to be politically or socially active in the community outside of work, especially if addressing controversial issues. It is important to clearly understand administrative expectations of nonworking conduct and institutional conflict of interest protocols within one's individual library culture.

Mediator and Counselor

Another major new role that middle managers frequently find themselves in resembles a personal advisor. Many libraries have moved away from Type X management with punishment-based motivation to programs of positive performance reinforcement with increased awareness on quality of worklife issues. By definition, this means spending more time trying to use positive motivation techniques to develop an employee's strengths and working to understand what makes a particular employee tick. As a consequence, managers are more aware of the natural personality of the individual and the personal issues that are important to the employee and may find themselves in the roles of mediator or counselor. These are roles that new managers should take on very carefully, especially if they are young or have had limited experience guiding or encouraging others in achieving goals.

Professional counselors and mediators maintain a certain degree of detachment even as they are helping patients/clients work through their personal or financial issues. It is important that the workplace manager does the same, expressing empathy to a situation or employee problem but not becoming sympathetic or getting drawn into taking responsibility for solving the employee's problems or into taking sides. Empathy requires the manager to understand the employee's situation and respond to it by making sure the employee understands the options and resources available. Sympathy implies that the understanding includes agreement, approval, commiseration, and a certain degree of emotional bonding. If the manager in question tends to be a problem solver by nature, it can be personally difficult to be unable to "fix" every problem situation. New managers must recognize that individuals themselves are the ones that must take control of and responsibility for their decisions and situations. The manager may listen and help to identify available options, but it is the employee who must take ownership of the situation and acknowledge the responsibility and commitment to the workplace expectations.

Mediation Expectations

Often called upon to mediate between an employee and her supervisor or two employees who report to different supervisors in the unit, the middle manager's role as mediator should focus on the issue of communicating expectations between the individuals. Generally, this is the real source of the conflict: Employee A said something but Employee B interpreted it as something totally different, and subsequent actions or behaviors caused an explosion colored by frustrations, remarks taken personally, and hurt feelings. Depending on the degree to which the situation has been building and the dynamics between the individuals, the situation may be resolved quickly in a single discussion session or through a series of progressive discussions with outside-action items.

The first step for the middle manager in any mediation process is to focus on the facts surrounding the specific event and to defuse the emotional responses. Getting a clear picture of the problem may require individual meetings with each party and possibly other employees, prior to the mediation discussion. A second key factor is to avoid choosing sides or assigning blame when mediating. Redirect the comments away from a discussion of who was right and who was wrong to focus on resolving why it happened and how to prevent the problem from recurring. In addition to not assigning blame during employee-supervisor mediation meetings, the manager should take care not to undermine the supervisor's authority to assign tasks and evaluate the performance of the employee. If there are recommendations or reprimands that need to be made to the supervisor, they should be done outside of the mediation meetings.

In an effort to do well and minimize conflict in the work environment, new managers may lose sight of the fact that mediation may not provide the solution to every problem. Similarly, a situation may have deteriorated so badly that a mediator with more experience and training may be needed and actual work assignments adjusted to allow for a cooling-off period. Sometimes in the course of the mediation process, the manager will need to transition into the counselor role.

Counseling Expectations

The middle manager's role as counselor should focus on whether or not a personal issue has an impact on job performance and if the impact is significant. If an issue does not meet this criterion, then the manager should be polite but resist getting too deeply involved with the issue. If there are problems that significantly impact job performance, the manager should discuss the observed job performance problem with the employee. If accommodations can be made with minimal overall impact on unit operations and user services, this offers a chance to build an employee's morale and loyalty. However, it must be clearly communicated that the accommodation is being made based on the individual set of criteria presented with this particular event. Each situation must be assessed, taking into consideration that the current environment and different circumstances may dictate a different manner or degree of accommodation. Also, new managers should take care that the employees do not abuse the privilege or manipulate other staff by announcing to others that they get "special" treatment, either perceptually too generous or too strict.

There may be times when a new manager may feel the need to be more sympathetic and emotionally involved with an employee, such as when faced with an employee being diagnosed with cancer or losing a family member. Unfortunately, even as the sympathetic bonding occurs, it can lay seeds for future problems to come to the surface. Suppose while the manager is acting in a sympathetic and friendly role, an employee, whose father has passed away suddenly, confides some personal information such as having escaped a sexually abusive situation at home. In the following months, as the employee is dealing with the aftermath and resurgent emotions associated with the event, she starts expressing opinions that create a hostile environment for her male colleagues. As the manager tries to address the situation, the employee, who had bonded with the manager, can try to call on those ties of sympathy and friendship.

Another issue that comes out of this particular example is the importance for managers to recognize when they are in over their head. At the point of the initial confidence, the manager should have been reaching for literature on the institution's employee assistance or counseling program. If there is not an institution level program available, managers should familiarize themselves with what psychological/psychiatric counseling opportunities are available in the various employee health plan options. Managers should also find out where they can turn to for support and advisement in handling individuals who appear to be experiencing severe emotional problems. Start with contacting the organization's employee assistance program or human resources department; they will identify if advising managers is within their mission and objectives. If this is not productive, managers should look to their own supervisor's experience, a respected mentor, or counseling through their own personal health plan coverage. The main thing is not to personalize the employee's problems into one's own life.

Lone Ranger

There is a natural inclination for all new managers to embark on a crusade to seek out inefficiency, fix all of the errors, right all of the wrongs, and immediately begin making judgments on how operations can be improved, both in their own units and in peripheral areas as well. Work in libraries very long and you will inevitably hear a frontline librarian say, "they" should be doing something differently, or "I could have told them that if they had just asked me." As these individuals first become a part of middle management, they see it as an opportunity to make a difference and show their peer group that they will be "better" managers who are knowledgeable about front line issues and who see them as extremely important.

With a "Hi-yo Silver, away!" philosophy, the new manager may perceive administrators, peer managers, and even other library employees as apathetic, mired in routine, or afraid to make change and become combative or disillusioned and frustrated. The truth is that others do care, but experience has shown them that organizations have a lot of momentum and enacting change takes time and is best done in transitional steps. During the past several decades, numerous waves of change have swept libraries; most decisions and new directions have been positive ones, but not all. It is that small group of bad decisions or coming full circle over a span of time, that lead people to resist change.

To effectively enact change, one cannot just barge in guns blazing at all targets. Rather the manager needs to have a plan and identify what is really worth using a valuable silver bullet to accomplish. The term *silver bullet* applies because one needs both a purity of vision of what one is trying to accomplish and recognition of the true cost, in the form of financial support, good will, and emotional energies, to carry it through. Chipping away at "injustice" will lead to overall improvement if one chooses the targets carefully. Jumping in with blindsiding emotional attacks will only create a real mess and burn bridges with managerial peers.

Chapter Summary

As new managers settle into the aforementioned roles, they will realize that, though they may look the same in a mirror, others now see them differently. They are no longer just "one of the gang" and their words or comments carry a different weight to others. They are now part of a different team, and the transition of going from being a big fish in the frontline pond to a small fish in the administrator's pond is not one that always happens easily. As managers, they are now responsible for better understanding their department's role in the overall library and the library's overall role in the academic institution and working for the greater institutional good rather than their own personal goals. Keeping the new roles in mind can help as a guide for doing well with these new responsibilities.

To Learn More

There are numerous project management resources published, with each having emphasis on different aspects of the process. Three books stand out as especially appropriate introductions for librarian managers. The first, *The Project Manager's Partner* by Michael Greer, is very readable with significant sections focused on project definition and planning.[1] The examples tend to be familiar activities such as home improvement projects. This allows the reader to focus on the technique rather than trying to decipher the project being presented. Another good text for interdisciplinary readers is *Project Management: Step-by-Step* by Larry Richman.[2] This book presents similar concepts to the Greer book but with more depth and details. In addition to a thorough section on planning, this book goes into project team management strategies. Each chapter includes case studies and some application exercises. For public librarians, Sandra Nelson's *The New Planning for Results: A Streamlined Approach* offers an excellent overview of organizational planning with relevant and familiar examples.[3] Greer and Richman go into significant detail on the analytical and tracking tools of the process, whereas Nelson focuses more on the qualitative-thinking aspects of planning and assessing the impact aspects of implementation. Another good reference source for better understanding the terminology is *The Project Manager's Emergency Kit* by Ralph L. Kliem.[4] Finally, for the librarian who wants to seriously delve into project management, the *Project Management Institute: Project Management Handbook* offers a thorough development of project management methodologies and techniques for the most complex of projects.[5] Microsoft Project is a fairly sophisticated computer program that compliments the Microsoft Office suite of applications. It includes the ability to create detailed specialized diagrams, called GANTT and PERT charts, for managing time and resources through a project.

Some of the essays in *Leadership and Academic Librarians* explore the nature of leadership opportunities, both as an administrator and as a nonmanager. The book offers a good introduction to leadership for those who are still struggling to define it.[6] Some managers may find it useful to look to the business literature on leadership and empowerment. Tom Peters is a prolific author in the area of corporate leadership and employee empowerment. The main thing that new middle managers must keep in mind as they consult resources and develop their leadership philosophy is to understand how it fits within their current library's hierarchical environment and specifically their middle-manager role.

Case Study: Leader/Planner/Implementer

Alex – director of the library
Sam – Kate's supervisor, associate director
Kate – internal middle-manager promotion (eight months ago), access services head
Setting: near the end of a weekly status briefing between Kate and Sam

With a sigh of relief, Kate continues, "So, I think that wraps up the latest staffing crisis for the moment. The last thing on my list that I wanted to go over with you was the problem we are having with the book drops. They are not working."

"Can you define 'not working'?" Sam responds.

"In reviewing the appeals on the overdue fines, I am seeing a lot of comments where students are saying that they tried to turn their books in on time but couldn't because the book drop was full or jammed. I know it isn't a really strong basis for forgiving the fine, but I feel like I am seeing a pattern of frustration on the part of the users."

"Are they actually jamming or are they automatically locking because they are full?"

Kate pulls out her notes. In the eight months she has been reporting directly to Sam, she has learned to get as many facts together as she can before bringing a problem to his attention. "I suspect it is because they are full and the patrons don't understand the auto lock feature. I've had the drops checked a couple of times and they seem to be working OK. The student workers who empty them report that the Student Union book drop and the drive-by one on Annie Oakley Lane are usually totally full, but the other two, by the Hot Dog Shack and the south dorm quadrangle, are usually only about a third to a half full each day."

"What time do we empty them each day? And do the appeals give enough information to gauge when the students are trying to return the books?"

"Currently, we empty all the drops once a day, seven days a week, at about 2–3 P.M. in the afternoon. I couldn't really see any patterns regarding problems the rest of the week."

"So what do you think needs to be done?" Sam queries with a smile.

"I knew that was coming. Well, there are several options that I can think of and some are more expensive than others. We could empty the drops more frequently, but that involves hiring another crew of student workers and either getting a dedicated vehicle or tying up the library truck in the morning as well as the afternoon. The other units would not like that at all. They already grouse that they have to work around circulation's book run schedule in the afternoon. One idea, which I'm not too sure how to accomplish, would be to better publicize the other two drops and convince students to use them more. Or, we could relocate the two lesser-used book drops to the heavier use locations. But since they do get some use, this would probably seem insensitive to those users. Another option would be to buy bigger book drops for the two heavy-use locations. But that would be fairly expensive. To go the next size up would cost about $3500 per book drop."

"Actually, even though it has the biggest financial cost, that last suggestion might provide a solution for an issue that came across Alex's desk just the other day. The dean of arts and sciences would like a book drop put somewhere near Da Vinci Hall for the convenience of the liberal arts faculty. Alex hasn't really decided how he plans to respond to the request, but if we bought larger book drops for the heavy-use locations, we could relocate a smaller one there and keep the other one in storage for emergencies or the next college-level request."

At these words Kate winces a little as she realizes how this will impact her unit operationally. "Uh, Sam, between adding another book drop location and increasing the size of the current two, we are going to have a lot more books to empty, which is going to take us longer. I'm guessing at least 30–45 minutes more each day. It won't affect the student budget significantly, only about $40 per week. But, I will need to make sure they can work longer and it will keep the van longer, which will go over like a lead balloon. Also, *where* precisely are we talking about? Da Vinci Hall is huge. On two sides, it faces onto major campus thoroughfares and I don't think a third side is van accessible."

"We'll have to contact Campus Planning, do a site visit with them, and work out the details . . . hmm . . . but I think this might work. I will explain to the other associate deans and unit heads about the van needs. I'm sure they will understand."

"They may understand, but I promise that is not going to keep them from griping. Oh well, such is life. So what do you want me to do next?"

"Go ahead and submit a request to the Operational Supplies Committee and see if they will pay for the two book drops. If they've already spent their money and deny it, we can explore other avenues. Though being this early in the fiscal year, they should still have the funds. I will let Alex know about the Da Vinci Hall solution so he can get back to the liberal arts dean. That part of it will take a lot longer to get worked out, probably the end of the semester at least, since we have to go through Campus Planning. This gives you a little longer to look at your student wage budget and student schedules."

"OK, I'm on it. I'll send you an e-mail once I hear back from the committee on buying the drops," Kate offers as she closes her notebook and gets to her feet.

Case Study Observations

- Be prepared: Kate did not just hand the problem to Sam. She had already investigated the situation, verified the source of the problem, and come up with tentative solutions. She had also done her homework to anticipate and answer the obvious questions about the problem she was presenting.

- Expect the unexpected: What Kate thought would be the least-popular solution, actually turned out to be the most favorite because of additional information that Sam had.

- Stay flexible during problem solving: Remain positive and do not get thrown by the unexpected. Seldom will the final solution match the original one that was proposed.
- Follow-up: Frequently, fixing one bigger problem will create other secondary challenges or inconveniences that require follow-up planning to resolve.

Thought and Discussion Exercises

What Do You Do Now?

1. Your current method of circulating reference books out of the building as exceptions is a clipboard with a handwritten form. The information on the form includes the person's name, ID number, book information, and due date. Library administrators have attended some briefings on preventing identity theft, privacy issues, and the Patriot Act. The information your supervisor brings back indicates that the clipboard is a legal disaster waiting to happen. What do you do now?

2. The library has decided to add a new Information Desk near the front door to better handle directional questions. The desk will be staffed by student workers/minimum wage staff, and your unit will be responsible for it. Library administrators have asked you to identify additional resources that you will need and prepare an implementation plan. What do you do now? (Hint: Do not forget that someone will have to supervise and train the students for this service.)

3. Two staff employees in your unit who report to two different first-level supervisors have a major miscommunication over some football tickets that one was going to give/sell to the other. By the time you become aware of the problem, the two employees are totally hostile, each feels that he was the injured party, and other employees are taking sides. The two supervisors, who are the same rank, are at an impasse. What do you do now?

4. You are having an operational planning meeting with a librarian who has seemed a little distracted lately. As you are talking about volunteer coverage during the upcoming holidays, the librarian suddenly starts crying and confides that she discovered her husband is having an affair, is moving out this weekend, and has filed for divorce. She just doesn't know what she is going to do. What do you do now?

Notes

1. Michael Greer, *The Project Manager's Partner: A Step-by-Step Guide to Project Management,* 2nd ed. (New York: AMACOM, 2002).

2. Larry Richman, *Project Management Step-by-Step* (New York: AMACOM, 2002).

3. Sandra S. Nelson, for the Public Library Association, *The New Planning for Results: A Streamlined Approach* (Chicago: American Library Association, 2001).

4. Ralph L. Kliem, *The Project Manager's Emergency Kit* (New York: St. Lucie Press, 2003).

5. Jeffrey K. Pinto, ed., *The Project Management Institute: Project Management Handbook,* Lewis R. Ireland, Foreword (San Francisco: Jossey-Bass Publishers, 1998).

6. Terrence F. Mech and Gerard B. McCabe, *Leadership and Academic Librarians* (Westport, CT: Greenwood Press, 1998).

CHAPTER 2

Your Time Is No Longer Your Own

One difficult acclimation that new managers frequently encounter pertains to their daily work schedules. Compared to the managerial environment, most frontline librarians have significantly more schedule predictability and control over their workdays. The world of the manager is much more fluid and ad hoc. No matter what you think or how you balance your worklife issues, being a manager frequently will mean working or thinking about work more than 40 hours per week. Depending on your individual area of responsibility, this might mean taking work home, being available to staff during off hours, or simply spending more time in the office by coming in early or staying late. In the latter case, this is due to the fact that some managers say that it seems like the only time you can actually get work done is when everyone else is gone. Seriously, the demands of others on your time significantly increase in proportion to managerial responsibilities.

Meetings and More Meetings

One time-consumer that most new managers do not appreciate until it overtakes them is meetings. As a frontline librarian, one probably attended a weekly unit meeting and a couple of additional committee or team meetings each month. As a manager, one now has the responsibility to actually conduct the unit meeting and attend a multitude of broader organizational meetings where the information for the unit meeting is delivered or developed. Depending on an organization's size and hierarchical arrangement, examples of this might be a weekly unit head meeting, a meeting of peer managers across the library, and one-on-one meetings with the manager's supervisor. Additionally, attendance of public forum meetings held by library administrators or operations personnel that were previously optional are now effectively mandatory. The purpose in a manager attending these is twofold. First, one needs to set a good example to the staff and communicate the importance and acceptability of attending. Second, it is important to verify that nothing has been changed by circumstances or interpretation since the staff heard it from you in a unit meeting, and also to be aware if new information is globally released in this forum. Additional meetings will come from a multitude of new cross-organizational teams or special interdepartmental projects that a manager will often be assigned to attend, with the role being that of an expert on unit operations and process change impact.

Engaged Participation

Based on their personal attitude toward meetings, managers tend to take one of two possible approaches in the plethora of meetings that they must attend: passive listening/recitation or active participation/guidance. In most cases, the nature of the meeting will define the level of participatory opportunity. One can see this by contrasting a routine monthly employee recognition/director's briefing type of meeting with a discussion-based/problem-solving meeting of peer department heads. The key to effective participation is recognizing and taking advantage of what each meeting offers. It is important to stay mentally engaged, even in the routine update meetings, in order to avoid passing along inaccurate or incomplete information to staff and peers. Managers who profess to hate all or most meetings and consistently see them as a waste of time will almost always lean toward the passive or disengaged role, regardless of the opportunities provided. Because they are not paying attention to the content and are resistant to the meeting on philosophical grounds, the meeting becomes a self-fulfilling prophecy and truly is a waste of time for them. Other managers, who can identify and isolate individual meetings based on the purpose of the meeting and potential opportunity for input and outcomes, are able to better prioritize which meetings are appropriate for prior preparation/research and be more effective when given an opportunity to contribute.

One deterrent to effective meeting participation may be stamina. Because they deal with fairly broad and complex issues, many managerial discussion meetings exceed the traditional 30-minutes or 1-hour meeting time. Maintaining one's concentration in excess of 90 minutes can be difficult, especially for the new manager. In most organizations if one is new to keeping this pace in a meeting, it is appropriate to ask for a brief break at the midpoint of any meeting that hits the 2-hour-plus mark or bring an energy-boosting snack for the midpoint. Similarly, meetings with many managers in attendance can be tricky to schedule and end up at moderately unpleasant meeting times, such as right after lunch, early in the morning, or late in the afternoon. If you know a meeting time coincides with when you are not at your best, address this as part of your pre-meeting preparation. Suggestions to improve alertness might include getting to bed earlier the night before a morning meeting, allowing an extra 15 minutes to wake up, getting an extra caffeine boost from another cup of coffee, taking a refreshing walk outside the building or around the stacks, or sparking creativity by reading an inspiring poem or checking out a favorite Web site. Some people who have very active minds that multi-task well find that they can actually concentrate better if they are keeping their hands busy and bring craft projects to work on during meetings. Unfortunately, this is often negatively perceived by others as disinterest or rudeness and is not appropriate once one reaches managerial ranks. More discreet activities that keep the hands busy, such as random doodling or playing with a worry stone, are viewed with a higher level of tolerance. The important thing is to identify the source of personal distractions and actively work to maintain meeting effectiveness.

Another aspect of being an engaged participant is to be prepared for the meeting. Many administrative teams will be based on projects that require a significant amount of work outside of the meeting. This "homework" may include doing background reading, taking a topic to departmental units for discussion or feedback, or preparing and reviewing draft statements or preliminary Web pages. This approach allows the valuable meeting time to be used more effectively and reduces the overall project timeline significantly. Team members who do not do their homework are considered to be dead weight. Initially, they will drag down the progress of the team. Eventually, the team will simply ignore their inane or backtracking requests in order to maintain forward momentum. Ultimately, the cost they pay is losing the respect of their peer managers and librarians.

A final key aspect in engaged participation pertains to attitude and behavior toward others and their contributions. Modern meeting techniques consistently support the importance of contributing with a positive perspective toward others and their suggestions. Even if one thinks a proposal is a really stupid idea, contemporary meeting etiquette requires that it be given thoughtful and respectful consideration to ascertain whether it introduces any essence of value. Negative remarks without accompanying dispassionate supporting facts are considered inappropriate. Additionally, the discussion of the idea should be disassociated from the person who has proposed it. A participant should avoid ever saying that an idea has no merit because the person who contributed it does not have sufficient background or knowledge in the concept. In fact, the person's distance from the concept may offer better insights into the real problem being solved.

Effective Leadership

Even as engaged participation is important, effectively running a meeting is a true opportunity to demonstrate and develop leadership skills. The understanding of the different nature of meetings is especially important when one is responsible for running the meeting. One of the challenges when leading or facilitating a meeting is to find a balance that allows others an opportunity for constructive participation but avoids deteriorating into anarchy and chaos. This can often be accomplished by having some structure to the meeting. It is also important to start and end meetings on time, though this may be subject to organizational culture and whether one is bringing together individuals who have back-to-back meetings and need opportunities for restroom stops or coffee refills while in transit.

Meeting structure takes the form of an acknowledged purpose or theme behind having the meeting. To better define the structure, one can use a formal or looser, informal agenda; a list of goals and objectives to be addressed; or bulleted milestone points to relate. The purpose is to provide some type of tool to keep a meeting flowing smoothly, to recognize what has been accomplished, and to identify when it is time to adjourn. Even open brainstorming meetings need to have structure to help the person leading the meeting keep one individual from dominating the discussion and identify when sufficient data have been gathered. In keeping with the concept of structure, the literature resources unanimously support the need to take some style of minutes. Even casual planning or brainstorming meetings should produce written action items or decision points. These follow-up notes/minutes validate having accomplished something in the meeting and serve as a record for referral, both as one is accomplishing the assigned action items and during subsequent meetings.

Another important aspect of conducting a meeting effectively is maintaining the integrity of the moderator role. The challenge of dealing with individuals who tend to monopolize discussions or repeat themselves can be a difficult one for new managers, especially if the individuals tend to be disorganized in their presentation of a suggestion or have a long history or seniority within the organization. One has to weigh the cost of antagonizing them or undermining their voice of experience by cutting them off against the importance of allowing others the opportunity to contribute. A good rule of thumb is to let them continue so long as they are contributing an original statement, no matter how rambling or convoluted. However, once the person has obviously started becoming repetitious, the manager should express appreciation for the opinion, paraphrase what was suggested to give a feeling of validation, and ask for ideas from other participants. Another effective technique in responding to this individual is to assign a follow-up action item or create a sub-team to explore the issue presented and bring back a recommendation.

As mentioned in the section on engaged participation, a critical role as the moderator in charge of the meeting is to disassociate the topic being discussed from the personal feelings and emotional investment of the individual involved in the dialogue. It is important to guard against the situation in which the person who suggested the idea becomes defensive to modifications or constructive criticism. One way to accomplish this and make the idea less personal is by combining comments from several people to compose the item put on the table for discussion. Similarly, it is important to prevent or quickly defuse any personal attacks toward another person in public meeting sessions. Although the idea of having a "venting" or unstructured issues meeting appeals to some new managers, these are usually counterproductive to morale because they can subliminally reiterate to participants the limitations in their sphere of authority or control in the organization as a whole and the futility of wishing things would be perfect in their work environment. A more structured meeting environment can acknowledge the limitations but not allow participants to wallow in a depressed state by segueing into focused discussions on what the individuals do have the authority to improve.

New Teams and Special Projects

In addition to the meetings associated with the primary role of unit manager, there are other meeting demands that will be placed on one's time. Many library-wide initiatives may have lengthy planning and implementation cycles that require ongoing input and representation from the operational area represented by the middle manager's knowledge base. Examples of this might include the selection and implementation of a new integrated system, the redesign of a Web site, the selection of vendors for approval plans or serial management, the development of computer resource allocations and initiatives throughout the organizations, or the updating of a disaster plan. In some cases where the area is constantly evolving, such as Web design, these may be lifetime rather than short-term appointments, at least so long as one is in the unit manager position. One way to moderate the load associated with these responsibilities is to recognize why one is on the team and evaluate whether the need continues to justify the appointment. Taking the development of a disaster plan as an example, managers may be the appropriate personnel to participate in writing a new plan. They have the knowledge and understanding of their facilities and personnel resources that need to be incorporated. They also have the authority to modify position descriptions and reassign oversight responsibilities as appropriate to make the plan successful. However, once the plan is written and has entered a state of periodic review/updating to maintain organizational and staffing accuracy, the manager's expertise is no longer required. Assigning a staff member who has been given the background information and who plays a role in the implementation of the plan to the ongoing maintenance team is a more appropriate use of personnel resources.

As when one is leading meetings, there are certain false expectations one keep in mind as an organizational team participant. The first false expectation is that the perfect solution will be achieved. In reality, what will be developed is the best solution given the input of all interested parties. It probably will not be the best solution from any one individual's perspective, but instead a compromise that is acceptable to all. A senior manager once offered this humorous analogy about teams: A camel is a horse designed by a committee. A second false expectation is that because the team is composed of senior staff or managers, everyone on the team has the same background knowledge and clear vision of the objective. In fact, the thing that makes a team effective is bringing different priorities and bases of experience to the design table. This is how true innovation can occur, by engaging one to think about something in a totally new way or poking holes in assumptions. A third false expectation is that the team will be a harmonious and efficient one. Actually, there will be a wealth of interpersonal communication challenges that impede the efficiency of the unit. Because the team is composed of peer managers, issues of collegiality and mutual respect are more critical than among peer librarians who occasionally interact with each other. The team may even include upper management with roles separate from their organizational authority. Consequently, it may take several meetings for individual participants to develop their comfort level with the team environment being neutral ground, relax to their natural communication style, and be willing to offer up farfetched or even idiotic suggestions. In those suggestions may lie the kernel of a really innovative development.

Data Requests and Crises

Other competitors for a manager's time are the disruptions associated with high priority data requests and crises events. Unlike group meetings, which are somewhat predictable, these events are usually structured around a need to drop everything and formulate an immediate response. The events vary widely and the manager's response must be flexible to the identified need. Responding to a crisis requires the ability to shift mental and priority gears to focus on the new objectives of the moment, execute a recovery or catch-up type of effort, and then shift back to previous routine and priorities after the event has passed. Some of these events may be perceived crises, such as the example played out below. Others may be more visible crises that place people or library materials at risk to injury or damage. Unfortunately, it is difficult to know how one will handle true crisis management until a few scenarios have been played out. Chapter 9 presents more detail on developing crisis management skills and expectations. The important point is recognizing that these disruptions do happen and that the ability to roll with them effectively is an important facet of being a successful manager.

Some crises are defined as such because they involve a library administrative need within a relatively short window of time. Frequently, these perceived crises involve a sudden financial windfall or disaster where there is a specific deadline for feasibility data to be accumulated and transmitted through the appropriate channels. An example might be the university's acquisition of a new warehouse building with uncommitted space. On many campuses, space is a premium commodity and the distribution is a fairly competitive process. In order for the library director to make a case for the library's need for this resource, he or she has to incorporate data from others in the organization. Enter the middle manager. This particular example might require an access services manager to provide data about personnel resource needs to implement remote storage retrieval, shelving requirements and whether any supplies can come from a current inventory, identifying targeted materials, and estimating how much floor space would be required, all within a three-day window. So the manager and other designated staff members drop everything they were currently working on, put in some overtime to prepare the data within the deadline, and route it appropriately to the library director. Several weeks later university administrators allocate the space for purposes other than the library. Depending on the enthusiasm and effort put into the project, this can be a serious disappointment for those who participated. It is very important for new managers not to become frustrated over the situation and dwell about all the energy expended with nothing to show for it. Similarly, they need to recognize sincere staff efforts even if the initiatives are unsuccessful. Feasibility studies and implementation estimates are very important exercises. Depending on an institution's particular hierarchical structure and dynamics, this may occur quite frequently. There could be 20 proposals that fail for every one that is successful. Unfortunately, there is no way of knowing ahead of time which one will be the successful proposal, so each must be treated with equal diligence, sincerity, and enthusiasm.

Open-Door Accessibility

The last time-eating monster discussed here that new managers encounter has a direct correlation to their availability to their staff. In the past, managers tended to be more isolated from their staff. This isolation may have been physical in the form of a more distant office with a clerical staff member guarding access to the closed door, or it may have been an emotional distance based on dictatorial or mandate-based managerial practices. Though contemporary middle managers may have retained an office with a door, that office is more likely to be integrated more closely to the open workflow or cubicle-defined area, and the door is more likely to be left ajar. Additionally, the personal secretary has gone the way of the dinosaurs and been replaced by a clerk or staff assistant who responds to the entire unit's needs. In addition to being available when needed, contemporary management theory encourages managers to get out of their offices and be a visible presence among the staff. This familiarizes one to all of the staff, rather than being isolated by a layer of lieutenants, and better enables one to spot conflict or physical resources issues before they become a problem. A good example might be spotting a petite staff member standing on an unstable surface to reach the top of the networked printer. Investing in a good stepstool or relocating the printer to a lower surface is a lot easier than dealing with a workers' compensation claim after an accident occurs. It also allows one to better assess whether there are other workplace factors, such as noise, that an individual may not complain directly to you about but is still irritating and hinders productivity and effectiveness.

At the core of accessibility is the shift in management philosophy presented in Chapter 1 in the section on mediation and counseling. The net result is the development of a closer professional relationship with the librarians and support staff in the unit and a perception of increased access and availability. This really is a good thing in terms of improved employee performance and teamwork objectives and is philosophically well-suited to the expectations of many new managers.

Unfortunately, being accessible can backlash on less experienced managers and morph from being available when truly needed to being available at each individual's beck and call anytime there is a question that needs answering or a concern to be addressed. These may include trivial questions, such as "Can I take a break now?" to more interruptive issues of "How should we do this?" This is a bad situation for several reasons. The staff members have effectively formed a dependency on the manager to make all decisions and can begin to choose to deny responsibility for their work performance. Additionally, it is inefficient for the manager who, unable to stay on topic for any length of time, gets less of his or her own work accomplished. It also disenfranchises staff as individuals and diminishes efforts to develop empowerment among the frontline staff. Finally, it derails innovation by undermining participatory decision-making. If the manager is always the one handing down how to do something or solve a problem, then other voices and ideas for a better solution go unheard. One technique to restore balance is to point out to staff those areas that you perceive as their responsibility to follow process or make decisions on, such as taking a different lunch hour or the next work task to do. Another way to cut back on interruptions is to route staff to email for routine or future style queries, such as an annual leave request three months away. Finally, encourage them to "hold the thought" and allow you to add it to the agenda for the next regular meeting for open discussion. The tricky point to the latter is making sure you understand the issue so as to accurately present it up for discussion. Adjusting the staff behaviors in this area can take several weeks or even months but employing these techniques should reduce the open door interruptions down to those issues that truly do need immediate attention by the manager. This is a tricky balance to maintain and requires open communication with staff members to keep it from going too far the other way, with the manager becoming the last to know.

Chapter Summary

In case you have not already gathered, if you are a structured person who dislikes interruptions, disruptions to routine, and drawn out team-based decision making, you may have a difficult transition into becoming a middle manager in the current organizational culture found in many libraries. The key is to recognize where the schedule flexibility is in one's schedule and use it effectively. Developing good time-management skills and being able to multi-task and shift gears midstream will be an asset to coping with the chaos. It is also important to self-evaluate one's commitments and daily activities in order to avoid slipping into a habit or routine pattern that undermines one's ability to be both effective and efficient.

To Learn More

There are many books available with tips on effective meeting participation and leadership. With the *Academic Administrator's Guide to Meetings*, Janis Chan offers a good introductory text that is short, readable, and focused toward the academic sector. It takes into account the tendency of faculty to think independently and bring differing perspectives into a meeting.[1] For managers trying to lead participatory meetings with a comatose group, Mel Silberman offers some excellent tips and strategies. Unlike many books on meeting engagement techniques, almost all of these suggestions treat meeting attendees as adults. Additionally, each strategy shows a graphical meter rating indicating whether it is a "serious" or "fun" technique.[2] This can be a critical factor when dealing with meetings that include academic faculty, civic leaders, or library administration. Finally, the manager who wants to become a meeting guru and is involved in group decision making on operational and business-style issues should look to John E. Tropman's text. This book goes specifically into Total Quality Management (TQM) style meetings and detailed group dynamics.[3] All of these resources help one better understand the qualities that make meetings more effective. Understanding this makes one a better participant for most meetings, even if one is not the actual convener. In warning, as you become more adept at understanding the dynamics and using meetings effectively, you will have less tolerance for poorly led meetings. Keep this in mind as you read Chapter 3 on interdepartmental issues and interactions.

Case Study: Meetings Management

> **Beth** – recent middle-manager new hire (six years prior experience elsewhere), general reference head
> **Kate** – internal middle-manager promotion (eight months ago), access services head
> **Bob** – experienced middle manager in library, head of acquisitions
> **Sam** – Kate and Beth's supervisor, associate director
> **Setting:** casual chatting after a Web team redesign meeting

Beth groans as she closes her calendar. "Well I just finished the math and it is official. By adding two more Web subcommittees to my plate, I am now officially spending more than 20 hours per week in meetings."

"That's horrible. How are you going to keep up with what is going on in your unit if you are spending 50 percent of your time every week in meetings? I mean I know you don't tend to have a lot of crises with your staff or major operational issues. But still, just keeping up with the paperwork takes some time. And then, if you do end up having to start up a virtual reference service, you are toast," Kate responds.

"Well admittedly it is not more than 20 hours of meetings *every* week. Some of the meetings happen only once or twice a month. But I'm still locked in for at least 13–15 hours of meetings every week. Not to mention all the preparation time for them."

At this point Bob, who has been at the other end of the conference table, comes up and addresses Beth. "Sounds like you need to sit down and review your meeting schedule a little to see where you can free up some time. Otherwise, you are either going to turn into a workaholic or burn out. I can't believe Sam would have assigned you to that many special committees."

"But they are all equally important," Beth protests.

Bob chuckles. "Beth, when you've been here as long as I have, you will come to realize how humorous that statement is. Would you like some advice, or should I just stay out of it?"

"No, as hard as it is to admit it, I do need help. With trying to keep up with everything, I haven't gotten out of the office before 7 P.M. the last three weeks. My exercise routine is shot and my husband is not a happy camper."

"OK, looks like no one else is using this meeting room so if you don't need to be anywhere else, why don't we work on it now," Bob offers.

Kate, who had been quietly listening to this interchange speaks up, "Do you mind if I stick around on this? I think I might learn something that will benefit me in the foreseeable future." Bob and Beth nod agreement to Kate's request.

Bob and Beth sit down at the table and begin looking at Beth's appointment calendar. "Okay, the first thing you need to do is look at the types of meetings you have got. How many of them are standing meetings based on organizational structure, such as your department heads meeting? How many of them are groups or committees? How many are meetings with individuals? And how frequently does each one occur?"

"I've got weekly status meetings with Sam, the public service managers meeting, my general reference department meeting, meetings with each of the four librarians and two senior classified staff that report to me, a meeting with the facility manager, and a monthly operations meeting with the senior subject reference librarians from the three branch libraries. It rotates between the branches and means driving across town. I've got Friends of the Library committees twice a month, along with the book sale subcommittee. Then I am on the strategic planning committee, the disaster planning group, Information Desk Implementation taskforce, the Web redesign team (now with the virtual reference and the database access subcommittees), the electronic licensing committee, chairing two search committees for branch librarians, and the downtown revitalization committee." Beth blinks a few seconds as the length of the list sinks in. "You know, I think I may be a little over committed."

Bob chuckles. "Just a little. Seriously, I'm willing to bet that you established a lot of these meetings and got on some of these committees when you first came here and were trying to really get to know your staff and how we did things here. But then when you had gotten up to speed, you didn't cut back. For example, do you really need to meet every week for a full hour with each one of your six direct reports? From my perspective, it seems to me that either you are micromanaging them or they aren't pulling their weight. Think about the meetings. Do you actually accomplish anything in them?"

"Now that I think about it, we did when I first came here but now, more often than not, we just rehash some of the stuff from the week's department meeting or talk about general stuff. They don't seem to be bothered when I have to cancel the standing meeting. In fact, usually if there is a real problem that needs immediate attention they catch me in my office or stick a 15-minute meeting on my electronic calendar. OK, so I can scale those back pretty dramatically." Beth pauses a moment. "I bet I can do the same with the meetings with the facility manager and cut that down to one meeting a month. But I am stuck for the monthly branch heads meeting across town. Still that does trim it down a lot."

"Exactly. For your direct reports, you do not want to drop them altogether but you could do them as a rotation. Since there are six different people, set up two 30-minute meetings each week. See a different two people each week of the month, with the fourth week being free. That way you stay somewhat connected to catch little concerns before they truly blow up, but you free up 5 hours of your workweek. Now, what about all of those committees, task forces, and so on. It is an extensive list. I know that Alex and Sam probably tapped you deliberately for several of them such as strategic planning, electronic licensing, and Web redesign. However, do you really need to be running both search committees? Also, have you thought about giving some of the younger librarians a chance to work with some of your senior staff and do some of the legwork on the Information Desk Implementation task force? It is generally known as delegation." Bob smiles slightly as he makes the last statement in a deadpan tone.

Beth looks thoughtfully at her calendar for a few minutes, thinking about what Bob has suggested. Then she looks up at him sort of ruefully and says, "I thought it was this library that was giving me fits on my schedule, but actually I was contributing to the problem myself. I think delegation may actually be tougher when you come into a new place because you don't really know at first who is capable of what. But you are right, I do have some people that I can trust to do a good job and who might benefit from working on some of these groups. I'll run it past Sam before I bail out, but as long as I've got someone good in mind as my replacement, it should not be a problem. He's been telling me I might want to think about prioritizing more; maybe this is what he meant."

"One final word on the Friends of the Library and downtown revitalization committees. Those are important too. But don't forget to share the load with others. I know you might be a little hesitant to speak up because you haven't been here as long. But don't let them push you into doing everything. At the book sale committee meeting, make sure others leave with action items too. Even if it means sitting still for several minutes until it dawns on them you are not going to volunteer, or politely telling them no if they try to give you more to do. Now, I've got to get back to my office."

"Thanks, Bob. I really appreciate your help," Beth smiles as he leaves the room and she closes her calendar. "That was interesting," she wryly comments as she turns to Kate.

"No kidding," Kate replies. "I think I had just started down the slippery slope with the appointment to the Web redesign committee assignment. After hearing what you guys had to say, I am going to go ahead and start streamlining my meetings now rather than wait until I'm overloaded."

Case Study Observations

- Delegate: This is something many new managers forget to do once they have gotten past the initial settling in period. Giving others responsibilities that bring them into contact with peers or teaches them more about the organization is a good thing to do.

- Committees may not be life sentences: Groups change over time. As some objectives are met, new ones get created. Do not forget to step back periodically and reconfirm that you are still the most appropriate person to be on the team because of specific skills or roles you can bring to the table.

- Learn to let others be the volunteer, or if you have already fallen into the pattern of being the first that comes to mind for a new responsibility, learn to say no, diplomatically of course.

Thought and Discussion Exercises

What Do You Do Now?

1. You have a staff member that drops by your office any time he has a question that comes to mind. Occasionally, the issue he is addressing is critical and needs and immediate response. However, usually, it is something that can be deferred. This is happening four to five times each day and is starting to impact your own productivity. What do you do now?

2. The associate director has contacted you that the library may have a chance to receive a large collection of books from a cooperative law library that is being closed down. The books have not been cataloged and some my already be duplicated in the collection. She would like you to take the lead in preparing a summary of the impact to staff and space resources ASAP. This means collecting and summarizing data from four separate people/units (subject collection development staff, acquisitions, cataloging, and shelving). What do you do now? [Hint: You do not have to chase down every single bit of data yourself, you are just pulling it together.]

3. Your normal schedule is to work 7:30 A.M.–4 P.M. Recently, you have been appointed to a new high profile committee that deals with the use of technology in the library (both staff and public computer issues) and is composed of other library managers. The committee meeting time (which has been the same for several years) is Tuesday, 4–5 P.M. What do you do now?

Notes

1. Janis Fisher Chan, *Academic Administrator's Guide to Meetings* (San Francisco: Jossey-Bass, 2003).

2. Mel Silberman, *101 Ways to Make Meetings Active: Surefire Ideas to Engage Your Group*, assisted by Kathy Clark (San Francisco: Jossey-Bass, 1999).

3. John E. Tropman, *Making Meetings Work: Achieving High Quality Group Decisions*, 2nd ed. (Thousand Oaks, CA: Sage Publications, 2003).

CHAPTER 3

Communicating as a Manager

One area of adjustment that may surprise new managers is the importance of diplomacy and discretion in their communications. As a consequence of their position in the organization, they will often be expected to interact in a different manner with upper administrators, peer managers, and staff in other units. As frontline librarians, individuals might have dealt with interdepartmental issues, either cooperatively with a frontline peer or by going through their own manager. In the latter case, their manager would consult with other managers and come back and advise the individual about what had been decided. Because one has assumed the role of middle manager, it is important to understand how to communicate effectively within this new dynamic, where you are the one approaching a peer manager with an issue or bringing back a decision.

One other area where managers should hone their communication skills is very situational, depending on the library, the community it serves, and the political or sensitive elements in the environment. Though applying a library policy equitably to all is fine in theory there are exceptions, and addressing these exceptions often falls to the middle manager. Holding firm to overdue fines accrued by the city mayor or university president while they were out of town on official business is generally a bad idea. Few administrations will uphold such a fine, given the perceptual cost and potential loss of goodwill. It is important for managers to be aware of who the influential individuals are within their community and take their cues from administration on how to defuse a situation before it can become a major incident. Depending on whether the organization has dedicated public relations support, managers may also find themselves talking to the local media, such as a reporter from the regional or campus newspaper or the local television morning show host. There is a technique to interacting with people in this format. One should choose words carefully, think in terms of impact-to-users sound bites, and not get bogged down in too much detail. One should also avoid throwaway quips or humorous comments that could be seized upon and misinterpreted by the reporter. If one has an unusual name (anything other than John Smith or David Jones) it is advisable to provide the reporter with a business card. Above all, recognize the fleeting nature of news and do not be too distressed the next day when one's name is misspelled and comments taken out of context and distorted.

The Myth of Power

One initial topic in this chapter addresses why adaptable communication skills are so important for the middle manager. Many frontline librarians and staff have an image of middle management as a position of power. After all, the manager is "in charge" and "controls" a department. They "tell" staff members what to do. They "decide" how raises are distributed. All of these verbs reflect a concept of power. In some organizations, there may be a long-established manager who has built a power base and wields that power in a personally motivated manner. This may be strongly or tacitly supported by administration because of historical issues or other factors that make it easier to allow the individual to maintain an image of absolute authority. However, in time these individuals will either push an issue too far and force a situation that the director must address through a rebalancing of power, or be overtaken by events and choose to retire. The assessment movement mentioned in Chapter 1 can play a role in this occurring. For most new managers in contemporary management environments, the concepts of power or authority occur within many constraints.

In truth, most new managers today are surprised by how little actual power they hold in a middle-manager position. True one is in charge. This means being the one who gets called anytime anything goes wrong, or being the one staff members go to whenever they have a complaint or problem. One does control what happens in a unit, in so far as it supports the organizational level initiatives and follows institutional policy and procedures and written operational guidelines of service or practice. One can tell an employee in the unit what to do, so long as it is supported by an appropriate business operational reason and falls within the policies, guidelines, and rules for the position as established by the library or institution as a whole. One can decide raises, but within the availability of funds and evaluation framework established by the organization. One can address a performance problem with a negative evaluation but without significant tangible incentives for excellent performance, this lacks something in terms of motivation. In actuality, the power of most middle managers is surrounded by a system of checks and balances that is designed to maintain a level of consistent management through the organization as a whole.

What middle managers do have is the authority to exercise judgment in daily operations-related interpretations of policy and represent the unit's staff and operations to others. The authority to make judgments is addressed in later chapters, with the current focus being the representative role. This representation of the unit occurs through communication with administrators, other managers, and even other frontline staff members to define staffing needs or operational concerns. Administrators do not have time to learn and retain every operational detail in every unit; instead they call on the middle manager at point of need to clarify an issue. Peer managers will have no idea what a particular staff member does but will expect this knowledge to be held by the middle manager. As the unit representative, one has the responsibilities to provide a clear picture of the unit to others and provide to the unit an understanding of larger organization issues as well. In today's world of empowered staff, the middle manager is the bridge that can connect individual frontline staff together to share ideas and problem solving, connect with other middle managers to form inter-unit collaborations, and connect administration's vision for the future organization to frontline operational improvements and new directions. It is in this role, which is based on authority and responsibility more than power, where a middle manager can be successful. Effective and diplomatic communication, persuasion, mediation, and negotiation skills are some of the most critical tools a middle manager can have and can never be too refined or polished.

Engaging Other Managers

Manager to manager interpersonal dynamics are in some ways quite open, but there are inevitable land mines that should be watched for and avoided. Middle managers tend to be interested in discussing issues and will have a better grasp of the impact and scope of projects or problems. However, even as they better understand issues and are open to dialogue, their focus will be on their own unit and they may not prioritize concerns in the same way. Whereas one manager will be quite ready to implement an organizational change tomorrow, another may be more cautious and want to gather more data, wait until other projects are completed, or phase in the change more slowly to allow a longer adjustment period. When this happens, there are several options: Accept that the other manager needs more time to adjust to the idea and establish a longer timeline for implementation; gather more data for the other manager and continue to work on the proposal within your areas of control; push the other manager with hopes of getting her to understand and support your perspective; or go up a level to your administrator and seek intervention at that level. Discussed in more detail later in the chapter, the latter approach should be used sparingly and with the conscious awareness that there are costs to this approach. The other options are situation dependant and should be chosen based on developing an understanding of the reasons behind the other manager's reluctance. Chapter 8 discusses issues related to managing organizational change in more detail and can help one to understand what other managers may be encountering. Alternately, it may be that the issue can be explained from a different perspective that will provide a more obvious mutually beneficial solution, or with a workaround that will allow progress with the other unit's participation phased in on a different timeline. The important thing is to stay connected to the facts and how they relate to organizational priorities.

During frontline interactions, librarians who have a frustrating experience in a peer interaction may just decide not to deal with that individual anymore and disengage. They may work through other team members or their supervisor to mediate future interactions. Managers do not have this luxury. They must stay engaged with their peers, listen to concerns, and continue to work on developing the relationship and seeking solutions. This does not mean that one cannot disagree with other managers. Seldom will a middle manager walk into a room of peer managers, present an idea, and get unanimous approval. The other managers will always raise questions or concerns. It is important to recognize the validity of these concerns and be willing to work with the other managers. Similarly, it may be a situation where both managers agree to disagree and defer to the majority decision of the other managers or work toward a compromise that is acceptable, if not optimal, for both. Whatever the managers decide to do about the impasse, it is critical that the disagreement be kept at a professional level. One must avoid making personal attacks against others or taking comments made by others personally. Similarly, as part of the ongoing relationship it is important to follow-up in a friendly fashion to reconfirm with the other manager that you are able to compartmentalize specific interactions and do not carry a grudge.

Even as it is OK for managers to disagree, new managers should be careful not to become the one who always makes demands, takes other managers or their staff to task, finds them uncooperative, or goes to administration. Part of understanding the importance of this is to recognize that as a new manager, one has a limited sphere of influence and a limited amount of goodwill among the other managers. During the initial "honeymoon period" of the appointment to a managerial position, many peer managers will recognize that one is learning the organizational dynamics and a few faux pas or poor judgment calls will be overlooked. However, as one matures in the position, there will be less tolerance for perceived hostilities or end run maneuvers. Peer managers can become evasive or unavailable to work with a manager who they perceive as uncooperative. They might decide to simply ignore the combative or complaining manager, thereby reducing that person's influence in the organization. Eventually, the situation will come to the attention of the appropriate administrator and may be resolved through direct coaching of the new manager or organizational restructuring that reassigns the manager into other roles.

Living in a Glass House

There is an aphorism about not throwing stones if one lives in a glass house. This is quite applicable when one is a manager and addressing interactions involving frontline staff from other units. When dealing with specific procedures, it is very easy for frontline staff to engage in finger pointing and assigning of blame for small mistakes to their peers in other units and to disregard their own lapses from perfection. As the manager one's staff come to about another unit's deficiencies, one must think first, act later, and weigh several issues before being caught up in the emotional reaction of the staff. Because one is trying to establish a rapport or trusting relationship with one's staff, one may want to provide something that will be an obvious symbol of support for them. However, managers are not meant to be sledgehammers manipulated by frustrated staff members. As a manager it is critical to have a realistic understanding of one's own staff and any bias an individual may impart to the report. One should recognize that one is getting a single perspective of the event. Many times there may be more to the overall situation than the perspective that has been reported. One of the biggest mistakes a new manager can make is to go into another operational area overseen by a different manager and try to coach or counsel a staff member in that unit. Almost as bad would be to confront the manager of that unit with reports that his staff are doing things wrong. In either case, the other party will likely react emotionally and immediately become defensive to perceived criticism of his actions or the management of his staff. Inevitably, the manager will recite a litany of past mistakes made by your own staff, with nothing having been accomplished except relationships and future opportunities getting damaged.

By taking a more deliberative, thoughtful approach, one can work toward engaging both units in a constructive and collaborative problem-solving relationship that will better open and establish peer lines of communication. In evaluating the problem and deciding on the best approach to use, the first issues to consider are identifying the actual core of the problem and determining whether the problem was a one-time error or represents a pattern of possible misunderstanding of procedure or disregard of best practices. One also has to assess the potential impact if the error continues. Finally, one has to look at the history of interactions between the involved units and individual staff and managers. Based on this assessment, one might decide to treat it as a one-time issue and choose not to act pending future reoccurrence of the problem. Alternately, one may decide that it is a problem caused by confusion over interpretation of a policy or procedure. Approaching the erring staff member or the other manager under this assumption can go a long way to smoothing away initial defensiveness over the error and may lead to appropriate retraining and coaching.

Sometimes there will be a problem that does such a significant disservice to library users and continues to occur even after repeated low-key intervention that the manager feels that it absolutely has to be resolved. At this point, one should engage one's administrative supervisor for intervention, providing extensive substantiating data and some suggested options for revising process to address the problem. Even after taking this step, one still has to be prepared to work around a negative response from the other unit's management and possibly accept that given the current environment the problem is not solvable. This is a difficult situation for new managers. The main thing in reaching closure is to make sure your own staff understands that you tried to resolve the situation and to try to prevent any of the involved parties from emotionally personalizing the event. By personalizing the problem and fostering a feeling that their efforts were wasted, staff members can fall into negative behaviors, such as disengaging as change agents, constantly finding fault on any interaction with the other unit, or becoming martyrs as the only unit upholding the organizational standards.

Seeking Administrative Interventions

As a manager, administrators expect one to be a problem solver who can work well with others. If a manager is constantly alienating one's peers and looking for administrative intervention or mediation, administrators are likely to perceive the individual to be a less effective contributor to the organization. Consequently, the manager will be passed over for the more challenging opportunities that might allow one to develop more experience for future growth or promotion. However, this is not to say there will not be occasions when you will need support from an administrator. Organizations are made up of people and people see and react to things differently. There will definitely be occasions when another manager has dug in his or her heels or is pushing hard for a change that has a significant impact on one's operational area, and will not listen to concerns or be willing to work toward an alternative solution. Similarly, you may have been assigned by administration to take responsibility for implementing something and cannot get a peer to engage on the workflow issues. In these circumstances, it is totally appropriate to look to your administrative supervisor for support or intervention; just make sure it is as a last resort after trying other communication techniques that try to explore why the peer manager is not engaging.

When asking for administrative intervention, it is critical to provide the administrator with as much background as possible on both sides of the issue, the tone of the interactions that have already occurred, what are the absolute key points you see as non-negotiable, and which are negotiable. It is important to discuss alternate solutions and make sure you are in agreement with the administrator as to the importance of the activity to the organization. It is also critical to realize that in turning an issue over to an administrator to resolve, the solution that arises may not be what you expect or desire but that it will be binding and you will be responsible for supporting the decision.

The biggest mistake some new managers—and even some experienced managers—make is a failure to realize that the solution reached by the administrator may be a decision to defer or to not address an issue. This can come about because the administrator has a better understanding of the organizational consequences or is privy to information not available to the middle managers. Unfortunately, this can involve confidential knowledge that cannot be shared as part of the decision. The administrator may also be able to take a longer view of the problem and recognize that something phased in over a longer time period may be less disruptive organizationally. Finally, there are times when it is easier to wait and see if a problem resolves itself over time through staff turnover or attrition than to take action in such a way that will diminish organizational trust. In these situations, the challenge is to weigh the immediate costs versus the long-term benefits of the decision. Instead of looking behind the administrator's decision to try and understand it, some managers may perceive this decision as a lack of validation toward the problem and a lack of support for their concerns and will continue to nag the administrator to fix the problem. They take every opportunity to bring the issue up so that it almost begins to appear to be an obsession or personal vendetta. What is at the heart of the conflict is a lack of trust by the middle manager in the administrator. Unfortunately, depending on the behavior of the manager, this attitude can easily be communicated down through the unit, leading to significant morale issues and undermining support for future administrative initiatives. Every interaction becomes a battle and there is a tendency by others to tune out the manager's concerns on other issues as well.

Communicating the Administrative Message

One primary role of managers is communicating and interpreting administrative visions, directives, and decisions downward through the organization. Some of these will be easy to communicate as everyone understands and agrees with their importance and the approaches being taken. Even as individual staff members have questions, the middle manager understands the issue in sufficient depth to provide knowledgeable and effective responses. However, it is common for middle managers, upon being briefed on a new initiative, to wonder why a particular direction is an issue. Then a few days later, they open an institution-wide e-mail, read about a government mandate, or learn of a budgetary change that will reflect directly on the recent decision. The most challenging message for middle managers to communicate effectively is the truly visionary or controversial one that brings radical change and seems counterintuitive to most in the organization. However, even as middle managers have difficulty understanding why an administrative decision has been made, it is important to support the official positions on issues when presenting them down through the organization.

In the latter difficult scenario, conscientious managers may have to fall back on generic remarks and acknowledge their own fallibility without abrogating their leadership role. Managers can use an approach that puts their role into perspective for their staff by saying "I don't have the complete background to understand why the library is moving in this direction but I know that the director and associate directors believe that this will be important in the future." Other supportive comments might be a recognition that something is going to be a difficult adjustment but we need to be open to change, give it a good try, and see what happens. Whatever specific words used, the message should always be one that looks to the future and challenges staff to continue to do their best in what can seem to be an imperfect, illogical, or confusing world.

Even as middle managers support administrative positions and recognize their own fallibility in understanding all aspects of an issue, it is important to avoid setting up unreasonable expectations among staff that administration is making a perfect and permanent decision. Library administration is not staffed by omniscient entities. It is staffed by human beings who, given the information at their disposal and initiatives set at the institutional level, try to establish a vision and plan for the library. Sometimes they seem forward thinking and make great decisions. Other times, they miss something relevant and make a bad decision. In this case, decisions must be reconsidered and changes implemented based on new information. Unfortunately, without middle managers effectively communicating the issues behind their decision and vision, and what went wrong, frontline staff can feel confused over why they are being asked to make changes and are battered by seemingly random decision reversals. Chapter 8 offers additional resources for effectively communicating as a manager in a changing organization.

Managers who have lost confidence in administrative decisions will communicate to staff in a manner that sends the message "Don't shoot me, I'm just the messenger and I don't believe in this either" and will undermine confidence in the leadership team of the organization. This conduct shows an unwillingness on the manager's part to actually be part of the administrative team and take responsibility for the future of the organization. At its worst, this attitude can be unethical, given that sharing responsibility for the organization is an expectation of one upon assuming a managerial title. Ironically, staff can interpret the fact that administration allows managers to use this approach as evidence of apathy toward their situation, further undermining hierarchical respect.

Chapter Summary

It is often necessary for new managers to adjust their communication style and expectations in their managerial role. Because a middle manager's role is based more on authority and responsibility rather than power, diplomacy and negotiation techniques are critical for interacting with peer managers and staff in other units. You have to invest more into long-term professional relationships with your peers and communicate based on a platform of mutual respect, even in the face of disagreement about issues. Additionally, you must pick your battles carefully and not waste emotional energies attacking a problem that does not have a current solution but is supported by the organization. It is important to communicate trust and support of administrative decisions, even as one disagrees with the decision.

To Learn More

There is an extensive body of literature that covers the broad study of workplace communication and interpersonal skills. One can find popular or readable introductions as well as in-depth texts. Two examples of books that offer a thorough yet easily readable introduction to workplace communication issues are *Communicating at Work* and *The Complete Guide to People Skills.*[1] One text among the introductory works is Lucile Wilson's book, *People Skills for Library Managers: A Common Sense Guide for Beginners.* The fact that it focuses on communication in the library environment and has a chapter that introduces some of the issues of communicating with peer managers and administrators sets it apart from most of the books found in the general business or psychology literature.[2] The individual who wants to delve into the world of communication and understand it at many levels can look to two styles of books. Several books are available that explore communication from purely psychological perspectives. In using these resources it is important to stay with more current texts that will include communication issues in contemporary workplace environments and between culturally diverse populations. Two titles, *Building Bridges: Interpersonal Skills for a Changing World* and *Bridges Not Walls: A Book about Interpersonal Communication* are good examples of textbooks that will provide additional understanding on how and why people communicate the way they do.[3] Another style of book is one that explores communication within the context of organizational structure and workplace dynamics. Two examples are *Interactive Behaviour at Work* and the *Psychology of Behaviour at Work: The Individual in the Organization.* Though neither would qualify as light reading, they do provide considerable depth in understanding the subtleties of employee and managerial communications in complex hierarchical and team-based environments.[4]

Case Study: Coordinating Across Departments

> **Kate** – internal middle-manager promotion (two years ago), access services head (previously five years at Mid State Library doing instruction/outreach activities)
>
> **Sam** – Kate and Beth's supervisor, associate director
>
> **Ellen** – senior circulation staff member, main library, reports to Kate
>
> **Melissa** – senior circulation staff member, Smith Branch Library
>
> **Monica** –senior circulation staff member, Jones Branch Library
>
> **Craig** – senior circulation staff member, Anonymous Branch Library
>
> **Pete** – senior circulation staff member, Davis Branch Library
>
> **Setting:** weekly status meeting between Kate and Sam

Working down her list of items to go over in the meeting, Kate introduces a new topic. "Ellen was cleaning out the e-mail notice reply mailbox and brought to my attention some of the e-mails in it. They were replies sent by the circulation branch units in response to student queries. I think we've got a problem. There was a lot of inconsistency to what the people were being told about our official circulation policies. Also, several of the outgoing e-mails had really poor readability, wrong verbs, misspelled words, run together sentences, and so forth. I put some better-worded template e-mails in there and dropped an e-mail to the branch circulation heads but they seem to be ignoring the templates and still writing on the fly. I was going to go ahead and try to set up a meeting to try and find out why they don't want to use the templates. Given how touchy and territorial they can be, I thought I would focus on having discovered that we are giving out inconsistent instructions about returning the books and what might work better. I definitely will keep the fact that Ellen found the errors out of the picture, given the history of conflict between her and Pete."

Sam rolls his eyes upward as he says, "Sounds like it is worth a try. Why don't you send a prescheduling e-mail summarizing the problem and cc the branch heads. I will mention it in the directors meeting that you are going to facilitate this and let them encourage participation."

Kate smiles her appreciation. "You know, I've come a long way in the past 2 years. When I first started as a manager, I would have been tempted to fire off incendiary e-mails denouncing their performance and telling them to shape up or ship out. These days I realize it may be more time consuming to use the soft-pedaled approach but with a better chance of overall success. I will probably cc you on my e-mails, just to keep you in the loop in case anyone flies off the handle or just digs in their heels altogether."

Setting: library conference room, Kate convening, Ellen, Melissa, Monica, Craig, and Pete present

Kate opens the meeting with a positive approach, "I really appreciate you coming over for the meeting. As I mentioned in my e-mail, now that the electronic notices process has been running for a few months, it seems appropriate to start working out some of the little glitches that are still hanging around. The most important one that I've noticed currently impacting patrons is the e-mail replies. We didn't really spend a lot of time on this when we first did the implementation planning because we weren't sure whether patrons would call the library or reply to the e-mail. Now that we've discovered they do tend to send middle of the night e-mail replies, we need to make sure we are all telling them the same thing about returning the books, especially when fines may be involved."

At this point, Craig interrupts, "Are you trying to say we haven't been doing our job? My boss told me I had to come to this meeting but you do not have any say in my annual performance evaluation."

Patiently, Kate replies, "I'm not trying to point fingers at anyone. I just know that I've been getting some really odd things showing up on the fines appeals that suggest patrons are getting e-mails from the library notice address with some instructions that are sort of vague and open to interpretation. If anyone wants specific examples, I've brought copies of a few with the names of the staff member who sent the message and the patron identification removed. Unfortunately, in the appeals the patrons are interpreting this in a way that benefits them. Given that consistency of service is a stated goal in the library's strategic plan, I thought it might be a good idea for all of us to get together. With the extensive procedural changes over the past few months and because we don't spend much time in each other's libraries, I thought there might be some confusion about what is the best response."

Melissa speaks up, "I still don't understand why the branches had to go to the e-mail system anyway. I know postage went up again but we really don't generate enough notices to cost that much and it has really been difficult learning to work with the electronic reports rather than the individual paper versions. Just because the 'big gorilla' main library did it, why did we have to?"

Kate responds, "Again, it has to do with the current administrative initiatives to improve consistency of service and make us look more like one library rather than a bunch of disconnected libraries. As shown from the data on the user service questionnaires this past spring, consistency is a really important service issue for the patrons. Plus, we are trying to find dollar savings wherever we can and even small batches of notices from each library add up over the course of the year.

"Coming back to the issue at hand, I looked at some of the e-mails that we have been receiving from patrons and was able to group them into several basic categories. It seems like we might be able to use some e-mail templates with standard answers to respond to most questions. This would save everyone the time and energy of writing each e-mail from scratch. I drafted up some templates to start with, but I'm sure they could benefit from your input. How about if I bring them up on the demo computer projector for us to discuss? In looking at the e-mail account, it also looks like some questions are getting answered by more than one person and others are never getting answered by anyone. We need to develop a process to organize and distribute the e-mails to make sure that we know each one is getting to the correct staff member for the specific library."

Pete nods. " I saw that e-mail where you talked about using templates but couldn't figure out what you meant. As far as the second issue goes, I'm not clear on which ones I'm supposed to answer, so if I know the answer I go ahead and send a reply but leave it in case someone else wants to reply as well. I guess that could be confusing to get a bunch of different e-mails. But I don't want to be responsible for all of them. I'm too busy."

Monica dryly offers, "Yeah, makes us definitely look like we don't have our act together. But I don't think anyone has time to go through all of them."

Moving to the demonstration computer, Kate brings up the e-mail software and logs into the e-mail circulation notices account. She explains how each library has its own folder where the appropriate staff members can customize a response with their signature lines and how to use the e-mail templates. She also works in comments about the e-mail netiquette training class that computing services offers and the importance of turning on the automatic spell checker. They bring up the actual templates and, working together, make changes to the wording so that everyone is comfortable with what it says. During this process, the group discovers that some of them had misunderstood some aspects of the other's facility. The group also decides to use a triage approach with Ellen reviewing all of the e-mails in the inbox, acknowledging receipt to the patron and forwarding it to the appropriate branch library's electronic folder. Since the main library has more staff, Kate offers to adjust workflows to free up Ellen to do this.

After saving all the changes to the templates, Kate begins wrapping up the meeting. "I really appreciate all of your help on this. I hope this will actually make this part of the process easier. Do you think it was helpful getting everyone together like this?"

Melissa speaks up, "I think it was helpful. I didn't realize that Anonymous Branch didn't have any way of returning the books after hours and that the book drop at the Jones Branch was actually behind the library to face the visitor parking lot."

As the others nod their heads in agreement, Craig comments, "I didn't realize that Davis Branch charged higher fines because of the law materials."

Kate looks thoughtful as she offers a proposal to the others. "Do you think it would be worthwhile for us to get together, maybe once a month or so, and touch base on problems we have been encountering?"

Pete enters the conversation, "Prior to this meeting, I would have said no. But even I learned some things about what is going on at the other libraries that is good to know about. We could always give it a try."

Kate smiles. "Agreed then. I will set up the meetings on the calendar and if you have particular issues/questions that come up between meetings, send them to me and I will keep a running agenda so we don't forget something. Thanks again for coming, I think we accomplished a lot today."

Setting: weekly status meeting between Kate and Sam

Summarizing the changes, Kate tells Sam, "I think this may really qualify as a breakthrough moment. Getting everyone in the same room and focusing on the facts with an actual agenda and desired outcome really defused some of the defensiveness and territorialism between everyone. In a way it is funny. If I had initially proposed having Ellen triage the messages, it would have been seen as Main dictating to them and been met with resistance. But because I waited and gave them the opportunity of refusing the task, they were much more amenable to Main taking it on. Hopefully, I can build on this to gradually address some of the other operational consistency issues that have been sitting in the strategic-plan parking lot for a couple of years."

Case Study Observations

- In facilitating discussions across departmental lines, it is important to stay focused on problem solving and deflect or defuse hostile remarks or attempts to assign blame. One must not become defensive or assign blame outside of one's unit.
- Focus on engaging rather than dictating.
- Praise collaborative performance and build on positive interdepartmental experiences.

Thought and Discussion Exercises

What Do You Do Now?

1. You do not work in cataloging but discover that some records for new books are being done incorrectly: no subject headings or authority control, incorrectly keyed ISBN numbers, and so forth. What do you do now?

2. Your request to replace a vacant position as an in-unit staff training librarian has been denied by administration. Admittedly, your proposal lacked some substance because you feel the position could be redefined more effectively. However, the staff in the unit feel this is a very important position and will likely be very upset at the news that it will not be filled. What do you do now?

3. You have been assigned to a team of peer managers working on a new Web site design. You believe you are being an effective contributor to the team, but one manager in particular has started making snide comments anytime you make a suggestion. The comments focus on personal issues such as your age, appearance, mannerisms, style of speaking, and so forth. What do you do now?

4. You have been given an administrative directive to change an interdepartmental process. However, the other managers and their staff have all told you they are too busy to work on this. What do you do now? Even if they finally get the message they have to do this, they may come to the meeting with a "shoot the messenger" attitude and resent your leadership role. What do you do now?

Notes

1. Tony Alessandra and Phil Hunsaker, *Communicating at Work* (New York: Simon & Schuster, 1993); Sue Bishop, *The Complete Guide to People Skills* (Brookfield: VT: Gower, 1997).

2. Lucile Wilson, *People Skills for Library Managers: A Common Sense Guide for Beginners* (Englewood, CO: Libraries Unlimited, 1996). Also available electronically through NetLibrary at http://emedia.netlibrary.com

3. William Gudykunst et al., *Building Bridges: Interpersonal Skills for a Changing World* (Boston: Houghton Mifflin, 1995); John Steward, ed., *Bridges Not Walls: A Book about Interpersonal Communication*, 8th ed. (New York: McGraw-Hill, 2001).

4. Maureen Guirdham, *Interactive Behaviour at Work*, 3rd ed. (New York: Prentice-Hall, 2002); Adrian Furnham, *The Psychology of Behaviour at Work: The Individual in the Organization* (Hove East Sussex, UK: Psychology Press, 1997).

CHAPTER 4

Understanding Department Makeup

Even without exploring the detailed human relations and interpersonal dynamics of your unit, it is important to understand several issues on department composition that create challenges for new library managers. As organizations, libraries are culturally different from other operational groups. There is higher percentage of female employees at all levels, both administrative and frontline, many juggling job and traditional family roles. Additionally, library employees face a dual mission of service and education and have undergone a significant amount of environmental changes and redefined jobs during the past 15 years. Some of the conflicts that arise, such as office support staff versus library paraprofessionals versus professional librarians, are unique to library environments and the culture of the profession. Any degree-based ego associated with the MLS must be tempered by compassion and a recognition of the need to connect with others within the organization as colleagues working toward a common goal, rather than focusing on rank and title. Other broad concerns, such as gender, race, ethnic, and generational conflict issues, are common throughout the world of work. Even as one has an awareness of the potential for bias and conflict, becoming a manager requires one to look at such concerns from different perspectives. Some of these issues are addressed in Chapter 7 in the context of human relations within the department. This chapter attempts to explore several significant issues that are pervasive in most libraries from a managerial viewpoint. Many of the techniques are applicable to locally specific communication breakdowns and group-based conflicts as well.

Staff Role Conflicts

Often the functional operation of the unit dictates the mix of professional versus nonprofessional staff composition. Some units that require a significant level of expert knowledge, such as reference, have generally had a higher percentage of librarians. Other units that have a more routine task structure, such as acquisitions or circulation are more likely to have large complements of nonlibrarian staff. Yet others, such as cataloging, consist of mixed staffing with both librarians and nonlibrarians. The introduction of computer-support technical staff and the restructuring of clerical positions into office support/business roles have increased the complexities caused by staff mix. To further complicate the issues, the manner and tone of interactions between various groups differ from institution to institution and may often be a function of organizational history.

Tension between professional librarians and library support staff has been around for many years. Most library schools touch on the issue during introductory classes. The tension has been fueled by periodic historical challenges to recognizing librarianship as a professional career with a unique knowledge and skills requirement. Over time, nonlibrarian staff who support library-specific tasks have been given different labels, including paralibrarian, paraprofessional, and the more generic term of library support staff. In this chapter, the term *support staff* will be used to identify non-MLS library employees engaged in library operational tasks. Separate from support staff, *systems staff* will describe those staff with technical computer expertise. Office staff will describe those employees engaged in office administration or tasks that are considered more clerical in nature (scheduling, correspondence, supply ordering, etc.).

The specific techniques for improving communications overall and resolving problems arising from different individual communication and motivational styles are discussed in the context of developing human relations and interpersonal skills in the workplace. Challenges associated with internal one-on-one interactions between staff within a unit are covered in more depth in Chapter 7.

Librarians and Support Staff

Different academic institutions have a variety of staffing models that address the similarities and differences between librarians and support staff. The largest problems occur when there has been a clear pattern in the past of support staff being denied the respect of the organization. Other catalysts are staffing cuts, which blur the defined responsibilities of each employee group, and changing organization service priorities from in-building to remote access and desktop delivery, which may involve reevaluating the need and importance of current roles. Additional misunderstanding can occur based on different perceptions or job expectations. For librarians, working in a library is a career decision with expectations of long-term growth and career development. However, even in institutions with career ladder opportunities, many support staff perceive their work in the library as "just a job." Although these individuals will do a good job and take pride in doing their work well, they have less personal investment in the overall success of the organization. Conflict also occurs when the supporting employees do not have a clear understanding of the librarian's role and contributions to the overall organization's mission and objectives, as well as their own contribution to the daily operations that support the mission and objectives. In many institutions, librarians may be expected to take on complex committee or leadership responsibilities, project planning, original cataloging, collection development, or liaison roles. Many of these assignments are less visible contributions than working many hours at a reference desk, copy cataloging large numbers of books, or being in an office from 8 A.M. to 5 P.M. Trying to explain the subtleties of developing original cataloging standards to a member of the support staff whose experience is centered around copy cataloging work using OCLC records may be actually quite difficult. Similar disconnects can occur on the public services side. Time spent interacting with a teaching faculty member or community literacy group, especially when it happens away from the library, can be perceived by the staff member, who is answering repetitive term paper or scavenger hunt questions behind the reference desk, as invisible contributions. It is not uncommon for support staff to use their own job responsibilities and experience as the ruler to measure all contributions of the unit. As an example, a support staff employee may believe that one's value to the organization is based on the number of hours spent at the main reference desk and become frustrated by the sense that someone doing "less work" actually gets higher status and pay.

The situation can be further strained by the introduction of faculty status for librarians in academic settings. Even within the faculty librarian role, there is wide variance in performance expectations, depending on an institution's faculty bylaws. Some institutions direct the faculty performance more into leadership on professional assignment responsibilities and performing service activities within the institution. Other institutions have quite rigorous expectations of additional research and publication efforts and/or service to the profession through national and state professional associations. The latter environment can be especially difficult for staff to understand. They might see librarians going away to professional conferences in interesting places like New Orleans or Washington, DC, but are often unaware of the hectic pace and long days spent attending meetings and programs, engaging vendors, and networking in large exhibit halls. Additional complications arise if the same institution offers both tenure and nontenure librarian tracks.

Technical Systems Staff Challenges

Another area of conflict that may arise between types of staff is that of librarians versus technical systems staff. Traditionally, librarians have thought of themselves as the ranking staff within libraries. They generally had higher salaries, better office space, upgraded office equipment, and more freedom than their support or office staff colleagues. Into this picture comes the technology-focused network infrastructure and computer support staff. They already have professional recognition and certifications within their own discipline, are in high demand, and can negotiate higher salaries than many librarians. Unfortunately, nonlibrarian technical systems staff hires do not have the experience to understand about library services or the complex background operations, and can encounter difficulty understanding and adapting to the library culture. Similarly, they may not be prepared for their representative roles as change agents. Chapter 8 addresses change adaptation in more detail. At this point it is sufficient to point out that it is much easier for a library employee pushed to embrace technology to personalize frustrations toward the computer support staff who performed the upgrade than to express frustration toward the actual inanimate device.

Contemporary libraries have become fairly complex organizations that exist on the edge of chaos with multiple high priorities and complex direct and indirect user service expectations. Within this fluctuating environment, the role of computer technology in delivering resources electronically and remotely has become a totally integrated part of library services and stable performance a critical part of user expectations. For those who enjoy working with computers, this world of constantly evolving client expectations and conflicting multiple priorities can be neither a natural nor a comfortable working environment. Unless someone familiar with library operations provides the technical systems staff with sufficient background information on internal and external customer service expectations and operational complexities, they can mistakenly perceive the impact of a problem to be negligible and prioritize it incorrectly. This can lead to librarians and support staff feeling their needs are being ignored and personalizing their frustrations. Suddenly, the systems staff, which thought their priority was to develop a stable and streamlined network, find themselves tarred and feathered for poor communication and customer service within the organization. Unfortunately, their introspective and analytical response to this situation is to withdraw rather than engage in emotion-laden dialogue, or become protective of their systems. This can continue until each side feels hostile and frustrated toward the other and interactions totally break down.

Building the Bridges

As a frontline librarian with a more limited sphere of engagement within the unit, one may have stayed on the edges of these conflicts or participated in the groupthink of immediate peers and colleagues. However, as a manager responsible for fostering an effective and productive environment within and across departments, one must be much more aware of these conflicts and the negative impact they can have on productivity. It is important to address concerns before a situation deteriorates to an uncooperative or hostile level. As with most problems based on an individual's perception, using communication, education, and coaching approaches with individual employees can go a long way to resolving the misunderstandings.

Librarian and Support Staff Resolution

In addressing the conflicts that occur between librarians and support staff, it is important for managers to explain how there are different roles and different manners of contributing to the library's organizational mission, and that everyone is a valuable contributor. This may mean taking a few extra minutes in unit meetings to acquaint staff with larger organizational issues and then engaging them to stretch their thinking beyond their immediate job tasks toward how those job tasks fit into the organizational whole. This understanding is not something that develops overnight or can be discussed once and dropped. It is something that is best introduced in bite-sized pieces over a period of time, much like planting a seed and letting it grow.

Another important element to resolving conflict requires maturity and discretion on the part of the higher-ranking employee, which in the case of the librarian–support staff conflict, is the librarian. It is important for librarians to take their responsibilities seriously and not play up the accompanying privileges of their rank at the cost of staff respect. On the surface, there are the typical business situations of pulling rank on office tasks or playing favorites with individual staff. An example is the librarian who expects to check out library materials without a library card or expects to be exempt from fines or normal processes. It may also be a librarian who monopolizes an especially conscientious shared office staff member. Other examples of inappropriate professional behavior among librarians could include making comments about "off-site research time" being "free to run errands, take a nap, catch up on house responsibilities, and so forth" or conferences being a chance to "attend lots of open bar receptions and see old friends." Even if the librarian is saying this in a joking or self-deprecating manner to another librarian, it can easily be overheard and misinterpreted by a staff member if the office environment is open architecture or open door. If the librarian is serious, then there is a more serious discipline and ethical performance issue that must be addressed. Either way, within days, the grapevine will be flourishing over the fact that librarians do not really work at conferences; instead they have an expense paid trip for a fun, carefree visit with out-of-town friends and party in vendor hospitality suites.

In addition to verbal misunderstandings, action-based and nonverbal behaviors can also be perceived inappropriately. Suppose most of the staff in a unit work 8 A.M. to 5 P.M. They will not be there to see the librarian who arrives each day sometime around 9 A.M. and usually stays well past 6 P.M., putting in more than an eight-hour day. Depending on how chafing the timesheet/hourly wage system is to the support staff, the staff member's personalized conclusion could be a negative one toward both the individual librarian and the organization for allowing the perceived abuse of not putting in due time. At this point, employee morale and positive attitudes are under attack as staff members react negatively to perceived inequities. The cycle continues as librarians become defensive and disgruntled over the lack of staff respect and consideration, and on it goes.

Some managers tend to take a bandage approach to these problems. They address the incident in a manner that may address a specific complaint but does not engaging the group to discuss the underlying issues. A bandage solution to the previous example would be to dictate that all staff, regardless of title/rank, must now work an 8 A.M. to 5 P.M. shift. In addition to being impractical from an operational perspective and taking self-control away from everyone, it does not solve the real problem. The solution is not to make all librarians punch a time clock and look like staff. The solution is to put comments or actions in perspective and explain the institutional expectations of the different groups with the message that difference is not a measure of better. One key to doing this effectively is to keep in mind that one is explaining, not defending, a situation. Putting the situation in fair but matter-of-fact terms will make a difference in how it is received by all parties. In conclusion, the same dignity and respect factors that are important between a person and his or her supervisor often need to remain in place across the institutional staff–librarian boundaries as well.

Collaborating with Technical Systems Staff

Though the interpersonal dynamics between technical systems staff and librarians may be a bit more challenging, the resolution again lies in the realm of communication and education. Obviously both sides of the issue will need active coaching to improve communications and find a compatible middle ground. One common problem that comes into this area is that traditionally computer science and engineering have been male-oriented careers and many of the communication skills of the profession follow the traits associated with gender-based verbal communication, including brevity and a tendency to make statements rather than ask questions. Additionally, the computer science profession tends to attract people who think very analytically. In contrast, librarianship has historically been populated with a preponderance of women, often with less-structured liberal arts and education backgrounds, who expand conversationally and use open ended canvassing of opinions. This is a classic scenario for the "he said, she heard/she said, he heard," analytical versus amiable, or feeling versus thinking (Myers-Briggs) mismatches. Both systems and library staff are going to have to be aware that this can happen and work on more actively listening, on over-explaining concerns, and being willing to learn from the other. This includes learning the jargon and language of each group. While working on developing the long-term solution based on mutual understanding and respect, there are several proactive things library unit managers can do to reengage with the systems staff in a positive manner.

The first thing managers can do is to encourage all nontechnical staff to develop basic computer troubleshooting skills. This means learning to do some simple checks before reporting a problem. Often such a check-list will include cycling through the shutdown and restart process a couple of times to clear and reset memory and processor components. Another common problem that is easily fixed is a loose plug, either on the individual component or where it plugs into the CPU or power strip. Once all staff can check the basics before reporting a problem, managers should work to understand more advanced technical language so that they can better communicate problems and facilitate troubleshooting. The manager can help translate between the frontline user and the technician, and encourage staff to use designated methods of reporting problems. Few things are more frustrating to systems staff than to be told "my computer isn't working." This could mean everything from the PC not powering up at all to a password is not being accepted to being able to log into the local network but having problems with a particular software program. Precise and accurate language in reporting is important because it allows better routing of the problem to the specific technician. Related to this, many systems units use a computer based "ticket tracker" style of software to triage, assign, and follow-up on reported problems. Unless a problem represents an actual crisis, staff should be encouraged to use this reporting mechanism rather than reach for the phone to call in every little problem. It allows systems staff to handle problems in a more efficient manner and collect necessary data for long-term improvements.

Next, new managers should learn to communicate problems in terms of impact on common organization concerns (i.e., customer service) that are understandable to a nonlibrarian. Simply saying that the shared tag tables need fixing for accurate MARC record fields has little meaning to most systems staff. Explaining that without a particular file (that contains the tag tables) being updated no one in cataloging can change or create a single book record gives a better operational impact to the problem. Given our automated world, it is true that anyone is going to have trouble doing a job when the desktop computer is malfunctioning. However, as with any workflow concern, everything cannot be a number one priority that must be fixed immediately. There is a difference in priority and operational impact between a total computer failure at a main service point and one on an individual's desk, especially if there are other computers in the nearby vicinity that could be used instead. It is the manager's responsibility to establish and communicate these priorities. Many staff personalize the computer on their desk as theirs. Having to go to a borrowed workstation pushes both the individual using the computer and the individual whose desk is being used out of their comfort zone for a temporary period. However, it is a better solution than having to over-allocate dollars into systems staffing because of unrealistic expectations of immediately responding and resolving all problems.

Another area managers should address is establishing realistic expectations of automated systems. Depending on the individual library's rate of technology advancement, library staff may still be enamored by computers and expect their use to resolve larger organizational workflow issues. For example, suppose a new program is purchased to assist in creating desk schedules in an easily updateable format. If an effective process for setting up the base schedule using availability lists, voluntary participation, and absentee reporting is not already in place, the workflow itself will still be flawed and purchase of the software package will not make a lot of improvement. Staff members who do not recognize this tend to be more easily frustrated with computer tools and correspondingly the staff who deliver them. Finally, managers need to recognize when the system staff responsiveness has not met realistic expectations and take appropriate action. As highly trained and analytical problem solvers, computer technicians enjoy tinkering with hardware and software coding and find the challenge of figuring out a problem mentally stimulating. Unfortunately, this can sometimes lead them to get so absorbed in troubleshooting a particular problem that they are can lose track of passing time and may not realize the need to bring in someone with more experience who can offer a new idea or perspective. A manager who has to bring this problem to a systems supervisor should do so with a realization that performance is more a function of the personality type and generally not an indication of incompetence. A dispassionate and factual approach will be much more effective in their world than an impassioned and frustrated rant.

Generation Gaps

Another aspect of departmental makeup that managers should work to understand is how generational issues can impact personal interactions. The commercial business sector has been grappling with these issues for several years and offers a wealth of resources to learn more about the challenges of a department with a mixed complement of Silents, Boomers, Generation Xers, and Millennials. To some degree, academic institutions as a whole, and academic libraries specifically, have not yet been impacted as dramatically by this problem. Perhaps, working with students on an ongoing basis gives one a preview of what is coming and allows for some subconscious preparation or adjustment. However, the potential for conflict is increasing as Generation Xers makes inroads among the professional librarian and managerial ranks and Millennials are introduced into student worker and office support roles.

Currently, the biggest workplace conflicts are between the Baby Boomer generation, born approximately 1943 to 1960, and Generation X, born approximately 1961 to 1981, and originally called the Thirteenth Generation. Most upper- and middle-management ranks in libraries are populated by the Boomer generation. Many new librarians and young managers are Generation Xers. These two generations have experienced extensive societal and cultural change. Based on the various concepts and detailed examples provided by the resources cited in the To Learn More section at the end of the chapter, it is possible to arrive at some broad generalizations that characterize Generation X. They went through different educational methods and grew up under different stimuli, family support structures, and learning environments. As a consequence of this, researchers have observed measurable differences in intelligence and social adaptation skills between the two generations. Generation X is very intelligent and has a greater ability to multitask effectively, but their socialization skills are usually much less developed than their Boomer predecessors were at the same age. They are extremely independent problem solvers and lack patience for working within bureaucratic environments.

The two generations also express significantly different viewpoints on workplace motivation, attitudes toward change, and life priority issues. Generation X employees are much more focused on improving themselves and expect, even crave, constant change. Boomers tend to connect more with the identity and successes of the unit than their individual skill developments and are less enthusiastic about change, especially when it is not tied to an obvious problem. Boomers still perceive long-term stability as a valuable job commodity. Generation Xers expect to change jobs and careers and are usually looking to invest in themselves more than their organization. On salary issues, Boomers often came up through the ranks and seniority is recognized as the significant salary determiner. Generation X defies this and seeks to be recognized based more on current accomplishments and contributions. These perspectives often make it more difficult for Generation Xers to adjust to the traditional organizational culture as defined by Boomer administrators.

Unlike the Boomer generation that was plentiful, Generation X is a smaller population. Using basic supply and demand theory, this means that organizations wanting to recruit and retain them into the profession will have to be more creative and competitive in their offers. Because of this, organizations must invest in the Generation X employee and work to develop, challenge, and grow them within the organization; otherwise they will leave for better opportunities and there may not be a replacement immediately available.

The Millennials, born after 1982, are just now entering the workforce, primarily as student workers or entry-level staff. They are the subject of many sociological studies, the most complete of which are referenced in the To Learn More section. In many ways they have more in common with the Boomers than their predecessors, Generation X. In other ways they are a unique and complex blending of the two. Their motivation and value structure mirrors the Boomer with its emphasis on family and long-term concerns. However, they keep their feelings on serious issues very private and do not engage well in large group settings. Born during the boom of digital technology, their multitasking, multimedia, and computer skills come naturally to them. How they will actually impact the workplace interpersonal dynamics is unknown but there is no doubt that they will have a significant impact.

Chapter Summary

It would be ideal, if a bit boring, if everyone worked in harmony with one another. Unfortunately people are different and even as a new manager will have to work to understand personal characteristics of individual employees, there are broader issues that one must frequently address as well. This chapter has introduced several of these issues for consideration. Depending on the individual institution, there may be additional areas where bias occurs based on other issues, such as educational background, marital status, family structure, or geographic background. In all cases, the key to resolving conflict is encouraging communication and fostering an environment of mutual respect and collaboration to common higher-level goals and objectives.

To Learn More

There are a number of resources available to educate oneself on these issues. A search of the business periodical literature through ABI/Inform or EBSCO Business Search Premier retrieves many vignette and anecdotal-style articles on the conflicts that can arise and the frustrations that are created with an intergenerational workforce. Though providing less depth than the resources cited at the end of the chapter, they are a good and quick introduction to the topic. There are also several good texts that will allow a manager to gain an awareness of generational behaviors and sources of conflict. The best-known scholars in the area of defining the different generations have been William Strauss and Neil Howe. Their books, *Generations: The History of America's Future 1584 to 2069* and *Millennials Rising: The Next Great Generation,* are considered required reading for one studying the issues. *Generations: The History of America's Future 1584 to 2069* introduces the theory behind characterizing behaviors and attitudes as part of generational identities and provides brief overviews of the past and predictions on future generational groupings.[1] *Millennials Rising: The Next Great Generation* presents an in-depth look at the youngest generation and what they will be bringing to the workforce and society.[2] The books are quite readable and introduce one to understanding the basis for the differences between the generations without requiring a strong background in the social sciences. From a more practical and applied perspective, there are several very good books on managing generation issues in the workplace. Some, such as *Managing Generation X* by Bruce Tulgan and *Twenty Something: Managing and Motivating Today's New Workforce* by Lawrence J. Bradford and Claire Raines, focus on the integration of a particular new generation into the workforce.[3] Others, such as *Generations at Work: Managing the Clash of Veterans, Boomers, Xers, and Nexters in Your Workplace* by Ron Zemke, Claire Raines, and Bob Filipczak and *Beyond Generation X: A Practical Guide for Managers* by Claire Raines, address more of the intergenerational problems that can develop and methods for improving tolerance and understanding between the generations.[4]

Case Study: The Boomer and the Gen Xer

> **Beth** – recent middle-manager new hire (six years prior
>   experience elsewhere), general reference head
> **Keith** – science reference librarian, early 50s, 18 years in library
>   (had applied for Beth's job and did not get it)
> **Debby** – new science reference librarian, mid-20s, hired five
>   months ago, spent two years working for a Silicon Valley IT
>   venture before getting her MLS
> **Setting:** reference department staff offices

Beth had just accepted a vague meeting request from Debby for
later that day when she hears a firm knock on the casing of her
open door. She looks up to see Keith. Tight-lipped and standing
rigidly in the doorway, he does not look happy.

"Can I talk to you?" he asks.

Beth lays down her pen and glances down at her day planner
and answers, "Sure, I can give you about 45 minutes before my
next meeting. What's up?"

Keith comes in and closes the door behind him. As he sits down
across from Beth, he bursts out "You have got to do something
about Debby!"

Beth is not totally surprised at the outburst, but wonders what
the details are that have triggered both the visit to her office and
the appointment she had just accepted moments earlier. She had
noticed some tension between Keith and Debby at the staff meeting the previous day but had hoped they would be able to work it
out between themselves.

"I noticed something seemed to be wrong yesterday in the meeting but couldn't tell what. What is the problem?"

Keith bursts out, "Better to ask what isn't a problem, the list
would be shorter. She is absolutely impossible. She has no respect
for my seniority in the unit. Every time I turn around she is asking
why we do something and is insubordinate and trying to tell me a
better way to do it using some kind of fancy computer program-
ming stuff. Also, when I sit down and try to go over something with
her, she bounces from topic to topic without ever letting me finish
what I was going to say. I asked her to pull together some data on
the number of users of the Wilson and EBSCO electronic
resources, expecting that would keep her out of my hair for at least
a couple of days. The next thing I know she is putting it on my desk
4 hours later. Then after giving it to me, she informs me that she
needs to leave early because it was the first night of dog obedience

school and she wanted to make sure she had all the necessary paperwork on her puppy. Here she is leaving work early for a dog! Plus, she has no sense of office decorum or behaving like a professional librarian. Have you seen her today? She looks like she is wearing a pair of pajamas and her hair looks like she just got out of bed, too. I feel like I am working with my six-year-old granddaughter." Keith pauses and looks to Beth for her comment.

Maintaining eye contact with Keith, Beth leans back and looks thoughtful. Keeping her tone moderated and neutral, she comments to Keith, "Well, there is definitely some conflict happening here. How long has this been building?"

"She hasn't really fit in since she got here. The first couple of months she was always just watching and listening, not saying too much. Then the real problems have cropped up just in the last month or two. The last straw was this morning. I was showing her the sheets for logging in the classes we teach and she actually asked me why we haven't automated the process into some kind of database. I told her the current system works just fine and our philosophy here is 'if it isn't broke, we don't need to fix it.'"

"What happened then?" Beth asks.

"Nothing, I left her sitting there and went out to the reference desk," replies Keith.

Beth sits forward and makes eye contact with Keith as she begins to talk. "I will be honest here. Debby has already asked to meet with me too and I am going to need to hear both sides to know specifically what direction to take in resolving this. However, I don't think this is going to be an absolute right-or-wrong issue for either of you. Part of the reason Debby was hired is that she has very extensive computer skills and can bring new ideas to us all on how to be more effective with the tools we have. She is also going to be a key player in implementing our Chat Reference service later this year. With the staff positions we have lost due to budget cuts, we need to be open-minded to streamlining workflows and improving procedures. However, it is also important to make sure that all employees are treated with dignity and respect for their knowledge and skills, so if Debby needs coaching in communicating with her peers, I will follow-through with her on that.

"In the meantime, I'd like you to think about some of the comments you just made while your emotions were taking the lead. First, you compared Debby to a child; do you really perceive her in this way? You don't have to answer at the moment, just think about it. If so, is it because she is a peer in age to your own children or is it because she is enthusiastic and defies the cynical outlook that often comes with age? About her asking "why?" stop and consider that her generation is one that has gone through the school systems under a model that teaches them to challenge ideas, participate in discussions, ask questions, and become problem solvers. Since you mentioned the dog class issue, I can tell you that I have heard Debby say to others that she is not ready to start a family and for her, the puppy is her child. Think of it as someone taking her child to the first day of kindergarten. This is something that can be difficult for some people, who have a different take on pets, to understand. Similarly, professionalism and competency are more than attire and appearance. The library does not have a dress code, just an expectation that staff will follow good hygiene and avoid offensively obscene or revealing clothing. The fact that she tends to dress consistent with the latest trends has little bearing on her capabilities as a librarian. In fact it might make her more approachable from the students' perspectives. These are all aspects of Debby's personality that are probably not going to change and are out of your area of control. However, what *is* in your control is how you perceive and respond to her. As much as we may try to avoid admitting it, we live and work in a world where things are going to change and at a faster rate than most of us are comfortable with. Debby is a visible representation of that change. You need to keep in mind that she is not questioning you personally even if she does question something you contributed to developing.

"I was wondering if you have watched the video on change that Sam made available in media services? If not, I think it might be a good idea and could give you some insights into what the next few years are going to be like around here."

Keith looks skeptical as he responds, "I honestly think most of the self-help video stuff is a waste of time, but if you want me to watch it, I will. I'm not against change where I can see an actual problem and the change will actually be a solution. I just don't like the idea of changing everything because you can."

"Please do watch the video, I think it might offer some insights for you. In the meantime, I will work with Debby about building colleague relationships and not being the bull in the china shop."

Setting: Picking up 3 hours later as Beth is meeting with Debby

"I have all these terrific ideas. And he just won't even listen to me as I try to explain how this could be so much better. I think he just views me as some kind of pest that he wishes would go away. But then when I did get out of his way by leaving early to begin puppy classes for my dog Merlin, I could tell he didn't approve of that either. I thought I was hired to update this place . . . so let me update," Debby says, gesturing wildly to emphasize her frustrations.

"As I was telling Keith earlier, this is not a simple right or wrong problem. In some ways, you both are right and in other ways you both are wrong. I won't deny that Keith can be a traditionalist and something of a cynic about the promise of change; his life's experiences have taught him that. Also, the two of you have totally different communication and thinking styles. You tend to multi-task and think big picture potential and he tends to think linearly at a detail-oriented level. However, he is a very good science reference librarian, is committed to the good of the library, and has a lot of skills and knowledge that are important to the unit. Disregarding his concerns and input because you perceive him as slow or unwilling to change is doing him a disservice. I have talked to him about seeing past your youth. On your part, you need to think about presenting a side of yourself that reflects a degree of professionalism and encourages dignified treatment when appropriate.

"Also, you need to better understand how change happens. Even though you may be right about seeing potential, you cannot cram change it down people's throats. You have to engage them to be participants in it, otherwise it will fail. Because you have less experience in the traditional librarian responsibilities but more experience in other business and technology areas, it may be harder for your peers to understand why you have these problem-solving insights. You are very intelligent, probably more intelligent than many people who work here. However, if you alienate them before you even start presenting your ideas, you've failed before you've even started and will not be very effective. Then you will discover real frustration. I was wondering if you have watched the video on change that Sam made available in media services? If not, I think it might be a good idea and could give you some insights into what the next few years are going to be like.

"In the meantime, I am going to put both you and Keith on the search committee for the new instructional librarian. Maybe by working together on a neutral project, rather than one that you both have invested in so personally, you can find a middle ground with some common interests."

Case Study Observations

- Generational issues often manifest themselves in offhand or emotion-based comments or behaviors.

- The differences caused by generational age and experience can be easily mislabeled with other causes.
- Often generational conflict is an offshoot of one's generational comfort level with changes implied by the introduction of the new generation's perspective.
- The key to moving past generational conflict is establishing mutual respect, finding some kind of common ground, and being willing to meet in the middle.

Thought and Discussion Exercises

What Do You Do Now?

1. A staff member comes to you and informs you that she cannot do her work because her desktop computer doesn't work. What do you do now?
2. A staff member comes to you and complains that the new social sciences librarian has taken over his job of ordering the books for the teaching lab collection. Following up, you discover that the librarian feels the staff member was not using good judgment in selecting materials that would be consistent with the purpose of the collection. What do you do now?
3. You overhear a pair of librarians comparing the merits of attending an upcoming ALA, PLA, or Digital Librarian conference. They are trying to decide which one they would rather go to. Based on the bit of dialogue you hear, neither one is really considering the conference offerings as much as the location and timing of the conference. What do you do now?
4. You overhear three support staff employees talking in a public area of the office suite about a senior librarian. Based on their comments, it is obvious they think the person is a parasite and does not contribute anything to the unit operational objectives because she is always out of the office. You are privy to the knowledge that the librarian is on three major university committees with considerable demands outside of the office. What do you do now?

Notes

1. William Strauss and Neil Howe, *Generations: The History of America's Future 1584 to 2069* (New York: William Morrow & Co., 1991).
2. William Strauss and Neil Howe, *Millennials Rising: The Next Great Generation* (New York: Vintage Books, 2000).

3. Bruce Tulgan, *Managing Generation X*, revised and updated (New York: W.W. Norton & Co., 2000); Lawrence J. Bradford and Claire Raines with Jo Leda Martin, *Twenty Something: Managing and Motivating Today's New Workforce* (New York, MasterMedia, Ltd., 1992).

4. Ron Zemke, Claire Raines, and Bob Filipczak, *Generations at Work: Managing the Clash of Veterans, Boomers, Xers, and Nexters in Your Workplace* (Chicago: AMACOM, 2000); Claire Raines, *Beyond Generation X: A Practical Guide for Managers* (Menlo Park, CA: Crisp Publications, 1997).

CHAPTER 5

Dealing with Budgets

Understanding budget issues can be one of the most foreign and frequently overlooked areas of training for a new manager in an organization. Budgeting is more than just adding columns in a spreadsheet. It actually encompasses the entire financial philosophy of an organization and how that philosophy translates into implementation. Understanding library budgets is complicated by the fact that different organizations may have different policies and use different jargon to express budget details. Budgetary sources, fund visibility, and flexibility between funds will vary from one institution to another. Even at a single institution, individual upper administrators may have different approaches in how they prioritize and manage their budget responsibilities. Such budgeting variance will have a trickle-down effect into the middle-manager's world. This chapter will introduce you to some of the budget issues that middle managers often encounter in academic libraries and offer some possible techniques to aid in developing an understanding of the financial behaviors at your institution. It starts at a local level and discusses typical funds overseen by a middle manager and broadens out to discuss types of organizational funding. The Mid State Library example offers a look at special project financial planning in an academic library.

Understanding the Basics

Finding reading material to help one develop appropriate financial knowledge as a middle manager in a library can be somewhat challenging. Within the librarianship profession, many of the publications and book chapters present budgeting from the perspective of the library director, who has more decision-making authority than most middle managers. Some resources tend to focus on the public libraries, which have different financial challenges than the academic environment. Even as a resource may provide coverage toward different types of libraries, they tend to be narrowly focused to specific topics, such as fundraising or charging fines/fees, and do not capture either small budget management or broader organizational perspectives. Unfortunately, the business literature is also less relevant because many library operations are part of the not-for-profit world and, relative to a large corporate entity, the library budget structure is quite different. However, to get some general understanding of budgeting practices and develop a knowledge foundation, some beneficial resources are suggested in the To Learn More section near the end of the chapter.

Figuring Out "Your" Funds

Middle managers are often responsible for several operational funds. They must monitor that the funds are expended for the correct purpose and in a timely manner. Almost any type of library department will have money allocated for office supplies and student worker wages, as illustrated in the examples used in this section. Depending on the size of the institution, individual department responsibilities, and organizational hierarchy, there may be numerous additional budgeted lines earmarked for particular purchases or projects. Some of these, such as overall facilities maintenance, may be managed at an upper administrative level. Others, like ordering barcode labels or overseeing expenditures on an approval plan budget, may be delegated downward into unit operational areas.

One aspect of managing budget responsibilities is finding the balance between monitoring and micromanaging funds. It is not an effective use of resources for a middle manager to make the decisions and prepare the paperwork for every pen and notepad bought by a unit. When dealing with routine unit operational funds, the role of the middle manager is to establish the framework of what is an acceptable and appropriate type of purchase, delegate the paperwork, mediate on items that fall outside the framework, periodically review the remaining funds relative to the anticipated needs for the remainder of the year, and make adjustments accordingly. The paperwork responsibilities and routine decisions of restocking basic supplies or hiring entry-level student workers should be delegated to a staff members with strong detail skills. Special projects or one time purchases may require additional hands-on participation by the manager in contacting vendors, reviewing competitive products, defining specific needs, or preparing bid proposals. Most institutions will have staff who assist in preparing, accepting, and reviewing bids in a manner consistent with legal fair trade practices and organizational guidelines.

Buying Stuff

Depending on organizational practice, there may be several ways of buying materials that support unit operations. Some libraries will have a business credit card, established charge account, or reimbursement policy that middle managers and designated staff will be authorized to use in order to make purchases directly from a retail store or vendor. Others libraries have more intricate procedures in place and require all purchases to go through a central ordering and processing office. In this model, most requests will go through a defined ordering and receiving/inventory process. For the latter scenario, there will be exception processes that allow a manager to check out a business credit card or get a prepurchase authorization form for local or urgent moderate purchases. No matter what the process, there is always specific paperwork that must be submitted. Though some of this can be learned from a current staff member who orders unit supplies, it is still a good idea to set up a meeting with appropriate business operations staff to get an overview of the process from their perspective and learn whether there are additional options available only to managers. Additionally, expressing an interest in learning to work within their current procedures makes a significant investment in developing positive future interactions with business office staff and establishes a position of mutual respect.

Most libraries operate on a postacquisition system where funds are actually paid out after a product is received. Business operations personnel use an invoice that is received with the item or a monthly summary statement. Some public institutions must process an invoice for payment within a certain time period to avoid penalties. This can be difficult if everyone waits until the last minute to place an order and the invoices arrive all at once. Because some products take longer to receive, institutions may use a process called encumbering to earmark funds as committed to a particular purchase. It is important to familiarize oneself with the available balance spreadsheets and understand whether or not encumbrances are represented. The advantage of the encumbering process is that it gives one a clearer picture of currently available funds, without having to figure out whether specific outstanding orders are represented in the available funds amount. One drawback of the encumbering process is that it may not take into account a vendor's pricing discounts. This means that the actual invoice amount will come out lower than the encumbered amount and the residual funds get released back into the account for use toward additional expenditures. It is a common mistake for managers to think a fund is exhausted only to discover several weeks or months later that it has available money in it again as encumbered funds are released.

It is important to realize that organizational culture may have a role in determining operational budgeting priorities with respect to goods and materials. Different organizations will have different perspectives on supply budgets and other "nonessential" costs. In some organizations, these are seen as ways to accomplish relatively painless savings during tight economic times and the budgets may be dramatically low. Other administrative viewpoints see the money spent on office supplies as a financial drop in the bucket relative to the overall budget and believe that it has more impact as a positive morale factor among staff. It is important to identify which philosophy is supported administratively when developing the framework for automatically approved requests. If supplies are supposed to be spent in a conservative fashion and everyone in the unit has expensive matching desk organizer sets, your fiscal responsibility and unit's budgetary need may be called into question. It is also important when delegating the routine responsibilities for buying supplies to periodically review the functional framework and process to make sure that the designated staff member is filling requests in a fair manner and not doling out supplies as a position of power over other staff in the unit.

Managing Student Worker Wages

In addition to buying commercial goods and services, academic library units often have designated funds for student worker wages. Large public libraries may have a similar situation based on hiring part-time or temporary hourly wage employees with limited benefits. Often the balance between using full-time staff and lower-compensated part-time/temporary employees is a function of organizational culture and administrative priorities. Retention and motivation issues can be especially challenging with this group of employees because their institutional investment is significantly less than for full-time staff. For a small library unit, such as instructional services or public relations, this may be a relatively small amount of money that is easily monitored and managed between two or three students. For a larger unit, such as shelving operations, that depends heavily on student or part-time labor, the amount of money and the time spent managing the budget will be more significant. Chapter 6 reviews issues associated with hiring student workers, but there are some aspects of student employment worth mentioning in the discussion of budgets as well. As nonbenefits positions, student worker and other hourly employee wages do not carry any hidden budgetary costs of retirement or health care benefits. Simply, the wage, multiplied by the number of hours worked, equals the budgeted amount.

Many academic institutions support Work Study programs that could affect a manager's use of the student wage budget. A Work Study student is one that has been awarded need-based federal or state funds to partially subsidize their working in an on-campus position to defray their educational costs. As the library's budget only makes up a portion, usually around 30 percent, of the student's wages, hiring Work Study students is an effective way to stretch one's overall student wage budget and get more students for the same cost. However, there are a couple of traps to be aware of when using this technique as part of the budget planning process. Work Study awards are made on an annual or semester-by-semester basis depending on the student's financial situation and available funds. Additionally, the awarded funds are a finite amount based on a formula and often cannot be used during intersession periods or non-enrolled summers. If a student's funds run out, the department will have to pick up the entire cost of the student's wages in order to keep him or her on the payroll. In most institutions, competition for Work Study students can be high. The students may be limited to working particular hours, thereby reducing the odds of attracting them to more repetitive or late-night tasks. In developing a plan or proposal for student wage needs, it is better to be conservative on Work Study expectations and account for essential coverage needs at regular pay rate levels. If a unit has been successful in recruiting Work Study students during the fall and spring semesters, the middle manager can look at hiring additional student workers for summer projects.

Unless you are the middle manager for a totally new unit or the organization has gone through recent budget restructuring, there will be past practices to review in understanding the student wage or temporary staff budget needs for your particular areas of responsibility and the library's convention for starting amounts and wage increases through longevity or merit. If documentation and justifications of past practice are not available and upper management does not offer specific objectives, compile a picture of the current practice from staff and try to set aside a full fiscal year to study the status quo in action. One important factor to recognize is that all student workers are not created equal. Student worker pay scales may have levels and flexibility to reflect the student worker's responsibilities. A student computer technician in a systems office may have a higher wage than a student worker who does basic photocopying and filing in administration. Additionally, there may be historical practice that students in one unit are paid more than students in others for the same work. This can create interdepartmental inequities and may be something to address with a peer middle manager or upper administrator once the details of the practice are verified.

Other Key Budget Concepts

Operational budgets are assigned and expended based on a fiscal year (FY), which may or may not coincide with a calendar, municipal, or academic year. Along with beginning and ending dates, the budget calendar will have deadlines for submitting specific purchases based on vendor and/or cost. Publicly-supported or publicly-assisted libraries usually have considerably more complex budget issues because of governmental regulations on how and when particular types of funds are used. Relatively large purchases, such as computers, office furniture, book drops, or library catalog systems may require significantly extra time to go through the purchasing process because the request will either have to go through a bid process to make sure the institution is getting the best possible price and product, or require extra paperwork to identify a particular source as being the only one to provide the required product/configuration. Many organizations go through a fiscal year closing process to reconcile all financial issues and prefer not to carryover a significant amount of operational funds into the next fiscal year, a restriction that may be either a local custom or a government mandate.

Depending on the organization's size and operational complexity, fiscal year closeout can be an intense period with frequent urgent fund inquiries and a flurry of eleventh hour expenditures or loss of funds. A fiscally conservative manager might prefer to keep funds in reserve until the end of the year "just in case something goes wrong." Unfortunately, there are several problems with this approach. As these funds sit unused, others in administration might perceive them as not needed by the unit and they could be suddenly reappropriated for other purposes. Additionally, last minute purchases create problems from an audit perspective. Some institutions must actually have received all purchased goods and services before the end of the fiscal year. For these organizations, a large number of last minute purchases will almost guarantee problems because staff will not be able to place all of the orders instantaneously and inevitably something will be backordered or delayed. This also can leave hard feelings with the financial staff who are placing or receiving the orders, because they must accommodate a spike in their workload as they are trying to conduct other fiscal closing reconciliation activities. A much better approach is to expend funds steadily throughout the fiscal year with a structured plan that leaves more modest amounts for the unexpected and urgent needs.

One area that contributes to budget complexity is the defined fund type and source of the money. Funds that come from a particular source of revenue may include significant restrictions in how the funds are used by the institution. Particular donors may only want books purchased that are noteworthy or support their personal area of interest. In academic institutions, faculty research monies may be dedicated toward purchasing material in a particular research discipline. Public funds allocated by state or local government may have limitations on use, such as stipulations that it can only be used on in-state professional development travel or restrictions regarding use on facilities-related expenses. Funds not committed to a particular purchase or operational support are generally referred to as discretionary or below-the-line funds and are generally utilized by library directors or their designates for special projects, collection enhancements, or unexpected cost overruns.

Another important concept to understand in organization financial basics is one-time versus recurring money. One-time money pertains to revenue or expenses that occur in a lump sum at a single time. An example of one-time revenue would be a single gift from a donor or allotment from a grant, whereas a one-time expense might be the purchase of a single paper-based book or stand-alone CD-ROM. This contrasts with recurring money, which is required for ongoing, repeated expenses, usually on an annual basis. Examples of recurring money are endowments that generate revenue based on the interest from an invested base amount, legislative-based allotments for salaries, or funds provided over a period of several years as mandated by a legal contract. Obvious examples of recurring expenses are staff salaries and journal or electronic database subscriptions. The majority of headaches associated with balancing organizational budgets are related to recurring costs. Even though the funds are recurring based on the source, the actual amounts may be subject to change. A primary example of this is serials inflation, where the recurring expenses have risen dramatically, versus the possible drop in recurring funding based on legislative directives or lower interest rates generating less interest revenue from an endowment.

Although most funds can be clearly defined as one-time or recurring, some will fall into a gray area and may have characteristics of both. One example of this is the purchase of an expensive set of books where revised or added volumes are offered every five to ten years. Some libraries might treat this as a recurring expense where during the non-purchase years the money can be spent like one-time funds. Other institutions might choose to treat it as a one-time expense and for a one-year period, when purchasing the books, reallocate some money from other discretionary funds. Another gray area is the desktop computer. Originally, treated as one-time expense by many libraries, Internet and office software technological advances now dictate replacing obsolete equipment every few years. Many institutions have developed recurring allocations that support a computer infrastructure replacement cycle. Another area that crosses the boundary between one-time and recurring money are programmatic enhancements. Most startup projects will require one-time start-up money, but most also need recurring funds for subsequent maintenance of the service.

Another type of funding that is used in organizations is based on salary savings. This is a term often used to describe the availability of funds that are created by not immediately filling a vacant position. Most libraries receive salary funding in an annual amount based on a certain allotted number of full-time and part-time positions. This amount is actually greater than the base salary because it includes the costs associated with employer's contribution to social security, health care, and retirement benefits. This is usually a formula that will be specific to an individual institution. Suppose a librarian leaves a position that normally costs the library $36,000 per year ($3,000 per month) and it is two months before the position is filled again. The library has freed up $6,000 in available one-time funds that can be reallocated to other needs. Sometimes referred to as *salary savings*, this can be a significant amount in larger library organizations. To a limited degree, larger libraries can have a feel for how much money will be available from salary savings each year and plan it into the budget. However, it is important to focus these savings on enhancements rather than use them to fund essential services because the amount of available funds can fluctuate. In economic downturns, when fewer jobs are available, even unhappy employees are less likely to leave current stable positions. Reduced turnover means less opportunity for salary savings to be generated. Also, if an academic institution decides to pull money back into the main coffers, salary savings are highly visible "free" money. It is a similar concept that supports the practice of providing raises by the elimination of positions. As with most budget and personnel tradeoffs, there is a point where an institution can become too stringent in creating salary savings and morale suffers because others feel overloaded with work.

Another revenue that figures into library budgets comes from fund-raising activities. Often these types of activities are routed through a Friends of the Library group of community supporters. They may include public events, such as a spaghetti supper, silent auctions, or book sales. In some libraries, these funds are a significant part of the main acquisitions or operating budget and a significant amount of staff time and energies must be spent nurturing the collaboration with the Friends group and helping out at the events. In other libraries, the monies may have less overall organizational impact and may be routed into a particular area, such as a rare books collection or dedication of an updated children's room decor. Learning the role of fundraising and the relationship with the local Friends of the Library group is part of adapting to an individual library's financial situation.

The last type of revenue discussed in this section is more common to academic libraries and nonprofit organizations than commercial ventures. This money comes in through endowments. Endowments create operational funds by investing a designated amount of money. Based on an institutional formula, the interest that is generated from investment can be used for specific expenses. Sometimes the funds may be targeted to a specific library purpose, such as enhancing a special collection of resources or supporting overhead expenses for a particular service. The endowment may also be established as a professorship or chair to supplement the salary, professional travel, or research expenses for a librarian faculty member and is generally tied to a particular position or awarded annually.

Organizational Culture

Once one has identified relevant budgets and gained an understanding of how funding comes into the library, it is important to understand the traditional budgetary practices and cultural philosophy of the institution. Some institutions routinely overspend a particular type of account as a political tool to identify where additional resources are needed. Others hold rigid expectations that one will come in under budget and to do otherwise is poor management. Regardless of whether overspending is anticipated or frowned upon, one wants to expend funds appropriate to the culture. Many administrations review funds annually and see unspent monies as available for reallocation to other uses. More than any other area of the library operation, budgetary allocations rely on historical data and justification of an identifiable need.

As mentioned earlier in the context of office supplies, it is important to understand how administration views different parts of the budget. This includes how the various budget components are prioritized and funding issues relevant to strategic initiatives of the organization. For example, a library with a significant student fee budgetary contribution would be more likely to emphasize allocations that support student users. One that is funded heavily from departmental allocations may focus on providing enhanced services to faculty members.

There are several ways to build an understanding of the institution's budget and budgetary culture. One initial way is to ask questions of the specific paperwork process, review spreadsheets that are available for review, and simply listen carefully anytime budget issues are discussed. Although this is a slow method to learn, one is less likely to stumble across a figurative land mine, disguised as someone's simmering irritation toward a particular administrative decision. If there is an established rapport with an upper administrator, sometimes an immediate supervisor, one can be more engaged and ask questions about the budgetary makeup and how decisions are reached. During the learning process, it is important not to back any administrator into a corner to defending administrative budget decisions. Often these decisions are made with an eye to the entire budget, with future planning and further-reaching implications, rather than within the knowledge base of the middle manager.

Chapter Summary

More than any other area of management, budgeting practices will vary from institution to institution. You can learn the basic concepts through reading, but learning the expectations, local jargon, and cultural practices are the real keys to being successful in these responsibilities. Identify those people who do understand the system and ask them to share their knowledge of the organization's budget structure. If math problems and using spreadsheets are not your strength, identify someone in your unit who is talented in this area. Then, reallocate responsibilities and empower the staff member to do the actual number crunching and provide you with understandable summaries.

To Learn More

Published by the American Library Association, *Basic Budget Practices for Librarians* was revised in the mid-1990s and provides a good overview to general types of budgets and working with revenues and expenditures. The author has packed a lot of content into 150 pages and written it toward the perspective of the practicing librarian, as opposed to a novice. Though many of the examples and practice experiences are directed toward the public library environment, most are general enough that the process is transferable to other kinds of libraries.[1]

To get an introductory understanding of organizational budgets, Terry Dickey's book, *The Basics of Budgeting*, is a quick way to bring yourself up to speed on budget terminology and how to think about budget issues.[2]

Another book by G. Stevenson Smith goes into significantly more detail on accounting practices and introduces some of the special concerns libraries face as not-for-profit organizations. Less relevant to the immediate needs of the middle manager, it is a good informational source for understanding the issues faced by business operations staff and upper administrators. The text includes chapters that explain accounting practices for capitol campaigns and large projects, such as a major renovation or construction of a new facility.[3]

Depending on individual managerial responsibilities and library culture, external fund raising may contribute a significant part of the library budget. For the fund raising newcomer, Steele and Elder offer a straightforward guidebook to understanding this aspect of fiscal activities.[4]

No matter how much one reads to learn about budgeting and accounting practices, most frontline librarians have limited opportunity to acquire experience in budget management. The nearest thing to budget management encountered by frontline librarians might be purchasing books from particular allotted funds. The middle manager's role in budgeting is considerably more expanded, both as one who oversees multiple funds and one who is more involved in the actual budget-planning process. As shown in the exercises at the end of the chapter, a lot of organizational budgeting is similar to old-fashioned mathematical word problems. If the previously mentioned works awaken a personal fascination for more study into the budgeting process, the *Complete Budgeting Workbook and Guide* offers 600 pages of financial knowledge, allowing an opportunity to develop specialized skills in this managerial area.[5]

Last but not least, even as they understand budgetary issues more comprehensively, new middle managers may be faced with an ongoing situation of an inadequate budget to meet the operational objectives. To address this, *When Your Library Budget Is Almost Zero* by Lesley S. J. Farmer offers a light-hearted yet valuable book of ideas and approaches to meet service needs within an inadequate budget. Though many of the specific examples seem more relevant to public libraries, the book encourages one to develop a more positive and creative attitude about a limited budget.[6]

Case Study: Preparing a Special Project Budget

Sam – Kate's supervisor, associate director

Kate – internal middle-manager promotion (one year ago), access services head

Ellen – senior circulation staff member (15 years in library); supervises unit student workers on various operational tasks

Scott – computer systems support (CSS) department head

Setting: Sam and Kate are discussing the budget for a proposed project to convert the main circulating collection from OCR (object character recognition) labels to barcode labels using a label-printing system to print a barcode label that matches the number on the OCR label. Circulation has been working on the project for the past seven months by putting barcode labels on books that come in to be discharged.

After handing Sam a copy of the proposed budget (shown below) and a two-page justification/overview, Kate begins summarizing how she developed the numbers. "Let me give you a brief rundown on the background to the numbers. In calculating the funds for the label and ribbon supplies, one of the experienced staff in technical services thinks that of the 2.5 million volumes in the stacks, about 2 million actually have OCR labels. We already have a back stock of 1 million blank labels. Ellen did a benchmark with the circulation student workers to find out how long it would take them to do a typical shelf of books. Given the one-year timeline and these other factors, I calculated that we will need to run at least nine simultaneous stations, preferably ten, 9 A.M.–6 P.M. Monday through Friday. Scott confirmed that we have enough old computers in storage but that we will need to buy printers, computer carts, and dedicated book trucks for each station.

"At this time, Scott has identified three nonallocated OCR scanning wands, six printers, and as many outdated PCs as are needed to set up stations in the stacks. Up to six desktop OCR scanning wands and one barcode printer could be reallocated to the project from circulation staff desktop computers. Others may be available from staff in other units. We will have to buy a few additional label printers and are not sure exactly what our replacement schedule on the printers will have to be since we have not actually worn one of these printers out yet."

"Remind me again, how we are going to do the staffing," Sam asks.

Consulting her notes, Kate replies. "Ellen agrees that the actual labor of converting an item from an OCR label to a barcode label is appropriate to student worker level tasks. We estimate that an equivalent of 10 students working full time for one year can complete the project. Since student employees do not work full time, a more reasonable figure is 30 students working a total of approximately 400 hours per week. Current operations staffing levels do not have the room to absorb this degree of additional supervisory responsibility, so an additional staff position will need to be identified for temporary hire or reassignment to the project. Possible solutions would be to expand two half-time positions into full-time for the duration of the project, hire a temporary staff member, or identify staff that could be spared for half-time/full-time reassignment to the project. To hire and supervise student workers, the position would have to be a Level 2 or higher on the library staff career ladder or a staff assistant or higher (based on the university's administrative support titles)."

As Sam ponders what Kate has said he looks at the proposal and asks, "What about books used in the library and left on tables?"

"It is mentioned there at the bottom of page 1. In addition to actually working through the stacks areas, we will need to more aggressively barcode those items currently in use during the project so they are not missed during the stacks sweep. Any item coming into the library will be barcoded, even during the heavier periods at the end of the semester. Any item picked up at a table (browsed) will be converted to a barcode before being reshelved. Any item discharged will be barcoded. Any item pulled for interlibrary loan purposes will be converted to a barcode before it is returned to the stacks."

"Looks like you have covered all the bases and this is a reasonable amount. Send a copy to the director's administrative assistant and have her put it on the agenda for the associate director's meeting near the start of the meeting. Can you be there next Wednesday at 2 P.M.?"

"Sure, I'll be ready."

Proposed Budget Needs For Barcode Conversion Project

The following identifies the necessary resource needs for the project and estimated costs:

9–10 portable printing workstations . . . . *equipment available*
    (Possibly purchase a few barcode printers at $500 each) *$1,500*
Student worker salaries *$100,500*
Temporary student supervisor for 1 year *$20,000*
    (Based on salary for Level II library staff or staff assistant)
Dedicated carts/book trucks *$4,000*
    (Mobile Computer Workstation $200 each)
    (Book trucks $200 each—37" wide to accommodate an entire shelf at a time)
Printer stock for barcode labels (1 million) *$13,000*
    (1000 labels/role, $13/role)
    (Ribbons ($10 each) are an unknown cost because we haven't worn one out yet)

Glitch buffer (unforeseen disaster) *$16,000*
  TOTAL MAXIMUM COST........................ *$155,000*

Case Study Observations

- Expect the unexpected: Some people estimate each line item high, others add in a glitch or SNAFU amount. Whatever planning technique is used, every detail cannot be foreseen.
- Don't forget staffing: Even if a task can be done by student workers, someone must coordinate those student workers. Sometimes this can be incorporated into current staffing, sometimes it cannot.
- Get input: Several people contributed information to the proposal that impacted the proposed budget. Do not assume everything for a project has to be bought new.

Thought and Discussion Exercises

What Do You Do Now?

1. You have 12 student workers in your unit who each work 10 hours per week for 48 weeks each year and earn $5.15 per hour. The composition is as follows: three currently in their first semester, three in their second semester, two finished their second year in the unit, one finishing her third year in the unit, and two leaving (to be replaced next semester). You have been told that the library is adopting a new wage schedule for the student workers. All student workers will now start at $5.25 per hour. After one full semester, they will get a $.25 increase. Each year they continue to work after that, they will get an additional $.15 increase. Your administrator has asked for an estimate of the increased cost to bring all of the student workers to their appropriate wage levels at the start of the next fiscal year. What do you do now? (Hint: Figure out the amount of increase for each student based on the amount of time and multiply that by the number of hours to be worked for each student.)

2. You have been told that all supply budgets are being cut by 20 percent. Assume that in the past, there have been no restrictions or guidelines on office supply orders; the unit bought anything anyone wanted, and looking around you see a lot of different supplies and some fairly frivolous purchases. You obviously need to create some guidelines or framework for ordering supplies during the forthcoming

year. What do you do now? (Hint: Bulk orders of a single item usually result in reduced per item cost.)

3. Spreadsheet software is often used to maintain budgets. If you are not familiar with this type of software product, you need to learn it. Most software comes with tutorials. Third party publishers also produce many effective books that use types of budgets as examples. As an exercise, develop a hypothetical student wage tracking worksheet that captures the amount spent each pay period with end-of-the-semester summaries. What do you do now?

Notes

1. Richard S. Rounds, *Basic Budgeting Practices for Librarians*, 2nd ed. (Chicago: American Library Association, 1994).

2. Terry Dickey, *The Basics of Budgeting* (Menlo Park, CA: Crisp Publications, Inc., 1992).

3. G. Stevenson Smith, *Accounting for Libraries and Other Not-for-Profit Organizations*, 2nd ed. (Chicago: American Library Association, 1999).

4. Victoria Steele and Stephen D. Elder, *Becoming a Fundraiser: The Principles and Practice of Library Development*, 2nd ed. (Chicago: American Library Association, 2000).

5. Jae K. Shim and Joel G. Siegel, *Complete Budgeting Workbook and Guide* (New York: New York Institute of Finance, 1994).

6. Lesley S. J. Farmer, *When Your Library Budget Is Almost Zero* (Englewood, CO: Libraries Unlimited, 1993).

CHAPTER 6

Learning the Legal Basics

This chapter is not meant to serve as legal counsel or turn one into a lawyer; rather it is meant to introduce new managers to an understanding of some of the terminology and issues associated with the world of personnel management relations and human resources. As with budgeting, this is an area often overlooked as one comes into a new managerial role. Even though managers may have come into a position having had previous supervisory responsibilities for a couple of employees, this is very different from being responsible for human resource issues in an entire department or unit. It is also an area that often presents itself as driven by policy with a right or wrong answer to any question. However, some of these issues have shades of gray based on interpretation, customary practice, and recognizing employees as individuals. The challenge for new managers is to understand what is acceptable and what is not and where a definite policy exists that must be followed.

One set of key resources that new managers need to develop early is at least a passing familiarity with the official policy and procedure manuals for their institution, both at the library and the academy levels. Though few middle managers will have the time or luxury to read them through from title page to appendix, it is worth the time to become familiar with the structure and organization of the documents. Many of these are now found on institutional Web sites rather than a row of dusty binders in administrative offices. If in doubt or if a decision is challenged, these documents are the core position to fall back on in defending a decision. Often difficult to read, as they present concepts in broad or legal terms, these documents define the institution's position on human resources issues such as use of annual leave accruals, sick leave, wages, and employee classification. At some libraries, staff members belong to a professional union with special contractual or collective bargaining agreements. Staff at other libraries, especially public library settings, may fall under civil service regulations. These will add significant complexity to the managerial environment and may have a direct impact on the material covered in Chapters 10 and 11 about employee evaluation and discipline procedures. Similarly, in an academic setting, professional librarians may be classified as faculty or classified staff. In the case of faculty, academic freedom and possible publication/service expectations must be taken into account in addition to normal work-for-hire issues. All of these parameters will have an impact on how one is supposed to manage the employee. Additionally, even as each institution will have different operational approaches to human resource issues, there is a body of common practice based on federal or state labor codes that crosses institutional boundaries.

One thing new managers of staff at any institution should expect is to have their life become ruled by forms. Even business operations that have embraced the paperless environment are not free from forms. Their forms will be in electronic format, which can sometimes be even more exasperating to use because the spacing will not work out correctly or insufficient comment areas are provided. Additionally, at all but the most sophisticated institutions that have adopted signature encryption systems, there will still be a number of forms that must have original signatures. These are usually kept in the appropriate personnel or business office files.

Basic Position Descriptions

Behind every position in a library will be a set of data that defines the position and the person in it. The data will include information about the job responsibilities associated with the position, the wage currently earned by the holder, the benefits associated with the position, and the rank of the position within the organizational hierarchy. In many institutions, background checks are often required for positions that involve handling cash transactions or driving library vehicles, as for bookmobile services or book-drop runs. Often position descriptions will be completed on a consistent form and filed in paper and electronically. When a manager is posting a vacant position or even completing an annual performance evaluation, he or she will be asked to review and update the position description to make sure it is current to the responsibilities of the job.

A position may be full-time, 40 hours per week, or part-time, as defined by a percentage of full-time effort (50 percent equals 20 hours per week). Additionally, a position may be based on an hourly wage or a monthly salary and exempt or non-exempt status. This status refers to whether a position is subject to the rules in the Fair Labor Standards Act of 1938, which addresses issues of overtime compensation, minimum wage, and the employment of minors. Exempt employees will be salaried and are not subject to the same time-and-a-half overtime rules after working 40 hours per week as are non-exempt, hourly wage positions. Used for managers, professionals, and employees with administrative responsibilities, an exempt, salaried position usually will not complete a daily time sheet and will have the same amount on their paycheck even if they work 45 hours one week and 35 another. A non-exempt, hourly employee must track specific work hours, account for any hours less than 40 with approved or unpaid leave, and receive either additional pay or compensatory leave for working over 40 hours during any given pay week. Excessive overtime pay can wreak havoc on budgets and is often limited to special situations requiring preapproval from an administrator. Half-time employees may or may not be eligible for compensatory overtime accrual depending on the state and local institutional rules.

Another key element of a position is what benefits are associated with it. Benefits fall into three basic categories: paid by employer, paid by employee, or paid by both. With some benefits, such as health insurance, it is easy to assign an associated dollar amount on a pay stub and see who is paying for it. Other benefits, such as annual and sick leave are more invisible benefits that are factored into the regular wage and do not usually appear on a paycheck with a dollar amount. Depending on the institution, the benefits for a specific position may be defined by the library, the academic institution, or the government and may vary for different types of positions and amount of effort. Private colleges and universities have the most flexibility in defining what benefits are provided and how they are financed. Public academic libraries or community libraries are usually constrained by state law or municipal rules to offer benefits in a specific manner and may have less room than private libraries for negotiation on relocation reimbursement or leave accrual rates. There are several different types of benefits that may be associated with a position. The most obvious are accrued vacation and sick leave, health and dental medical coverage, employer provided and optional life insurance, and basic retirement programs. Additionally, there may be a myriad of other benefits available to an employee on an optional basis. These can include academic tuition waivers, financial support and/or release time for continuing education, tax-saver options for additional medical needs or child care, long-term and short-term disability coverage, elder-care coverage for the employee or the employee's parents, or spousal job assistance benefits. As a manager, you must become familiar with the available benefits, even those you personally do not choose to activate, in order to be knowledgeable when interviewing potential future employees. Even as one does not have to be a procedural expert on all of the benefit options, one needs to know where to go or who to call in order to get expert information.

Another element of the position description is the rank or official title of the position and whether it is part of a career ladder. Career ladder positions offer employees an opportunity to move up through a series of titles with increasing levels of responsibility and wage compensation. However, they can also offer workflow challenges for managers. A career ladder position will be described by a set of generic descriptors that define what an employee at that level can and cannot do. Often an entry-level classified staff position, that is lower on the career ladder, cannot supervise other employees (especially in terms of signing off on documents) and emphasis is on the training of the employee rather than an expectation of demonstrated judgment and decision making. Some career ladders will allow employees to move up a ladder based on their own skill and knowledge growth. Other career ladders can define the growth in terms of movement into a particular position in the unit based on what the position holder is supposed to be able to do. Usually, in order to move to the next level on a career ladder an employee will have to meet a time-in-rank eligibility requirement and reflect skill and knowledge advancement based on a series of benchmarks. Understanding career ladders and their associated requirements and procedures for advancement can be one of the most complex things a new manager will have to master. Some positions, especially administrative and office support positions, may not be based on a career ladder. The only way employees in these positions increase their earnings will be through organizational merit or cost-of-living increases, across-the-board pay scale adjustments, or case-by-case negotiated increases. The different types of positions and opportunities associated with them can cause friction between staff.

Filling a Vacant Position

Gaining an understanding of the position description is essential to filling a vacant position. Depending on the size of one's institution and the layers of bureaucracy, this is often not a trivial task. There will likely be different procedures for filling vacancies at different levels of the organizations. Hiring managers will need to understand these differences and learn what they are expected to do. In some institutions, there will be staff support out of a central library business or personnel office that will handle a lot of the paperwork, possibly even checking references. In other libraries, more of the clerical work will fall on the hiring supervisor or chair of the search committee. It often seems that hiring processes are constantly being tweaked or adjusted per staffing support, the move to an electronic world, and specific institutional directives. When a new manager learns an employee is leaving, it is important to find and talk with a peer manager who has recently filled a similar type of position. Even experienced managers and administrators, especially if their unit has low turnover, may not be familiar with the current procedures. With the increased attention to hiring a diverse workforce that is occurring at many institutions, managers need to make sure they understand the current expectations, policies, and procedures of filling a position.

Librarian positions in academic settings, especially if they also have faculty status or are at a public institution, are usually posted as a regional or national search. Though some larger public libraries may recruit librarians at a national level, many fill positions based on a regional pool. This usually means advertising on targeted listservs, in the jobs section of trade publications, or even through direct contact to solicit interest from a librarian at another institution. The selection process will usually involve an actual search or recommendation committee, rather than just the hiring supervisor. Scheduling and coordinating the interviews, which often last a full day and have the candidate meet with many different people and make a presentation, can be difficult and lead to delays. Even after a decision is reached by the committee or library director, it may still need to be approved at a university administration or city governance level. It is not uncommon at many institutions for several weeks or even months to pass before a replacement is hired.

The process to hire nonlibrarian staff is usually a simpler one in terms of coordination but may be more complicated in terms of paperwork and process. The role of the hiring supervisor is expanded and the only committee that comes into the picture will be if the manager wants to bring in the person who previously held the position or a colleague who will work closely with the candidate to gauge whether there could be compatibility issues. Unlike professional librarians, who expect a certain amount of vagueness in job postings, staff postings must usually be very specific about the tasks and expectations of the position. They must detail any physical requirements and night/weekend/overtime expectations associated with the position. For example, if an area of shelving is not wide enough for wheelchairs and the person will need to work in the area, the posting should indicate that the employee must be able to walk and stand between shelves of books. Another issue that has come up in the past few years is the presence of allergens in the workplace. It may be appropriate to state up front that the employee will be required to handle books that may be contaminated with dust, dust mites, or microscopic mold spores. Hopefully, putting this information in the posting and possibly touching on it in the interview process will lead applicants to self-select themselves out of the candidate pool if there could be a problem and thus avoid obvious bad hires.

Fairness in hiring is a major workplace legal issue. Often the hiring manager must document what criteria were used to evaluate the candidates and how/why they were ranked the way they were. Some institutions may require that any criteria used to rank the appropriateness of the candidate for the position must have been explicitly stated in the position posting. For example if the posting does not indicate a preference for the candidate to be able to use computer office software, then the hiring manager cannot use it as a selection criteria or discuss it in the interview process. Similarly, there are many issues that legally cannot be addressed during an interview at all, or be taken into account when deciding which candidate will receive the offer. In addition to the obvious recognized discrimination issues involving race, ethnicity, religion, age, or gender, there are subtler lifestyle issues related to marital status that also cannot be taken into account during the hiring process. In addition to not asking illegal questions outright, part of a manager's role is to protect a candidate from having an inadvertent comment used against them. Even though most professionals realize they should not mention personal issues during an interview, many less experienced or less educated candidates may not be aware of their rights to fair consideration. For example, a manager should not react or engage in any follow-up discussion if candidates mention that they have small children. A good technique is a vague throat clearing or "how nice" and immediately moving on to the next interview issue. The manager can verify that all candidates understand the expected work schedule and ask if that will be a problem. But once candidates say that it will not be a problem, which is what usually occurs, the manager should move on to the next question. The manager absolutely cannot get into discussions of what kind of child-care arrangements have been made or belabor attendance issues more than for any other candidate because of this knowledge. The same is true for any health or physical issues. So long as candidates feel they can meet the requirements listed in the job posting, it is not for the manager to judge based on a visual assessment.

In the same way that managers are held accountable on these issues when they are actually the hiring supervisor, so must they hold their staff accountable for other unit hires. A staff member may want to only hire male candidates to work late at night because of what is perceived as safety issues. It is the manager's responsibility to explain that this is not legal and that if a female candidate applies for the position knowing it involves working late, and has better overall qualifications, then this is the person to hire. New managers should talk with hiring supervisors about their recommendations to make sure that appropriate qualifications are being considered. It might even be appropriate for managers, or their seconds, to briefly drop in on every interview for a new unit staff member. This allows managers to be seen as connected to the unit without being a hovering micromanager. It also gives managers an opportunity to go over their vision, philosophy, or unit management style and meet the person so that they are not in the dark when the hiring supervisor delivers a recommendation. This can be especially important if the unit is still going through change adjustment (discussed in Chapter 8). Once employees are hired, there can be more opportunity to get to know them but managers will already have formed a connection with them from the first day.

Daily Staff Management

Even when dealing with staff members who have been in positions for a long time, there are inevitable issues that the manager is expected to address. With these issues, it is important for the manager to develop an understanding with the supervisors in the unit about what is appropriate for them to make decisions on and what absolutely must be brought to the manager's attention. It can sometimes be difficult for new managers and their staff to find the balance between constantly interrupting managers with routine operational concerns and items that managers or administrators truly need to be aware of and address. Usually this will be an iterative process that is dependent on individual personalities. Inevitably something will explode, with the manager getting caught unaware. It is important not to overreact when this happens but instead to use it as a constructive example once the situation is resolved. Managers will have similar filtering challenges when communicating information to their administrators.

Time Sheets

It is the author's opinion that one of the true curses of management is the time sheet process. Every institution will have an organizational culture associated with defining how accurate and precise time sheets need to be. Some institutions may actually have a time clock that employees will have to punch as they go in and out of the workplace. Similarly, all types of leave must be coded appropriately and taken through a signature or approval process. Some types of leave, such as emergency leave for the death of an immediate family member, may require a signature from the library director. Holidays will be especially problematic for two reasons. Time sheets are usually due early around holidays with employees trying to predict the time they will be working, which is always a difficult bet to hedge. Also, staff who work irregular schedules of nights or weekends may have to make special adjustments to match their schedules, the needed coverage, and the awarded holiday hours. If a library is open on a holiday, there may be additional overtime or compensatory time that has to be documented, justified, and approved. In addition to being a complex maze of details and regulations, time sheets will have an institutional culture around them. Whether they are supposed to be absolutely precise or represent the basic work schedule is something a manager will need to learn. The tricky part is that verbal instructions may not match actions. For example, suppose the official message is that time sheets are supposed to reflect the exact time worked down to the minute, but time sheets are due to an accounting office one to two days before the end of the pay period for processing. If an employee gets in 15 minutes later than predicted and stayed an extra 15 minutes at the end of the day to make it up, does the employee have to go through the process of having the time sheet pulled and changes made at the last minute. In theory yes; however, after this has happened for the tenth time during a single month, accounting office staff may start getting just a tad bit snippy and start making snide comments about one needing to get staff under control. In truth the situation is a judgment call that needs to take into account the specific employee and time adjusted to determine whether there is an underlying performance issue. It requires the overall maturity to understand if an exception to the letter of the rule is appropriate. This is discussed in more detail in Chapter 10.

Health Issues

Another major area that managers should be concerned about from a legal perspective centers around workplace health and injury issues. Sick Leave accrual, Family Medical Leave Act (FMLA), workplace injuries, and workers' compensation claims are all issues that can have a significant impact for managers. Unlike vacation leave, absences involving employee health issues are much less controllable and must be handled carefully, especially if the health situation is one with long-term impact or one that was caused as a result of an injury in the work environment. The key thing for new managers to realize when confronted with these issues is that it is *not* their responsibility to make a judgment, validate, or render a decision on the actual health issue. Their role is to follow designated institutional procedures for reporting the concern and subsequently address appropriate unit impact issues.

This usually means having made sure that employees were provided with appropriate forms and given time away from their desks to consult with benefits experts.

In the library environment it is important to be aware of computer ergonomic and repetitive stress injury issues in addition to standard safety issues of slippery-when-wet floors or unstable stepstools. Because of the costly litigation in recent years, most organizations, either within the library itself or within the city or university human resources umbrella, have designated a position for an advisor on ergonomic/health/safety workplace issues. This individual can train employees and managers on the correct way to bend and lift when emptying book drops or reshelving books and advise on the correct configurations for computer workstations. It is important to make a reasonable effort to create a comfortable work environment and encourage employees to use breaks appropriately. Managers may need to be especially attentive if employees in a particular unit spend a significant amount of their workday at their desk using a mouse or a computer keyboard: It is important to make sure stretching and physical breaks are taken away from their desk and any reports of soreness or injury taken with serious concern.

One issue managers need to be sensitive to is the possibility of an employee having to produce evidence of having a long-term or serious illness or of having been injured on the job. Although you would not want to report every little paper cut or every tension headache, it is much better to have been conservative and referred too many employees to get FMLA packets for their doctor's consideration or to have reported an injury that does not have lasting consequences than to have an employee later accuse you of having denied them a medically-related benefit. It is especially important to be aware of offhand remarks that could hide on-the-job injuries. Suppose you are walking past an open work area a few days after a big collection shifting project and overhear an employee remark to a coworker that his back is really bothering him. It is important to immediately but casually follow-up with the employee as to when his back started hurting and whether or not he has visited a doctor about it. It may very well be that his back is hurting because he had company and slept on the floor at home the night before, in which case you do nothing. However, it might also be that he got a muscle strain on the job the previous week and he has just seen his doctor, who has recommended a reduction in his physical responsibilities over the next few days and ongoing rehabilitation. The employee may not be aware of how this is supposed to be communicated to you officially. As a manager, it is your responsibility to know the procedure. In the latter scenario, you need to make sure he is promptly provided with the appropriate contacts and paperwork for him to connect with human resources representatives who can make sure his legal rights are protected regarding timely notification of the claim and compensation for any lost work time.

The Family Medical Leave Act (often abbreviated FMLA and pronounced fem-lu) is a federal law protecting an employee's job for a period of time in the event of absence due to having a child or suffering from an extended illness. Most full-time employees are eligible for FMLA coverage. FMLA is most valuable for those employees who do not have sufficient accrued sick leave for the duration of the illness. Though FMLA does not equate to paid leave for the employee, it does prevent the employee from being charged for or dropped from standard benefits, including health care, during an ongoing absence that lasts longer than one month. One myth about FMLA is that once an employee files a health issue as FMLA, you are stuck with them forever. Because FMLA coverage expires after 12 weeks per year, this is not true. After FMLA coverage expires, if an employee continues to have problems that remove him or her from the workplace with no apparent future resolution, the employee can be terminated. Typically, libraries are compassionate places to work and invest in employees to such a degree that they do not wait with bated breath to terminate an employee whose FMLA coverage has run out. However, situations can occur where employees use up their FMLA coverage but their health has hit a long-term plateau. In a case such as this, the unit cannot afford to continue to have the position vacant, and termination is the only realistic operational option. This situation is more likely to occur when the employee already has a history of marginal performance or during budget-tightening periods when fewer employees are being asked to do more and the individual load on each employee has a more extensive overall impact.

In a simple world, employees who are sick take sick leave and are not in the workplace. When they feel better, they come back to work. Unfortunately, this is not a simple world and many people are working sick. Typical symptoms include sinus congestion, sneezing, coughing, headaches, muscle/joint aches, low-grade fever, and so forth. Employees may have different reasons for coming in while they are sick and new managers need to address this situation carefully. Unfortunately, many employees may have insufficient leave accrued and must choose between working sick and not being paid. Given this scenario, most managers in libraries will take the more humane approach and tolerate temporary reductions in productivity rather than send the employee home. It may be appropriate to encourage an employee with a cold or other virus to modify the workflow in a way that minimizes exposure and transmittal to coworkers or patrons. Another reason employees may come to work sick is that they have invested a significant part of their identity into their jobs and may want to perceive themselves as essential. This is a more difficult scenario to address. Some techniques a new manager might try would be to explain to employees that they would actually end up being more productive by taking a couple of days to rest and get better than to extend the illness with more days at reduced productivity. One may need to explicitly tell employees that it is all right for them to be out. Also, the manager can arrange for cross training within the unit and officially assign individuals to serve as backups for employees who are out. However, if the employee still insists on coming in and is not totally incapacitated, this is a situation that the manager must accept. Managers, especially newer ones, tend to fall into this category themselves and may even have been chosen for the position because of their reliability.

At the other end of the spectrum, some new managers may be taken aback at how regularly some employees use up their sick leave. There is a natural tendency to want to question the chronically sick employee who uses up the sick leave allotment as soon as it is accrued. This can be also be tempting to do when an employee calls in sick and uses sick leave, but does not sound sick or is then spotted a few hours later in public. However, questioning an employee about their health is something managers and supervisors should never do unless explicitly stated in an institutional policy manual and done in an equitable fashion across an entire unit. As an example, the employee may have had a temporary impediment, such as getting her eyes dilated, that enabled her to do other things but not her work tasks at a computer. Requiring proof or taking an employee to task for not scheduling the procedure in a manner that would be more convenient for the unit could be categorized as a form of harassment. Today's laws on employee privacy on health-related issues are stronger than ever, and until managers can document significant impact on the overall operation of the unit, they should avoid bringing up medically related absenteeism in any but the most general terms.

Privacy

Employee privacy is extremely critical in an organization and must be a consideration during all managerial interactions. There are different degrees of privacy that must be maintained. Depending on the situation, a manager can discuss a personnel issue with an administrator or human resources representative, a peer manager, or everyone. Knowing how to recognize with whom and in what situations privacy must be maintained is very important.

As one might guess from the previous section, employee health issues should be kept extremely private and only discussed with human resources personnel and senior administrators to make sure appropriate procedures are being followed. Only in rare circumstances is it the manager's position to announce a health condition to others in a unit or throughout the organization. This might occur when an employee has asked the manager to distribute the knowledge to help answer questions that make them uncomfortable. An example where it might be appropriate is that of an employee who has come back from cancer chemotherapy treatment that was kept fairly quiet during his absence. His changed appearance (hair and weight loss) will cause an inevitable reaction from his coworkers and rather than answer a lot of questions, the employee may ask the manager to explain why he has been out and remind his peers that encouraging comments are more welcome than morbidly curious questions.

Another issue that managers need to address carefully are those employees who have unacknowledged health concerns. Unless a health issue has an obvious and documented impact on an employee's performance, it should never be addressed at all by a manager or supervisor. Even when a medical condition is suspected, questioning should be put in a job-related context, such as exploring what might be contributing to the employee's performance difficulties. Managers and the staff they supervise should never suggest to the employee that there might be a medical reason underlying performance concerns. If an employee does confide privately about a medical or emotional condition, the manager should make sure the employee is aware of the resources that are available, but the manager should not share the knowledge with other non-administrative employees, including peer managers.

Another area of employee privacy that is important to maintain relates to performance issues. Even if one works in an institution with open records laws or public budgets, it is important that a manager never talk about the specifics of a particular performance review with anyone except the employee, manager witness, administrator, or human resources staff. Although one can discuss managerial concerns or conundrums with other managers, it is best to make sure this is done in a closed office environment and in case study or generic terms without identifying the specific employee. If one does feel the need to include a witness to a managerial interaction, it should always be another supervisor and absolutely not a peer to the employee being assessed. This issue is covered in more depth as part of Chapter 10.

Chapter Summary

There are many legal and official subtleties that one must master as a manager. For new managers, it is most important to focus on issues that have a direct impact on their operational areas and to know who among the senior managers or administrators can guide them during their first few years. If one's unit is primarily composed of long-term and stable staff members, you may not initially need assistance with interview and hiring processes. However, inevitably someone will leave and a vacancy will need to be filled. At that time it is quite helpful to have already identified the people who can help you and to have learned something of the local process. This will include determining if postings and applications are handled through paper or electronic means and what forms are used. New managers can build this knowledge by working with their own administrative supervisor, a managerial peer, a human resources representative, and experienced senior subordinates or by attending a workshop on the process offered at the institutional level. The most important thing to remember when dealing with employee personnel issues is to recognize the limitations in one's knowledge and experience and be willing to ask questions of the experts. This is not the time to apply the theory that forgiveness is easier obtained than permission, or to try to appear to know more than you do. Legal challenges are always messy and are sometimes unavoidable. Having made sure that basic procedures were followed, paperwork provided, appropriate confidentiality maintained, and events supported can make the difference between a resolvable situation and one that the institution has to address for years to come.

To Learn More

There are resources available to gain detailed understanding on many of the issues presented in this chapter. Some resources, such as *The Human Resources Glossary: A Complete Desk Reference for HR Professionals* by William R. Tracey, will give general definitions of terminology and overviews of legal milestones and key concepts.[1] Traditional library management textbooks, such as *Library and Information Center Management*, will give a good overview with relevant details to some of the issues presented in this chapter.[2] It is important to stay with texts that have been published or revised within the past five years or so as this information has changed dramatically with increasing emphasis on a diverse workforce and more legal challenges entering the work environment. Older works, such as *Library Personnel Administration* by Lowell A. Martin can provide a good background to issues, but should not be used to set current practice.[3] Other books that are more focused on a particular issue in the broader academic environment may also be quite useful for academic libraries. The *Jossey-Bass Academic Administrator's Guide to Hiring* is quite readable and goes into significant detail over some of the unique challenges of hiring, recruiting, interviewing, and retaining staff within the academic setting.[4] *The Academic*

Administrator and the Law: What Every Dean and Department Chair Needs to Know takes a little more concentration to read but provides a very complete perspective of some of the legal issues encountered in the academic environment. It includes issues that might impact student privacy issues as well.[5] The human resources textbooks presented in Chapter 7 will also include information about specific employee management issues. For those needing to learn more about ergonomic concerns, *Applied Ergonomics* and *Introduction to Ergonomics* are good examples of recently published, fairly readable texts on the topic. Directed toward a generic workplace, they go into considerable detail on various activities that might lead to ergonomic concerns in libraries.[6]

Case Study: Discussing the Candidates

> **Kate** – internal middle-manager promotion (two years ago), access services head (previously five years at Mid State Library doing library instruction/outreach)
> **Ellen** – senior circulation staff member, main library, reports to Kate
> **Mark** – interlibrary services (ILS) librarian
> **Maria** – senior staff member in ILS, reports to Mark
> **Dave** – staff member in circulation (six years in library, four years in circulation)
> **Annette** – senior staff member in reference department; 12 years in library, interacts heavily with access services staff on referrals and service desk training
> **Harriet, Deborah, Travis, and Ahmed** – candidates for access services administrative assistant opening, have interviewed during the past two weeks.
> **Setting:** meeting called by Kate to get input/discuss/evaluate candidates for the administrative assistant position

Kate opens the meeting by saying, "You have had a chance to meet with each of the four candidates to tell them about your particular unit support needs associated with the position and participate in the question and answer sessions. Even though everyone kept to the prescribed questions, I'm sure we all heard and noticed different things. I'd like to get some of your impressions. Anyone want to go first?"

Ellen jumps right in, "I *really* liked Deborah. She was so funny and easy to talk to and had a great sense of humor. She was telling some wild jokes that had all of us in stitches. I think she would get along great in the unit."

At this point Mark jumps in, "Deborah may have been a lot of fun but she really seemed clueless about what the job would require. I noticed when we asked her about using the various office software, she only has a little bit of experience with a word processing program and using e-mail, no spreadsheet or database knowledge. Also, it sounds like this is her first full-time job. I think we need someone who is more familiar with an office environment and knows how to work around red tape. Not to mention that I actually found some of Deborah's jokes to be in less than good taste. Personally, I liked Harriet the best. She has worked in an office before and had really good computer skills."

Dave adds his comments. "I found some of Deborah's male-bashing jokes and pregnancy stories offensive, too. I don't think she would be good for the unit. Harriet struck me as much calmer and definitely more professional."

Ellen responds, "Harriet was nice enough but I have concerns about her reliability. When we happened to both be in the restroom, she mentioned to me that she has two small children, one two years old and the other five years old, and her husband walked out 6 months ago. This means she is doing the single mom route and every time something happens with one of the kids that means they can't go to daycare, she won't be here."

Kate steps in firmly at this point. "Ellen, you know we cannot take that into consideration. I explained quite clearly to Harriet what our attendance and work schedule expectations were and she specifically told me she could meet them. The fact that she mentioned such personal things to you should not and cannot be discussed as part of our criteria or decision. Does anyone else want to offer anything substantive about Deborah or Harriet? Also, what about Travis or Ahmed?"

Annette enters the conversation. "I pretty much agree with Mark and Dave on Deborah, nice but no experience in an office environment at all. If this was an entry-level position with close supervision she might be fine, but as the unit administrative assistant, she would be expected to make judgment calls and I don't think she could do that. I really didn't get a clear read on Harriet. I know she has really good references and experience but she seemed nervous."

"I think she was nervous because she wants and needs the job so much," Maria offers.

"That could be." Annette continues. "I did have some problems with Travis and Ahmed though. If Travis had called me 'little lady' or 'honey' one more time, I would have slugged him. I noticed as I was doing the tour of the different service desks that he checked out every attractive woman that we passed. You know, the elevator eyes thing. On a couple he even tuned me out while he turned his head and watched them from behind, sort of whistling under his breath. I'm afraid this guy has absolutely no sense of what sexual harassment means."

Kate visibly winces at this report. "Did anyone else notice this type of behavior by Travis? He was a little folksy with me but nothing blatant or actually offensive."

Mark nods as he says, "I did. He commented on Maria's appearance and asked if she was 'available' and seemed really disappointed when I explained that she was happily married. Then, he followed up with some sort of comment about this looks like a great place to work because there would be a lot of opportunity to . . . I'm sorry but I'm not comfortable repeating exactly what he said in mixed company but it was with sort of a wink-wink-nudge-nudge approach."

Kate reaches a decision at this point. "OK, we nix Travis based on unacceptable conduct during the interview and inability to interact effectively with others in the unit. His overall computer skills and work history were definitely not as strong as Harriet's and it sounds like he is a sexual harassment complaint waiting to happen. Annette, you had also mentioned some kind of problem with Ahmed."

Annette seems tentative as she offers her remarks. "I can't say exactly what it is about him that put me off. I know that, even though he does not have a lot of work experience, his computer degree and organization skills look really impressive on paper. I just know he made me uneasy. It seemed like I would try to talk to him and he was just sort of tuning me out. Plus, I'm a little concerned about his communication skills. English is obviously a second language and I couldn't get a real sense to how much he understood."

Dave asks a question about Ahmed. "Do we know if he is an American citizen or not. If he isn't, I wonder what his visa status is? If he holds Middle Eastern citizenship, it could take forever for human resources to get hiring approval. Not to mention, the annual renewal issues and extra paperwork involved. Plus . . ."

"Hold on!" Kate interrupts him. "This is another issue we cannot include as part of the decision matrix. It is not legal to discriminate based on ethnicity or nationality. You know we have to stick to the posted skills desired. So far I have that he has really strong computer skills and Annette has unsubstantiated concerns on his communication skills. Anything else anyone has to contribute that is substantive, relevant, supported by facts, and *legal*?" she finishes in exasperation.

Maria looks up from the papers she was shuffling as Kate was speaking and offers a comment. "Well, I was actually a little surprised that we interviewed him. His official resume looked good but have you noticed how many typographical and grammatical errors there are on the actual application and the short cover letter. In the sections where he is describing his past job responsibilities and reasons for leaving, I can barely follow his sentences. Plus, he has put 'see resima' on a couple of questions and even left some entire sections blank. I wonder if he had a friend help him on preparing the resume and cover letter ahead of time and proofed it, but then he had to fill out the online application on his own." While Maria is speaking, the others are flipping to their copies of the application with audible mutters as the others see what she is referring to. "Do we really want to hire someone who can't do basic correspondence for this position? Also, on the side of his verbal communication skills, I noticed that he was having a lot of difficulty understanding the question or two I asked. I had to repeat them and even change my wording before he answered. The fact that English is not my native language and I do have a Latino accent could have been a factor, but he is going to be answering the phone for Kate and needs to be able to understand and respond to a variety of dialects and accents. I think he speaks English better than he understands it, especially the nuances."

Mark agrees that the position requires someone who can prepare memos appropriately with minimal revisions and editing; he is quite upset at the lack of quality control on the actual application form.

Checking the time, Kate begins bringing the meeting to a close. "We've got to vacate the meeting room but I really appreciate your input and observations. At least the legal ones." At this last comment she casts a stern look at the group. "I better not learn that any of you are using personal or discriminatory issues in filling your subordinate positions. Don't be surprised if I follow-up with some of you individually and recommend taking a refresher workshop in hiring procedures from human resources. Thus far, it sounds as though the candidate who best meets the combined criteria of relevant experience, computer skills, written and oral communication skills, interpersonal skills, and ability to interact with others effectively is Harriet. She was actually my personal first choice, based on the prior jobs she has had, which are quite similar to what I will be asking the person in this position to do. I will get a memo prepared for Dana in personnel based on our recommendation and probably offer her the position."

Case Study Observations

- It is extremely important during an interview process to follow procedure that is fair and equitable for all candidates. This may mean using prescribed questions or just making sure staff know what issues are appropriate and inappropriate to discuss.
- If someone mentions something illegal or unsubstantiated when discussing a candidate, the normal supervisory guidelines of avoiding public reprimand of an employee take second place. Managers are responsible for interceding and verifying that due process is followed and a hiring decision is not based on emotional bias or illegal issues.
- Hiring decisions must be based primarily on documented reasons that relate to the position responsibilities, advertised preferences, and work environment/interpersonal communications issues. Only when it comes down to a close tie between two candidates (which seldom truly occurs when a quantitative decision matrix is used) should a manager rely on instincts or feelings about which candidate will be the best fit to the position and the unit.

Thought and Discussion Exercises

What Do You Do Now?

1. An employee is in your office complaining about the recent erratic attendance and poor performance of a coworker. You know that the employee in question learned five weeks ago that her husband has an inoperable brain tumor and has only a short time to live. FMLA paperwork has been filed, but the employee has obviously not told anyone else in the unit. What do you do now?
2. From behind the service desk, you see an employee in your unit trip on the door threshold as he enters the library. He falls on his hands and knees and seems shaken for a minute, then gets up and walks gingerly into the office area. What do you do now?
3. You notice that an employee seems to be wearing looser clothes, is frequently eating crackers and drinking lemon-lime soda at her desk, and has been taking off for doctor's appointments every two weeks. You wonder if she might be pregnant. What do you do now?

Notes

1. William R. Tracy, *The Human Resources Glossary: A Complete Desk Reference for HR Professionals* (Boca Raton, FL: St. Lucie Press, 1997).

2. Robert D. Stueart and Barbara B. Moran, *Library and Information Center Management*, 6th ed. (Greenwood Village, CO: Libraries Unlimited, 2002).

3. Lowell A. Martin, *Library Personnel Administration* (Metuchen, NJ: Scarecrow Press, Inc., 1994).

4. Joseph G. Rosse and Robert A. Levin, *Jossey-Bass Academic Administrator's Guide to Hiring* (San Francisco: Jossey-Bass, 2003).

5. J. Douglas Toma and Richard L. Palm, *The Academic Administrator and the Law: What Every Dean and Department Chair Needs to Know*, ASHE-ERIC Higher Education Report, vol. 26, no. 5 (Washington, D.C.: George Washington University Graduate School of Education and Human Development, 1999).

6. David C. Alexander and Randall A. Rabourn, eds., *Applied Ergonomics* (New York: Taylor & Francis, 2001); R.S. Bridger, *Introduction to Ergonomics*, 2nd ed. (New York: Taylor & Francis, 2003).

CHAPTER 7

Exploring Your Inheritance

On becoming a manager, one seldom assumes responsibility for a new-born unit with no history. In truth, one is inheriting both operational processes steeped with familiarity and personnel who have already-established routines and relationships. The process of familiarizing one-self with the environment and understanding the process history and interpersonal dynamics is essential to being effective in enacting any future operational or organizational change. As one develops a sense of the issues and personalities in the unit, a manager can get a better gauge of how to prioritize and introduce new initiatives. One can also better recognize where the problems will occur and determine the cost trade-offs in emotional energies and morale. As one is exploring processes and personalities, the key in engaging staff during this exploration process is that even as the past impinges on the current situational assessment, the focus should remain clearly on the future of the unit. It is important to avoid getting bogged down in past practices or old grudges.

Predecessor Residue

Regardless of whether one is succeeding a saintly manager who is retiring after 20 wonderful years or a controlling micromanager who treated people like pawns, new managers always have to deal with emo-tional and operational baggage that is left behind. Even when the man-agement change represents improvement to the overall environment, it may not be immediately embraced by the employees in the unit. On the surface, the new manager represents significant change, which many people in the library environment may find to be a difficult adjustment. However, unlike some changes that can be embraced gradually, changing management staff has an immediate impact to the unit power structure and interpersonal dynamics. Unless given specific information from an administrator, new unit managers need to reserve judgment on the popularity and effectiveness of the previous manager. This may mean employing noncommittal, passive listening when employees make reference to the individual and avoiding getting caught up in first impressions based on a staff member's personal anecdotes. As managers work with the staff as a whole on understanding operational issues, a clearer picture of the previous manager's style will be developed.

In replacing "wonderful" outgoing managers, new managers face a potential situation of constant comparisons and being found lacking and less liked. This is easily demoralizing to the new manager's self-confidence and, over time, can cause the new manager to shy away from making changes or to become defensive when faced with the memory of the previous manager. There are several techniques new managers can employ to avoid becoming insecure in their initiatives or resentful of the previous manager's memory. If possible, try to engage the previous manager or a trusted administrator in a "passing the torch" event with all of the staff. Using this forum, the new manager can be given a public vote of confidence from the previous manager, and the staff can be reassured by a sense of gradual change rather than immediate disruptive change. Once in the management position, the best route to take is to communicate a tremendous amount of respect for one's predecessor. Depending on how rapidly change must be made, it may be important to emphasize that changes are coming based on external factors, rather than personal whim or the intention of tearing down the predecessor's accomplishments. Although new managers should not apologize for being different and making decisions that change things, they should acknowledge that they do recognize that they are asking employees to take a new direction and that doing so does not diminish the accomplishments of the previous manager. If appropriate, it may also help to remind the staff that their former manager spoke highly of them and had promised that they would be as supportive to the new manager as they were for the previous manager. Even as one tries to transition from the outgoing manager's style, it is important to avoid canonizing the previous manager. Although the perception may be that everyone liked the person, there are inevitably some staff members who were not as fond of the outgoing manager but found discretion to be the better part of valor and chose to remain silent instead of voicing dissent. If the new manager gives the perception of wholeheartedly approving of the previous manager, these staff members may continue to hold back on their opinions or contributions.

In replacing a "bad" manager who micromanaged or did not treat employees with respect, newly minted managers may feel that it should be obvious to everyone that they are bringing happier days to the unit. Consequently, they may be taken by surprise if they are not met with open arms but instead with suspicion, resentment, or passive resistance. What they need to realize is that during the time that the "bad" manager was in place, this individual hired and retained some staff who may have been content with this management model. Staff members may have been hired based on their ability to be followers and have very limited leadership skills or tendencies to question authority. Like any abused or victim personality, staff may have convinced themselves that they are inadequate and are not deserving of decision-making, trust, praise, and other positive management techniques. Another element the new manager will have to work through is lack of trust. Even as staff will respect the position of authority or power that is held by the new manager, they may not trust the person and will not easily engage in discussion and brainstorming of ideas. The staff may not believe that environmental change will last and may need to be given time to overcome their reluctance to hope that the new manager does represent a permanent change in organizational philosophy. The new manager coming into this type of situation will need a considerable amount of patience, time, and administrative support to effectively enact change. The best tools in this manager's resources will be facts, honesty, consistency, permission to fail, and the ability to allow the staff members to grow without extreme repercussions if an idea is unsuccessful. At times, it may be appropriate to employ more direct approaches to push staff outside of their comfort zone. The key is balancing their personal discomfort or uncertainties with reassurance on a job done well or maintaining familiarity in some other aspect of their work environment.

The manager who has come up through the ranks within a particular unit faces additional challenges. The transition of having a familiar colleague change from a peer role to a supervisory one is a situation that people adjust to differently. In some cases, where the manager was a senior librarian and had already been taking on unit leadership roles, staff accept the change as an obvious choice and make the transition easily. In other cases, where the manager may be less experienced or newer to the organization, staff may be surprised by the appointment and find the transition more awkward. In the latter case, there may be a tendency for staff to dwell on memories of the time that the new manager made a faux pas or on other shared personal experiences. The manager must gradually draw back from the familiar collegial banter to establish a better sense of the new role. This distance becomes critical when the manager must make the inevitable unpopular decision or unwelcome directive. In time, memories of the individual as a manager will replace the early peer memories.

One common theme to each of these situations is the importance of taking things slowly and allowing time to dull memories or heal wounds. During this time, it is important that the new manager be discrete and neutral during all references to the previous manager. One can afford to be generous, and this avoids putting staff in the position of defending the previous manager out of a sense of loyalty. Even if the previous manager was horrible, in time staff may convince themselves that the previous manager was not really that bad. If this rationalization enables them to bring closure to their emotions toward the previous manager and move forward, then it serves no harm. At some point the new manager may reach a point where most of the staff are on board to the new organizational philosophy and the remaining loyal traditionalists constitute only a few individuals. Dealing with this situation is covered in more detail in subsequent chapters, but should involve close discussions with administrators on deciding if it is more important from an organizational perspective to force change upon the individuals or just minimize their impact to unit operations and morale.

Recognizing the Cliques

A new manager coming into a department or library is somewhat analogous to being the new kid in high school, who has just moved to the area but has brought with him a reputation of being a really good football quarterback. Some students and teachers may be a little standoffish and suspicious, especially if a big deal was made of the person before he arrived. Others will connect immediately with him because they think he will be the "big man on campus." There is inevitable speculation of whether the person will live up to his reputation and what he is really like. The team will wonder how he will want to change their plays and strategies and whether he will be invasive to the friendly relationships between certain players, already in place from practicing and playing together. The fact that he is in a position that often serves as the team captain may additionally set him apart from some of the other team leaders. This is similar to the experience of new managers. As organizations, libraries tend to have very active, informal information networks or grapevines. Often new managers are hired or promoted through a process of negotiation and amid rampant speculation. The other managers will wonder how well the new manager will fit in as a colleague. The staff in the unit will wonder what operational changes the new manager will want to make and if it will disrupt their established working relationships with favorite peers.

Most library environments are favorable for the forming of close connections between small groups of individuals with similar perspectives or complimentary personalities–that is, cliques. The basis of the connections can be professional, personal, social, or a combination of these areas. Some examples of cliques might include a group of academic, tenure-track librarians who came in at the same time with similar professional hurdles or, more generally, a group of library staff members with similar family composition (single, recently married, small children, teenagers, etc.). Similarly, cliques among the manager ranks may come about through sharing professional experiences and overcoming challenges. As many support staff do not see their library jobs in the same career perspective as librarians, their cliques tend to be based on external factors. These would include socioeconomic, educational, and social or family structure similarities. Depending on the characteristics of the organization and the nature of the connection, the clique may cross librarian/support staff boundaries. Examples of this might be people who belong to a bridge or exercise group or participate in religious activities together. It is not the role of new managers to either immediately break into or breakup cliques. In time, the managers will integrate into the organization's interpersonal dynamics, consistent with being the new person in any setting. However, it is important to immediately start building an awareness and knowledge of the cliques to avoid making a faux pas or appearing to favor one employee over another.

There are some unique things to watch out for in recognizing relationships between professional librarians. It is also important to remember that many administrators have come up through the ranks or been active in the professional community. A manager should never assume that just because someone is still a frontline librarian, he or she does not have close personal ties to someone in an administrative position. It does not bode well for one's professional success to complain to person A about how difficult it is to work with administrator B, only to discover that they have a friendship that dates back to when both started in the organization. Similarly, there are many dual librarian marriages or partnerships, where the names are different and the relationships not immediately apparent. The author has seen up-and-coming librarians burn bridges by making unpleasant remarks about a person in the presence of the person's spouse or partner, not realizing there is a special personal relationship.

When dealing with cliques within units under your management, it is important to assess whether the effect of the clique is a positive or negative one. Positive cliques provide connections between staff that are supportive in nature by sharing experiences, developing solutions, or laughing over similar things. Negative cliques–intentional or unintentional–will be exclusionary in nature. They undermine the acceptance of differences and diversity in the organization or cause hurt feelings. Intentionally negative cliques have no place in the professional workplace and should be addressed in a direct manner by the manager. This may mean holding coaching sessions with specific employees and requiring clique partici-pants to modify their conduct as part of performance expectations. Unin-tentionally negative cliques may be more easily addressed by heightening awareness of the clique participants or encouraging moderation. Some-times, the office architecture and layout will have an impact on the clique tolerance level. Open office environments or cubicle arrangements that offer little aural privacy create an environment with lower tolerance for social cliques.

Positive cliques can become negative ones based on changes to envi-ronment or to the perspectives of either clique participants or the per-ceived outsiders. Suppose within a unit, one staff member has been trying to have a baby and another staff member, who already has sev-eral children, announces another one is on the way. There is the poten-tial for a strained relationship to develop based on social chatting. As others celebrate with the expectant mother and engage in baby discus-sions through the course of the pregnancy and formative months, the childless employee may feel excluded in a way that is social in origin but that extends into the professional environment. As another exam-ple, suppose several staff members in the unit are very active together in a staff association. They bond while working on fundraising events and planning office socials. However, one aspect of participation is being able to purchase a $10 per year membership and spend a few dollars here and there on food or silent auction items. For some house-holds, every dollar has significance and there is no spare money. In this case, a normally positive interaction is perceived as exclusionary by a staff member who cannot afford it. As the manager, one should encourage the group hosting the social function to consider whether a financial commitment is really required, and if so, is it appropriate if it causes someone to be left out.

There is a fine line between clique behavior and creation of a hostile environment. One example of this is a group of staff who attend church together and begin talking about personal Christian viewpoints in the presence of a non-Christian colleague or patron. Another example occurs when a group of women share graphic childbirth experiences or participate in humorous male-bashing in the vicinity of a male colleague. In both cases what was initially bonding behavior can be perceived as legally offensive and discriminatory or creating a hostile environment for someone else. It is the manager's responsibility to be aware of the possible impact of these behaviors and encourage employees to seek more generic and library-based topics of conversation before it reaches the level of formal complaints. Depending on the nature of the subject matter and the receptiveness of the staff members, it may be possible to simply bring the issue up in a casual manner in a unit meeting. If the manager does not see an improvement in the conduct of the individuals, a specific coaching meeting for the employees engaging in the unacceptable conduct should be considered. The purpose of the meeting should be to heighten the sensitivity of the employees to their environment and clarify expectations of appropriate professional conduct.

Discovering Questionable Practices

Even as new managers may discover some toxic interpersonal relationships in a unit, they may also uncover other questionable practices. These are processes or procedures that were put in place through tradition or arbitrary decisions made by the previous manager but that do not follow current institutional policies or effectively address individual needs. In addressing these issues, it is important to try and understand why the practice developed, its significance, and the impact of changing it. In understanding the history of questionable practices, one can better identify how entrenched the practice is and how much resistance there will be to changing it. It also allows the manager to better address the question of why it was acceptable then but now it is not. This does differ from trying to understand the logic behind the practice, which can be frustrating and futile. In some cases where the practice developed because of someone's whim or a miscommunication, there will not be a logical answer to the question of "why." Rather this is a situation that generates the response that it's "always been done like that." By understanding the implications of a questionable practice, a manager is able to prioritize it with respect to other change initiatives. A practice that is in direct conflict to state or federal labor laws, such as employees not accurately recording time worked, is extremely critical and must be changed immediately. Other practices that are less critical, such as shifting work schedules for better unit coverage and consistency with changing user needs, can probably be deferred and introduced gradually as part of the inevitable turnover process when the staff have gained more trust in the manager. Finally, understanding the impact of changing the practice will allow the manager to be better prepared for any repercussions caused by enacting a change. With many changes there may be a ripple effect that will impact several staff. As covered in more detail in Chapter 8, it is important that the manager try not to take the staff by surprise. A good example of the ripple effect can involve changing supervisory guidelines on taking annual leave. A previous manager may have told staff members, who normally work nights or weekends, that they can never take annual leave during much of the year or for several consecutive days because there is no one to cover their hours. The new manager may want or need to change this and allow the staff member to use their annual leave, but to do so must convince other staff to help cover the night or weekend shifts.

In the course of identifying and categorizing questionable practices, a new manager may run across issues that are sore points or sacred cows. These are things that one or more staff members may hold very dear or have personalized, and trying to enact change that impacts these areas can explode in the face of the new manager. Chapter 8 offers tips on addressing these types of issues as a change agent, but the focus here is to identify the hot issues and recognize when to pull back until they can be explored from a new angle that is less emotional. One way to recognize hot button issues is by listening to the staff. The phrases "over my dead body," "you can't do that," or "you can't make me" should be an immediate red flag that one has stumbled across something the staff member holds close at a personal level. In dealing with these types of scenarios, it is good to defer further discussion for another time and verify one's authority with an administrator or human resources representative. This is an approach that is not usually prescribed in the corporate environment, but is more appropriate in library settings, especially in public institutions under complex state employment guidelines. An example might be trying to change a staff member's scheduled work time. Depending on the hiring rules of the organization, there may be a due process that has to be followed, such as allowing someone else to volunteer for a shift change before dictating it.

Some managers might believe that they can focus solely on their subordinate and interunit collaborations and be successful. In truth, the development of a good relationship with the administrative team, and especially one's administrative supervisor, is even more critical to one's managerial success. These people must have respect for and confidence in the manager's judgment. This is necessary because managers need their administrators to trust them enough to be included in the decision-making process and to serve as the manager's advocate when taking forward ideas or proposals. Depending on the organization's size and complexity, this might be one or two individuals, such as the library director and a single associate, or a larger group of associate and assistant directors and administrative managers, such as a human resources head or finance officer.

Relationship Development . . . One Level Up

One key aspect of this relationship is identifying the administrator's expectations of a manager's performance. Part of the role of the middle manager is to support what the administrator needs. Does the administrator need someone to provide logistical background insights or just take the handoff on an idea and run with it? Is the administrator expecting the manager's role to be encouragement and validation of ideas or to play devil's advocate and find the weak areas of the idea? Does the administrator expect the manager to come in and enact heavy-handed change? Or is more gradual change anticipated to minimize overreaction and shock by the staff? It may even be that a manager is coming into a department that is efficiently and effectively meeting the current institutional objectives, and initial expectations are to maintain the status quo. Beyond these parameters, managers need to learn whether they are expected to be visionary and initiate new ideas or implement objectives previously identified by administrators. Only through understanding these expectations is a manager able to apply appropriately the roles referenced in Chapter 1. No matter how great a manager is, not doing the job expected by administration will only lead one to be unsuccessful within the organization.

Learning about administrative expectations is accomplished through establishing effective communication between the manager and administrator. Just as you have a particular natural communication style, so will your administrators. Learning and adapting to these styles will allow communication to be more effective and focused and help avoid misunderstandings or false assumptions. Some things to take into consideration are whether either the manager or the administrator is a multitasker who can handle interruptions and think on her feet. Or is either one less flexible, having difficulty communicating on the fly and needing to mentally prepare remarks? It is also important to understand how administrators offer and the managers receive constructive criticism. It is most important to realize that because a manager does not interact with an administrator on a daily basis, the criticism may seem less timely and occur after the manager has already moved on to other issues. Managers must be careful to interpret constructive comments as actual growth opportunities, rather than as suggestions of failure as a manager. Another expectation to clarify is how to handle status reports and one-on-one meetings. Does the administrator want to be kept updated with minutia or just engage in context of the big picture? Does the administrator think mostly in concepts and seem to move freely from topic to topic or prefer structure and logic in discussing issues. All of these play a major role in developing that relationship one level up, and while these expectations may be difficult to arrive at, they should not be neglected. As communication styles are very personal things, developing an effective communication relationship is a process that must be repeated anytime either the manager or the administrator changes because the new person will likely have different expectations or assumptions than the previous person.

This book is written with the assumption that you have a positive and successful upper administration that truly wants to see you succeed and is participatory in developing a new manager. Even as you may have different styles of communication and different understanding of organizational initiatives, you should be able to develop an open and supportive relationship. If you find yourself in a situation where this is not the case and the conflicts seem insurmountable, there are some books that address the issue of dealing with difficult bosses. In the Library of Congress classification system, they are frequently found at HF 5548.83 or under the subject heading "managing your boss." Depending on the specific details of the situation, you may be faced with the difficult decision of whether to tough it out, step back from management but stay in the organization, or move on to other opportunities. This is a personal decision that ties into your individual expectations and reasons for becoming a manager. If faced with this scenario, reading Chapter 12 may help you put perspective on the issue and engage in self-analysis.

Chapter Summary

In summary, exploring the background on the human relations issues and interpersonal relationships of your new managerial responsibilities is extremely important. Understanding and building the necessary relationships is something that will happen on individual timetables and require patience and a willingness to adapt on the part of the new manager. Even as an understanding of unit history and personal dynamics becomes clearer, it cannot be used as an excuse for not moving forward. Instead, it must be incorporated into timetables and leadership techniques.

To Learn More

Literature on human relations can be useful in developing an understanding of the professional personalities of the unit staff and the administrative supervisor to which the middle manager reports. Currently in its 10th edition, *Your Attitude Is Showing: A Primer of Human Relations* by Sharon Lund O'Neil and Elwood N. Chapman is an excellent resource for developing an initial understanding of some of the interpersonal dynamics and human relations situations in the workplace. It introduces issues relative to understanding motivational factors, informal communication networks, and bonding between employees, as well as the importance of developing the supervisory relationship.[1] Additional insights can be developed using textbook-style works in this area. Two sources that address issues in a contemporary manner with attention to social issues and diversity initiatives are *The Human Side of Organizations* and *Human Relations: Strategies for Success*. Both were published in the mid-1990s and address a wide range of issues relevant to a new manager. In its 6th edition, *The Human Side of Organizations* is truly introductory in nature and follows a traditional textbook style. It presents terminology and concepts, with less detailed case studies and exercises.[2] *Human Relations: Strategies for Success* differs in that it focuses more on an applied perspective, with extensive case studies and numerous lists of tips and techniques. It is more readable in content for the person who has the basics but wants to develop a stronger skill set in understanding the human relations issues in a unit.[3] To build a better theoretical understanding of human relations, George Henderson goes into considerably more depth than the other books. In addition to good coverage of the background and history of human relations research and its application to improving organizations, the book addresses selected issues, such as alcoholic workers or burned-out workers, in significant detail that enables to reader to have a better understanding of these difficult staffing situations.[4] All of the books discuss styles of supervision and the effects they can leave within a staffing structure and organization.

Case Study: Understanding the History

Beth – general reference head, (six years prior experience at another organization)

Kate – internal middle-manager promotion (eight months ago), access services head (previously five years at Mid State University doing library instruction)

Sam – Kate and Beth's supervisor, associate director

Allen – Beth's predecessor. Left for a position in another state after five years as head of general reference.

Patricia – Kate's predecessor. Retired at 65 after 25 years with the library, the last ten years as head of access services.

Setting: over coffee in Beth's office

After taking a sip of coffee, Beth looks thoughtfully at Kate and says, "You are probably wondering why I wanted to get together. Manager to manager, I need some background and thought you might could help."

"I'll be glad to help if I can. What's up?" Kate replies.

"How well did you know Allen?" Beth asks.

Kate looks thoughtful and a little wary. "I coordinated through him with some of the instruction scheduling involving the reference librarians and worked with him on a committee or two, but I wouldn't really say I knew him well. Why?"

"Well, I'm sort of confused about some of the stuff that the staff are telling me about the 'old ways' and am really having trouble getting a handle on what kind of manager he was. I know when I interviewed and was hired, Sam told me that they wanted me to focus on some future initiatives and be a change agent but I just thought he meant the unit had gotten into a rut. The stuff I've been hearing lately is making me wonder otherwise," Beth replies.

"I wondered how much they had actually told you about the recent history in the department. Most of it is locked up behind private personnel files, but I do know some of the stuff that was circulating through the grapevine." Kate sighs and looks thoughtful. "I do know from personal experience that Allen was really old-school management. TQM, empowerment, and consensus decision-making were not in his vocabulary. When I had a class that I needed a reference librarian to do, he would designate to me who would do it without even consulting the individual first. The few committees I was on with him were pointless in my opinion. He would state his viewpoint at length and in detail and anyone that tried to give input was cut off."

"OK, well that goes along with some of the phrases the staff were quoting. Cheryl, the student supervisor, was saying she had been told 'she could never have a new monitor' and Tracy was telling me that they were not allowed to call a patron back if it was long distance. The question had to be answered when the patron initially called on their dime. Keith has even said that because he was the only science librarian he was never allowed to be away from the office for vacation leave. If he was sick, Allen would call him at home to check up on him and berate him. I've even heard that he would make passes at some of the female employees and patrons. To hear a couple of them talk, he was every villainous, lecherous figure in history and literature all rolled into one."

Kate shakes her head ruefully as she says, "You know, I've gone through a few 'old manager' stories in my unit as well and have learned a few things from talking them out with Sam. It is really important to keep in mind that you are effectively hearing this stuff through a filter. Allen did run a tight ship and didn't give people a lot of freedom, but in some cases, I wonder how much of what they heard was what they wanted to hear. Take Tracy for example, I know that I have heard her say how much she hates doing reference via the phone. I know I once ended up with a question she was supposed to follow-up on, but she never got back to the person and it was an on-campus call. When I asked her why she didn't get back to the person, she told me he never answered and she didn't like to leave messages on machines. Why she ever became a reference librarian I honestly do not know. Another thing is that sometimes you can verify the story. For instance you might look at Keith's personnel file to see if he has ever used any sick leave or vacation time. If you do find something that looks fishy, you may have to step in and make Keith take some time off, even if it means messing up his martyr role." Kate sort of half-smiles at this last comment.

"Whew, heavy stuff. You might be right though about Keith, he has the long-suffering, unappreciated librarian role down to an art. It is just really hard to sift through it sometimes and know exactly how to respond when I never even saw this library until Allen had already been gone for six months," Beth replies.

Kate nods in agreement, "Even though my unit's previous manager didn't have some of the idiosyncrasies of Allen, I've found a few oddball things that make no rational sense to have been done the way she did them. Whenever, I stumble across one, I've found the best route to take, which Sam endorsed, is to respond rather matter-of-factly. I acknowledge what the person says but remind them that I'm not Patricia and things are different now, that we have different reasons for providing service the way we do."

"You said that Sam had endorsed this approach. Does that mean that you and he discuss the staff? I wasn't sure if he expects me to do it all or if he is OK being a sounding board to talk out different perspectives."

Kate's face lights up with enthusiasm as she replies, "He is definitely good as a sounding board for me. I learn a lot through discussions that update him on unit staff. He has a lot of positive management experience in understanding staff motivations and behaviors and really prompts me to think below the surface comment or reaction. Also, since he was interim head while the position was vacant, he knows your staff and may be able to offer some real insights."

"That's really good to know. I don't have much to cover with him tomorrow in our weekly status meeting. Maybe I should use the time to talk out some of this stuff. Thanks for the tips," says Beth looking reassured.

Case Study Observations

- Any unit has a history with personnel issues or operational decisions that will seem odd to the incoming manager. These may show up the first couple of months or out-of-the-blue several years later.
- Recognize that when staff tell you about past issues, they are colored by their personal perceptions and interpretations. Getting to the facts may be impossible.
- See your administrative supervisor as an ally in gaining understanding of the environment and for putting a professional interpretation on past events.

Thought and Discussion Exercises

What Do You Do Now?

1. You receive a complaint from a faculty member about a letter he received from a staff member in your department. You get a copy of the letter and discover it is full of errors and inaccuracies and is rather insulting toward the recipient (calling him an irresponsible and childish library-user) and was sent out under the name of the previous department head. What do you do now?
2. A staff member tells you that she was never allowed to take annual leave because she was essential to the unit. You check her leave balances and learn that she has an extraordinarily large amount of accumulated annual leave. What do you do now?
3. You cannot understand the behavior of a staff member. One day he is friendly to you and chats comfortably. The next day he freezes up when you try to talk to him and only answers in monosyllables. You also cannot get him to explain how he goes about gathering the information, doing write-ups, and posting updates to the Web site. You decide you need to approach your administrator about some insights into this person's conduct and discover he had a close working relationship with the previous manager. What do you do now?

Notes

1. Sharon Lund O'Neil and Elwood N. Chapman, *Your Attitude Is Showing: A Primer of Human Relations*, 10th ed. (Upper Saddle River, NJ: Prentice Hall/Pearson Education, 2002).

2. Stan Kossen, *The Human Side of Organizations*, 6th ed. (New York: Harper Collins College Publishers, 1994).

3. Lowell H. Lamberton and Leslie Minor, *Human Relations: Strategies for Success* (Chicago: Irwin: Mirror Press, 1995).

4. George Henderson, *Human Relations Issues in Management* (Westport, CT: Quorum Books, 1996).

CHAPTER 8

Being a Change Agent

The profession as a whole and individual library environments are changing at a rapid rate. Regardless of one's particular position or opinion about the future of librarianship, the factual nature of the above statement cannot be denied. The manner and pace in which change manifests itself in the academic library workplace may vary from institution to institution. It is often dependent on the larger organizational goals, the role and mission of the library, and the priorities and leadership of current library administrators. Often the responsibility of implementing this change and supporting it on a daily level falls on the middle manager. In this role, the middle manager may alternately become leader, cajoler, encourager, dictator, or defender of the staff in the unit. Moving between these roles and engaging staff in implementing change can be one of the most difficult challenges a manager may face. Handled well, it will place the unit in a good position for future challenges. Handled badly, it will result in disaffected staff and poor service.

How It Starts

Part of a library administrator's role and responsibility is to prepare the library to meet current and future institutional initiatives and expectations. Because of this, most widespread or major organizational change will begin with upper administrators and leaders in the local community, college, or library. They will establish strategic initiatives, define areas of perceived service improvement or redefinition, and lead changes in organizational culture and philosophy. This will usually come following a period of strategic planning and assessment that will lead to the development of an overarching mission or vision for the organization and its future role in the community. In the library culture, assessment tools can be national or regional rankings, results from user surveys, such as LibQual+ or focus groups, or a pattern of feedback from staff or library users. Upper administrators will address these areas in broad terms using the language of strategic planning. Concepts might include having access to information concerns, providing accuracy of service, or meeting user research needs through services and collections. Often they will be written to support even broader institutional initiatives, such as creating an inclusive and diverse workforce or addressing academic integrity.

Some organizations have experimented with bottom-up strategic planning where frontline staff and middle managers are heavily engaged in the strategic planning process. These efforts have been largely unsuccessful. What administrators find is that the ability to think in a global, systemic, and strategic manner is not intuitive to most people. Instead much of the input comes from an operational perspective and addresses narrowly focused perceived needs. As an example, a strategic initiative might be to develop the computer infrastructure for new remote-access service initiatives. Most staff would be more likely to arrive at the operational objectives such as more frequently upgrading desktop computers or offering more frequent training on application software. Feedback from the frontline staff might even be so detailed as to suggest that computer tech Richard needs to call back faster when paged. It is only when an organization is selective in its participants and provides them with extensive training and indoctrination to strategic concepts and an understanding of the organization as a whole that bottom-up strategic planning can have a better chance for success. Even in these cases, it will often be necessary for administrators to make changes to the plan before sending it forward to institutional leaders.

Going Public

Once the strategic directions and new organizational paradigms are established, administrators will usually engage middle managers to assist in identifying detailed level assessments and actual operational changes that evaluate and address these areas. This can include keeping service desk statistics that identify the types of questions being asked, evaluating current workflows, or brainstorming discussions. This is the point that staff, even those with a narrowly defined focus, begin to recognize that their immediate workplace is going to be impacted by these changes. Although some will embrace the change from the start, many will experience an initial response of uncertainty and change-anxiety. This anxiety can manifest itself in many ways and vary in intensity, depending on the individual. Some staff will have a strong desire to be a part of the development process and provide input at every phase. This allows them to maintain a sense of personal control of the situation and protect some of their own interests. Later, they will be the ones able to say, "I told them not to do that." Others may not want to take responsibility for changes and would rather stay distant from the planning process until presented with a fait accompli once all the glitches are worked out. They are reserving the right to say, "I didn't have anything to do with it." Finally, some may decide to actively resist change. This can be done through consistently expressing a negative attitude to any proposed changes. A few employees may be so resistant to change that they actually work to undermine the new direction and sabotage others' efforts. Do not be surprised if employees' concerns or frustrations lead them to transfer the emotions and associate the change with the manager leading it, instead of environmental and organizational factors. After all, it is hard to be angry at an inanimate object like the university budget and often chancellors or other financial officers are remote, abstract figures. The best response is to express empathy to their anxiety but reinforce that everyone has concerns and the important part is to accept that the change is happening, try to reengage, and move forward. Above all, try to avoid letting unit staff or yourself become the "victims" of change.

When dealing with the first two groups, it is important to encourage them to feel invested in the change and understand why it is happening. One of the challenges is not to lose their trust during the inevitably rocky shakedown and prototyping periods. This can be done by going through extensive preparation and letting them play out some "what if" scenarios. It is also critical that they understand that some mistakes and overall performance slippage while adjusting to new processes are normal and acceptable. Finally, as the manager, it critical that you stay positive, upbeat, and forward-focused. Do not fall into the trap of getting frustrated over the problematic details or things you cannot fix; instead focus on developing reasonable workarounds. The point at which the manager loses faith in the change or transfers fatigue or frustration to the frontline staff is the point at which the initiative will start to falter. Several of the readings in human resources and change management literature address specific techniques for fostering and maintaining forward progress and encouraging positive attitudes through the more dramatic changes. All agree that, because of the introduction of the human emotional element, there is no formula or magic wand to make organizational change smooth and easy. The rate at which staff members accept and engage in change is very personal and can vary depending on what is being changed.

When faced with staff who are actively resisting change, there are two possible approaches that can be used to address the problem. Middle managers are advised to look to library administration and personnel representatives for guidance on which approach is best supported by the organization. One approach, more often seen in privately funded environments, is somewhat confrontational and demands that the individual change rapidly. An ongoing unwillingness to change is carefully documented and disciplinary action taken, possibly leading to termination. Often perceived as insensitive to the employee, it requires significant micromanagement and can be very costly in terms of overall employee morale and trust in management. This approach will often result in employees filing grievances against supervisors and may cause good employees to resign in order to escape the combative environment. The other approach, more often seen in academic and public libraries, is to stage change much more slowly and try different techniques to engage the reluctant individuals. As more staff in a unit are slowly won over to the new paradigm after witnessing the new initiatives and improvements, peer pressure effects will come into play and encourage acceptance of the change. Eventually, the small group of naysayers will be narrowed down to one or two, and acceptable solutions of internal relocation, reassignment, or limited disciplinary action can be more easily explored. More guidance on dealing with this situation is presented in Chapters 10 and 11.

Making Progress

Chapter 1 discussed the role of many middle managers in planning and implementing operational changes and introduced project management techniques and resources. Integrating the human element into the plan is yet another challenge faced by the middle manager. Once one has a basic framework in place, it is extremely important to bring frontline staff into the process. This serves to recognize and validate the impact that change will have on them and helps to identify oversights and false assumptions. Often frontline staff will have expert knowledge of the current process and may be able to recognize real problems early on. Additionally, as new workflows are prototyped, an experienced staff member will instinctively identify errors and inaccuracies. It is important as their manager to recognize when individuals are communicating legitimate concerns and when they have not yet bought into the change and are creating invisible problems. When employees are identifying real problems, managers can often guide them to provide details and data that substantiate what they are addressing and provide specific examples or develop "what if" questions that are based on frequently encountered scenarios. The individual who is uneasy with the change will be creating "what if" scenarios that do not happen very often, if ever, and use these to sidetrack or delay the process. When faced with this, it is important for the manager to point out that even the current process is not all-encompassing and has exceptions that must be dealt with on a case-by-case basis. Even though the new process should be better, it will not be perfect all the time for everyone. Holding on to the expectation that the change will solve all problems in the library is an effective delaying technique. It may eventually fall to the manager to declare the project done and launch it, especially if several staff in the impacted unit or implementation designing process tend to be perfectionists.

One aspect of group- or staff-engaged planning and implementation has to do with gaining approval and consensus. In some venues a simple majority vote of a group or team overrules the minority dissenting opinions. However, contemporary management practices strongly encourage the use of consensus agreement to make decisions and move forward on them. In theory, a consensus agreement is an adjusted solution that satisfies everyone's concerns or issues and is more likely to be supported by everyone, not just the majority. In fact, consensus agreement usually occurs because of the different weight or priority that individuals give issues, rather than having succeeded by unanimous approval. An individual may still not agree with a particular idea but will have decided that it is not worth expending the energy or losing equity with others to push a dissenting viewpoint. In this respect consensus agreement change will craft a process that includes everyone's key issues of primary importance, but still may not be the most effective or efficient way of meeting the strategic goal or initiative. Most large-scale change will include a combination of directive decision making that keeps in mind the required end product and the set of absolute criteria that must be met along with consensus decision making with regard to filling in the details.

Stay Flexible

Elastic, flexible, adaptable, and agile all express a concept that is critical in the effective implementation of organizational change. These concepts are especially important in managers. Planning and scripting only go so far, especially when the change crosses departmental boundaries, impacts numerous workflows directly or indirectly, and involves technology. It is essential to recognize when something is not going according to schedule. As one recognizes that the plan is breaking down, it is critical to understand and explain to staff that although a sense of urgency or concern is appropriate, no amount of panic or hysteria is going to make any difference. It is critical that frustration over the change not deteriorate into hostilities between individuals or departments. Chapter 9 discusses the process of dealing with crises and may offer insights into managing disconnects or oversights during a change. However, it is equally important that one not see a crisis at every turn when implementing change. How you handle the unexpected roadblocks will say a lot about your leadership skills and areas of professional development.

One key technique to getting past these hurdles is to think near-term and long-term solutions. A near-term solution may be a few extra steps or a workaround that can be supported for a couple of weeks until the process can catch up. However, the long-term solution should always be kept in sight so that workarounds do not take on a life of their own. As an example, suppose you want to implement a process that allows library users to initiate recalls in the online catalog, but you then discover that you have a relatively small group of books that are going to be problematic because they have separate item records for pieces (tapes, CDs, diskettes, etc.). The way the turnkey form works, this may cause the student problems differentiating which items they are supposed to recall. A long-term solution would be to recatalog the problem pieces. However, the cataloging unit says they cannot get to it for at least four months. The rigid manager will simply say, "OK the project is stalled, we have to wait for cataloging." The flexible manager will explore whether there is any way to have a staff member keep an eye out for these kinds of problems and manually clean them up as they occur. This will allow the project to move forward but keeps track of the fact that the workaround is temporary and that cataloging staff must still try to recatalog the items in a timely fashion.

Occasionally, something will occur so that the workaround becomes the long-term solution. This may happen when a piece of software does not work as expected or a key staff position disappears amidst budget cuts. If this happens, it is extremely important to step back and reassess workflow and workload issues and evaluate the possibility of improving the workaround so it is less burdensome. This may mean redefining it as a routine operation and assigning it to a student worker or staff member with less expert knowledge or using technological tools to automate it. If the workaround continues to be a problem and an acceptable solution cannot be found, managers must consider cutting their losses and backing out of the proposed initiative or trying to look at it from an entirely different direction. Sometimes, this can actually be extremely difficult if one has personalized the project and feels that too much is invested in it, or if it is considered a high administrative priority. If the latter case represents reality, it may be necessary to look at letting go of some other aspect of the unit workload to accomplish the new priority.

Goals and Triumphs

When implementing significant operational change, it is incredibly important to tackle it in bite-sized chunks that have finite points of completion. Depending on the organization, these may be referred to as goals. Within these goals, milestones, or objectives, it is critical to set them in a way that moves people out of their comfort zone but that also are truly accomplishable. Vague or perpetually open-ended goals will only wear staff out and never offer an opportunity to stop and recognize what has been done successfully and reward those who contributed to the success. Being able to recognize the triumphs, and realize it really is working, will go a long way to relieving change anxiety and encourage staff to the next phase of change.

When recognizing the accomplishments, it is important to single out the shining stars but equally important to recognize the background contributors. As an example, suppose a library has completed a large project of converting materials to RFID technology. Obviously, the staff who handled the books should be recognized first and foremost for many hours of labor on the task. However, there are other staff whose contributions should be acknowledged as well. These would include staff who helped keep computer equipment operational, special-ordered supplies, or dealt expeditiously with bibliographic record problems, as well as the coordinator or supervisor who oversaw time sheets and set work schedules. There should also be some measure of recognition for staff who may have taken on a heavier routine operational workload to free-up others to work on the special project.

Along with knowing who should be recognized, it is important to think *how.* This is not the time to be understated, subtle, or discreet in praising employees. During periods of change, when many employees are at their most uncertain and insecure, public and detailed praise is more critical than ever. Managers should work on being effusive without being phony or insincere. Many library managers tend to be understated or so focused on problem solving that they overlook the praise that is especially appropriate during phases of change.

Chapter Summary

Leading an organization through a period of significant change is challenging for any manager, regardless of experience. For a new manager, it can be an even more difficult and rocky path. Staying grounded in reality and focused on the purpose of the change, while still allowing for detours, can help keep things moving forward. Make sure that you understand what administration's expectations are of you and what are their priorities. Usually this will be a balance between making apparent progress toward a goal but slowly enough that you have staff support, not total rebellion. Also, make sure that your own expectations of your staff are reasonable ones. Organizational change can be accomplished successfully, but it takes a lot of energy, positive encouragement, flexibility, innovation, and interpersonal communications. Generally, middle managers who are most successful spend significant time working with administrators to have a clear understanding of the issues and intent associated with the changes, and also with frontline staff "in the trenches" to understand the details from their point of view as well.

To Learn More

Many of the human relations resources, referenced in Chapter 7, will include a chapter on organizational change. Unfortunately, most books in the business literature that focus on change management are directed toward the upper manager's perspective, with emphasis on developing and sharing the initial vision that leads to organizational change. Employees are not examined as individuals; instead authors tend to deal with them in a rather abstract and global manner. A new manager may benefit from the case study approach. One reference that is more readable and relevant for an academic library middle manager is *Checklist for Change: A Pragmatic Approach to Creating and Controlling Change.*[1]

Another way to learn more about dealing with change as it impacts frontline staff is to explore the behavioral aspects of change from a psychological perspective. Lawrence M. Brammer's brief text *How to Cope with Life Transitions: The Challenge of Personal Change* provides a readable and thorough introduction to the study of change.[2] *How We Change: Psychotherapy and the Process of Human Development* by Richard L. Gilbert offers a more scholarly and in-depth understanding of the emotions and reactions associated with change, for both an individual and a social group.[3] Understanding why people react to change in a certain way allows a manager the insight to try different techniques to engage them. Both *Leading Change* by John Kotter and *The Heart of Change* by John Kotter and Dan Cohen offer some practical advice for leading change within an organization. *Leading Change* is a faster read that looks at why change stalls and fails and offers an eight-step process to sustain organizational change. *The Heart of Change* expands upon the ideas in *Leading Change* and offers many case studies and anecdotes to address change more effectively.[4]

Another way to learn about managing change is by joining professional societies and attending conferences. Currently a significant issue within the profession, many state and national library organizations are offering preconferences, workshops, and programs on effectively managing change in the library. Similarly, a search in Library Literature of "change AND manag*" produces more than 200 hits. Additionally, there are video resources that can help staff and managers recognize and overcome change-related anxieties. One fast-paced 36-minute video uses humor and a straightforward approach to both validate the concerns that individuals may have with change and offer coping methods for improving performance in a changing environment.[5]

There are a few resources that address change from a library operational perspective and apply many of the techniques from the other resources. The books *Staffing for Results: A Guide to Working Smarter* and *Creating Policies for Results: From Chaos to Clarity* address implementing change in a public library environment for two major areas. Both books provide tips for engaging staff in the change process and continuing to move forward in implementing policy or staffing changes.[6]

Case Study: Let's Go Chat!

Beth – recent middle-manager new hire (six years prior experience elsewhere), general reference head

Keith – science reference librarian, early 50s, 18 years in library (had applied for Beth's job and did not get it)

Debby – new science reference librarian, mid-20s, hired five months ago, spent two years working for a Silicon Valley IT venture before getting her MLS

Nancy – social sciences librarian, mid 40s, five years in library

Annette – senior staff member in unit; 12 years in library; in charge of desk scheduling and basic customer service training

Sam – associate director, supervises Beth

Setting: in a library meeting room

Beth looks up as the last two people arrive for the meeting. "Go ahead and close the door behind you and get comfortable. The reason we are meeting is to start looking at the issues involved in implementing a chat-based reference service." As she makes this announcement, Beth observes each person's reaction to the news.

Nancy looks rather surprised as she asks, "We're really going to do it? I had heard rumors but figured they were just grapevine chatter. Where did the money come from? Or are we going to try and half do it on a shoestring budget?"

Annette has an interested but concerned expression on her face. Debby seems really excited as exhales and exclaims, "Finally!" Keith looks glum but does not say anything.

Beth explains, "The startup money is left over from that general education grant that funded the replacement of the public computer workstations. We saved money by taking the hand-me-down PCs from the research labs. Since the grant has to be used for direct services to library users, the library director thought the chat reference service would be a good use for it. Once we get past startup, the product we have targeted has a fairly low annual charge. The contract for the software went through yesterday, so now we can start getting an implementation team together and look at how this is going to work at the detailed level.

"This is why you are here. I expect you to form the kernel of a larger team, and possibly subteams, to look at developing a workflow around this service and addressing operational issues. There are still a lot of details to be ironed out. At this point, the only definite is that we want to have the service up and running in a publicly visible manner in eight months to coincide with the start of the next budget year."

Annette quickly speaks up, "So will this be something that will happen while people are at the reference desk or will it be another entire schedule that I have to put together? And who is going to be on the schedule, everyone or only a few people? What if someone flat refuses to do the chat reference and tells me to take them off the schedule altogether, what do I do then?"

Beth responds in a calming tone. "These are exactly the types of things that you, as a group are going to have to discuss and decide. Since this is something every library does differently, there is no magic formula that automatically works and Admin feels it is critical that people believe they have opportunity to provide input and air concerns. Perhaps by addressing this in the planning process, everyone will feel more invested in making it a success."

Debby speaks up enthusiastically at this point, "But why would someone not want to do it? It is a great service that helps people outside the library and the software package we've bought has some great features. We will be able to do lots of remote control functionality, with full escort capabilities both to see where they go and take them where they should be going, pushing down handout instructional pages, scanning and sending pages from a print resources, providing them with transaction logs. It will be so much fun learning all the details."

At this point, Keith chimes in repressively, "Well I hate to disappoint you but I am one of those people who are not just jumping with joy at the idea of doing this. From my perspective, this is another complex computer program we all have to learn with a lot of confusing bells and whistles. I'm not even sure what some of those features you just named off will do. I've tried regular chat a few times when my daughter used it from summer camp. I couldn't understand half of what she was saying with all the abbreviations and shortcuts she was using. Plus, I am a hunt-and-peck two-fingered typist. A lot of times, I hadn't even finished my sentence for her first comment and here were two more piling up, and she is only twelve. I can only cringe at the pace some of our users would expect. Plus, I saw a demo at ALA last year and they were talking about queues that allow you to switch back and forth, helping several people at once. I'm sorry but when you try to help a lot of people at once, you don't provide good service to anyone. The first thing you know, you will be telling the person with the question on multiple personalities to use Agricola to find the information on the genetically enhanced corn."

About halfway through Keith's comments, Debby starts sputtering and trying to interject comments. Annette and Nancy also start inserting their opinion as well. Beth realizes she needs to regain control of the meeting before it gets totally out of hand and deteriorates into personal sniping.

Speaking firmly, Beth says, "OK, everyone, calm down a minute. Excuse me. Excuse me!" As the furor subsides, Beth continues, "*This* sort of reaction that each of you just had is why it is critical that we get input and work on a team-based solution if we are to have any hope of implementing this. However, I expect each of you to be sensitive to the other's concerns and perspectives. Already, I can see that training and orientation is going to be a huge issue, both on the software and on converting the reference interview to a new environment. There may be staff who truly cannot develop the necessary skills and make the transition, but I expect everyone to at least make a conscientious effort and not just dig in their heels or go in expecting to fail. Additionally, they will have to recognize that by not participating in the chat reference service, they may be asked to take on other responsibilities to free-up time for chat librarians.

"Also, we do not expect to implement this the very first day as an answer everything, 24/7, open-the-floodgates sort of service. It will take time for users to become aware of it. Also, some questions will still require a face-to-face interaction because of their complexity. The idea of chat reference is to help with simple factual information and get them started or point them in the direction they need to go with some key electronic resources or search strategies.

"Now, the next thing I want us to discuss is how we break this planning process down into manageable pieces, what satellite teams we need to set up, and who we should bring into them. . . ."

Setting: picking up two days later during Beth's weekly status meeting with Sam

Beth is referring to her postmeeting personal notes as she says, "Well, as we expected Debby and Keith were at each other pretty quickly. I predict that I am going to be doing some pretty extensive coaching with each of them independently, but hopefully they will both come out of this with a better respect for each other. Debby is good at the technical side but if she hopes to go into management someday, she must develop patience and understanding for different personality types and personal perspectives. She has also got to learn to work with people who may not be as bright as she is, have less ability to multi-task, and have difficulty learning new computer systems. Similarly, we really do need to pull Keith out of the rut he has established for himself. His intolerance to change was starting to create other problems in unit operation.

"I was a little surprised at Annette's response. I really expected her to be a little more tuned into the unit-wide issues. Unfortunately, every single area that she commented on seemed to include the concepts of 'impact on me' or 'my area.' I think I am going to let her be on two subteams. One will be the subteam that deals with scheduling, which does have a direct impact on her workflow. But I am also going to have her co-chair the training subteam. This will force her to communicate with the other reference staff and bring their needs back to the group. Compared to the strong reactions from the others, I really couldn't get a good feel for what Nancy's position was. I couldn't tell if she was just being thoughtful or wanted to think before speaking, or if she was just overwhelmed by the more outspoken folks, or if she just wasn't really engaged. I have assigned her to lead a subteam and will keep an eye on that progress. Anyway, we have started mapping out a timeline with some discreet objectives and milestones. I'll keep you updated on the interpersonal dynamics issues."

Case Study Observations

- It is important to keep staff focused on addressing an issue intellectually rather than getting too bogged down in personal emotions.

- Mutual respect for, tolerance toward, and understanding of coworker's perceptions and concerns are key facets for effectively implementing team-based change.
- It may be necessary for a middle manager to guide a team to develop effective interactions before sending them off with action items, especially when individuals have widely varying viewpoints.
- Recognize that a specific organizational change can have a domino effect and drive further change based on its impact.

Thoughts and Discussion Exercises

What Do You Do Now?

1. The library has decided to initiate an electronic desktop delivery service to patrons. Extra student workers or part-time staff will be hired to retrieve items off the shelf. Then they will process the request by scanning the requested pages and using a new computer tool to make it available to library users via a login ID and password. One long-time staff member is convinced it will not work. At every planning meeting, he reels off the reasons it cannot be done and succeeds in either demoralizing or upsetting others in the unit. As the manager of this person (and the unit implementing the change), what do you do now?

2. Library administration has decided to buy some wireless laptops that can be checked out to users for use within the building. As a whole, the circulation desk staff are rather skeptical about the idea and feel that it will be problematic for many reasons. As the middle manager in charge of implementing this, what do you do now?

3. The library has decided to switch from sending paper notices via the campus and U.S. Postal Service mail systems to an e-mail based system. This is a complex change that impacts a lot of operational areas. Things have been going along rather well when it is discovered, all of a sudden, that a fairly large batch of e-mail addresses have gotten corrupted in the patron database. The computer support staff have found the problem, but have told you that it will take a month to get a patch for the code from the software vendor. In the meantime, undeliverable e-mails are showing up in the departmental mailbox. What do you do now? (Hint: Accurate e-mail addresses are available by looking up an individual in a separate online directory.)

Notes

1. Thomas R. Harvey, *Checklist for Change: A Pragmatic Approach to Creating and Controlling Change*, ed. Lillian B. Wehmeyer, 2nd ed. (Lancaster, PA: Technomic Publishing Co., 1995).

2. Lawrence M. Brammer, *How to Cope with Life Transitions: The Challenge of Personal Change* (New York: Hemisphere Publishing Corp., 1991).

3. Richard L. Gilbert, *How We Change: Psychotherapy and the Process of Human Development* (Boston: Allyn and Bacon, 2002).

4. John P. Kotter, *Leading Change* (Boston: Harvard Business School Press, 1996). Also available through NetLibrary, Inc. at http://www.netlibrary.com; John P. Kotter and Dan S. Cohen, *The Heart of Change: Real-Life Stories of How People Change Their Organizations* (Boston: Harvard Business School Press, 2002). Also available through NetLibrary, Inc. at http://www.netlibrary.com

5. Ben Bissel and W.R. Shirah, *Facing the Challenge of Change* videotape (TAMCO–Training and Management Consultants, Inc., 2002).

6. Diane Mayo and Jeanne Goodrich for the Public Library Association, *Staffing for Results: A Guide to Working Smarter* (Chicago: American Library Association, 2002); Sandra Nelson and June Garcia for the Public Library Association, *Creating Policies for Results: From Chaos to Clarity* (Chicago: American Library Association, 2003).

CHAPTER 9

Crisis Management

Crisis management is the ability to stay in control of oneself and address the needs of a critical event in the midst of absolute chaos. There is never a good time for a critical problem to arise, but inevitably it seems that crisis events customarily occur at the worst possible time. Many managers will not truly know how effective they are dealing with a crisis until confronted with the need. The clichés *trial by fire* and *tempering* are nonetheless appropriate analogies. Some managers have naturally strong crisis-management skills, whereas for others it is an area that they have to actively work on in order to achieve a level of competency. This chapter will discuss the middle manager's role in crisis situations, explain what makes one manager better than another in a crisis, and present the crisis process, from reaction through response to recovery.

To develop an understanding of this area, it is important to familiarize oneself with the library and university's emergency response documentation. Most libraries should have a written and usable emergency plan. Though some elements are consistent, such as the information to gather from a bomb threat, emergency plans are unique to the individual institution and may include specific local concerns. For example, the plan for a library located on the coast of the Gulf of Mexico would probably address issues related to a hurricane. As a manager, one needs to be extremely familiar with the plan and may need to be an active participant in keeping it updated and visible in the unit though coordination with a facilities manager or an emergency plan team. In addition to knowing the basic plan, one should develop an understanding of the roles of the university and community law enforcement groups, facility maintenance support crews, and medical facilities. One area for academic institutions to clarify is whether on-campus health facilities are available to faculty or staff during an emergency or if they just serve the student body population.

Managers Get Called First

In most organizations, when faced with a true crisis, the frontline staff member and middle manager do not have the necessary decision-making authority to resolve the crisis. Depending on the decision being made, this control often resides with upper administration. However, it is the middle manager who will usually be the first managerial representative on the scene. This is the person who must make critical calls on identifying the crisis, determine who should be contacted next and how, and conduct first-response damage control. Similarly, as decisions are made, the middle manager must communicate them back to the staff and provide on-the-scene support in implementing appropriate follow-up activities.

Categorizing the Crisis

The first thing a manager has to understand is what constitutes a crisis. Crises are anything unexpected that has a significant impact on library operations. Crises can be categorized in a number of ways depending on scope and impact. Things to recognize in understanding crisis situations include an assessment of what has transpired to cause the crisis, short-term impact, long-term impact, loss/cost to the library, and the impact on people, both in terms of the emotional response to the event and in the workflow changes required. Some crises require minimal workflow adaptation to routine and staffing, whereas others can disrupt an entire organization.

Most people have encountered mildly inconvenient or workflow-disruptive crises, such as a network server crash or an unexpected failure of the library online catalog system. Inconvenient crises usually have limited impact within the service sphere, are resolved within a couple of hours or days, and require temporary process workarounds until the situation is resolved. The key role of middle managers in inconvenient crises is threefold. First, they should lead staff in the development of workarounds for common minor crises so there is a fallback plan to use. Second, they should act as contact person and make sure that the appropriate experts, such as system technicians, are aware of the problem and the scope of the impact, and communicate back to staff the estimated repair time. Finally, they should stay calm and encouraging to staff as they struggle to adapt workflows to the situation.

The introduction of the potential for permanent damage to equipment or materials takes a crisis situation up a notch in intensity. For example, a leaking window seal that only drips on a section of carpet is less critical than a roof leak right over a range of shelves loaded with books or a bank of computers. These crises usually require an immediate response, such as creating a protective barrier against the source of the damage or removing materials from the affected area, followed by an administrative response to prevent a future recurrence of the problem. The middle-manager role is in guiding staff through the immediate response needs. This means being aware of which staff members can be called upon and where the necessary supplies (plastic, tape, etc.) are kept. Following the initial protective response, the middle manager then conducts follow-through notification to facilities/operations managers and upper administration. Given how word can spread in a library, these individuals may show up at the site of the crisis during the initial response. Generally, they will understand the importance of protecting the collection before requesting a briefing on the situation.

The highest priority crisis situations occur when a library user or significant amount of the collection or property have been put at risk. It is fairly easy to cover one or two ranges with plastic to protect the books from a localized dripping roof. It is another story to deal with a major pipe burst that puts over 30 ranges of materials at risk of water damage. Similarly, how a library responds to the injury of a library user, especially in academic settings where a large part of the user community are minors, can make the difference from breathing a sigh of relief once the crisis is past and being able to laugh about it later to dealing with accusations and lawsuits of negligence with negative media coverage and publicity. The guiding principle in all crises is to be responsive and effective. The key for the middle manager is to make and communicate decisions and follow-up on administrative instructions immediately and thoroughly.

Decision Making

Generally, if frontline staff members encounter a crisis situation, they will follow the chain of command to the middle manager fairly quickly. The middle manager must then do a basic situational assessment and make the call regarding the best method of follow-up. This includes determining who needs to be notified and how critical is the notification time lag. Depending on the situation, it may be necessary for the middle manager to interrupt an administrative meeting or call an administrator at home. This is part of the mental decision matrix that must be developed by the middle manager based on the practice of the organization. It is something that managers going into a new library need to find out about very soon so that they will not be overtaken by events. One aspect of the notification decision-making is not to assume someone else has already called the administrators. Just because a procedure says that the police representatives are supposed to call the library director in the event of a bomb threat does not necessarily mean they already have done so, depending on where they are in the event investigation.

In order to be effective, good crisis managers should express a heightened level of emotional interest in keeping with the event, without letting it get away from them into panic, hysteria, or the inability to make a decision. If surrounded by others who are reacting with emotional extremes, one might need to become more emotionally withdrawn in order to do a thorough situational assessment and notification decision matrix. So long as one does not emulate Chicken Little with frequent claims that the sky is falling and calls to the library director, being conservative and over-notifying upper management of a potential crisis event, especially by a new middle manager, is generally considered acceptable. In time and with experience, one should develop a better sense of which crises are truly considered critical by the organization and how they should be reported within the organizational hierarchy. Bear in mind, it is a greater error not to report something, which then snowballs and blindsides administration, than to report a few extra mini-crises to one's administrator. If in doubt, go ahead and notify your immediate supervisor. But, debrief afterward to better define your decision-making matrix.

Regardless of whether it happens at the time of the crisis or in a later briefing, administrative notification should not be delegated downward to a subordinate. The reason for this is that the middle manager is already known to the library administrative staff and will be more trusted to understand the scope of the situation and possible repercussions. Also, because there is a previous communication relationship, the middle manager will be better able to explain the events to the administrator in a clear and understandable manner based on first-hand observation, even with underlying concern or excitement that might come with some events. The following example offers a parallel to this effect. Suppose, you were crossing a street and noticed a stranger yelling out to you that a car was coming. Your first thoughts will be "who is that guy?" followed by an effort to attune your ear to better understand what he is saying. Contrast this to a trusted friend yelling out the warning, which you are more likely to understand better and respond to faster. In addition, subordinates may have a less-clear picture of the facts and scope of the crisis. This could lead to an inaccurate or incomplete report.

Leadership Means Going the Extra Mile

In addition to relating the problem and what has been done thus far, the middle manager should always follow-up by asking the administrator, "What would you like me to do to help?" Similarly, getting a call for assistance from an administrator or peer manager in the midst of a crisis is not the time to say "I'm sorry but I'm busy right now" and suggest contacting someone else. Suggesting one is present but unavailable or avoiding further participation during a crisis can be interpreted as a serious lack of commitment to the organization as a whole. Involvement in crisis events provides an opportunity for real teamwork and bonding to form between the participating staff and managers. Even though a senior library administrator may have prior commitments that take them outside the library, middle managers should stay on the scene and be highly alert to the crisis situation and maintain on-call vigilance. Additionally, middle managers with good leadership skills will leave their job descriptions at the door during a crisis and will not hesitate to get hands-on experience along with the staff.

However, it is important to make sure that what one volunteers for or is assigned to do is appropriate to one's abilities and actually is a help, not a hindrance. As an example, suppose a group of staff members were trying to drape protective plastic over a range of books and one particular employee is significantly shorter than the others. This particular person might be of better assistance in doing other tasks, such as stringing caution tape, pushing in books on the bottom shelf (below the drip line), or staffing a phone to coordinate repair/cleanup response. Sometimes staying out of the way or making sure other library operations are continuing is as important as being in the middle of things. The key is to stay flexible and adaptable during a crisis.

This flexibility should extend to personal attire as well as time. Crises can get messy or require significantly more physical activity than most managers customarily encounter in a normal workday. To be better prepared, middle managers may want to keep a set of casual/grungy clothes on hand if needed. A mid-toned pullover style of shirt or sweater, some durable cotton slacks or jeans, socks, and exercise shoes are the perfect attire for the well-dressed middle manager during a crisis. The mid-toned shirt is more appropriate than white or black, both of which will show dust from books much more visibly. Being appropriately dressed will allow you to move around without being distracted trying to protect your favorite suit of clothes or looking awkward and just plain silly. It allows one to better maintain a perception of being in control of the situation, which usually has a calming effect on staff. If a crisis has required one to get physical do not overlook hydration issues. This is not the time to be enforcing a library zero-tolerance policy on beverages (especially water bottles). Most library buildings are effectively climatologically sealed and if the crisis event has involved curtailing heating or cooling utilities, the availability of warm or cool beverages is important.

One aspect of some crises, especially those that go on for a period of several hours or days, is that fatigue becomes an issue. In some careers, such as the military, emergency medicine, or endurance competitions, this is a recognized phenomenon that is covered as part of the education/career training process. It is not something generally covered in library science programs. As mental and physical fatigue begins to set in, try to be aware of them. They can lead one to become clumsy and make mistakes. This could include dropping things, tripping, or walking into things. Mental fatigue can lead to bad decision-making. When in a state of mental fatigue, do not rush decisions. You should stop to think and talk them through. It can also be helpful to rely on a team approach to head off an irrational idea before it goes to far. If someone in the group groggily says, "I know something is wrong with that suggestion, but I can't think what," stop immediately and go back through it again. This is a major red flag that something has been overlooked. Naps are beneficial and will serve to give a temporary boost and hold deep fatigue at bay a little longer. The key is to recognize when your cognitive abilities are starting to be impaired and take steps to counteract this. Unless contra-indicated by specific health issues (this is not the time to stick to your current diet), high carbohydrate energy bars and caffeinated drinks can help sustain a person through a crisis. Keep in mind that all these techniques are temporary measures. The next section on recovery issues deals with post-event expectations.

Post-Event Recovery

There are several things to expect once the crisis event has passed. Immediately after a severe crisis, those that have been in the thick of the efforts to deal with the situation may experience a physical and mental crash as the adrenalin in their system tapers off and the fatigue catches up. This can also manifest itself through emotional highs and lows. Rest and a low-demand environment for a couple of days should allow for full recovery back to normal operating levels. In addition to the recovery issues associated with personal needs, there are organizational recovery events that will need to be done as well. These may include replacing physical supplies used during the crisis, restoring access to an area of the collection, or making sure that materials have been put away appropriately. Upper managers may be dealing with budgetary reallocation issues in order to cover special expenses accrued during the crisis. There may also be several debriefing sessions and follow-up meetings to address the events surrounding the crisis.

This is a very important part of crisis management. If individuals or organizations do not follow-up on a crisis, then they are inviting it to happen again and for the crisis to become routine. The problem with routine crises is that people get tired of responding to them with the appropriate level of energy and enthusiasm needed to facilitate effective recovery. Eventually, the situation can develop where a crisis happens, no one responds, and the loss is extremely high. Post-event analysis should explore several areas. First, why did the crisis event happen and could it have been prevented through a particular facility maintenance or staffing behavior response? If the answer is yes, then someone will need to be assigned to evaluate and implement the feasibility of enacting preventative measures. The answer may be no, that there is not a way to effectively predict where or when a similar crisis would recur. In that case, it is important to move the discussion forward and focus on crisis identification, notification, and response procedures. Crises sometimes occur because a failsafe has actually failed. One example might be a server room monitor that is supposed to trigger an electronic page to a systems technician when the room reaches a particular temperature. This has obviously failed if the technician walks into the server room one morning and finds it above 100 degrees. The post-crisis analysis may prompt the organization to build-in a layer of redundancy or more regularly test a critical sensor. Another area to assess is the notification and response process. Were the appropriate people notified in a timely fashion? Did they respond appropriately? Were the needed response equipment or supplies available, and did the relevant staff have accurate knowledge of their use? Were there any times during the crisis and recovery efforts that respondents seemed truly confused and the atmosphere was actually chaotic, not just hurried and intense? Could anything have been done better in handling the crises? Answering these questions and engaging in follow-up discussion helps improve organizational response processes and will assist in developing individual crisis management skills and expectations.

Even as an organization and administration are going through the post-crisis analysis and identifying the areas for improvement, it is important to recognize the positives that people did and pat them, and yourself, on the back. Dealing with true crises is difficult. Unless one has a dominant glass-half-empty philosophy and always truly expects the worst-case scenario to occur, the crises announcement will always be a shock. Effectiveness as a crisis manager is defined by how quickly one recovers from the shock to take positive and decisive action in a manner that supports the response team and organizational objectives.

Losing an Employee

Another crisis that most managers will inevitably encounter is the death of a current, active employee. The death may be sudden and

unexpected, such as a fatal car accident one night, or it may be anticipated, such as when dealing with the terminal illness of an employee.
Both scenarios can have a significant impact on unit operations and
emotional morale. The first scenario will have more intense initial reactions of shock and denial. With acceptance will come a stronger grieving
process because of the inability to have had closure with the individual
and being confronted with the fragility of life. Additionally, depending
on the individual's responsibilities, there may need to be immediate
workflow reprioritizations and adjustments to cover critical services. The
terminal illness scenario may produce a different initial reaction because
employees may have been able to address workflow issues in a gradual,
interim manner, and may had had a period of separation while the individual was undergoing medical or hospice care. However, the final act of
giving up hope and accepting that the individual has actually died will
still be emotionally wrenching for all unit employees, both managers
and staff.

The manager's role through this is a difficult one. Even as one
wishes to grieve with others, the personal grieving process may have to
be postponed while addressing essential operational issues. This may
mean implementing workflow changes in a preemptory fashion. If so,
it is important to reassure the staff that everyone will go back later and
revisit the decision and adjust all of the impacted workflows with
opportunities for staff input. In other cases, it may mean confirming
that interim changes that were quietly put in place are now permanent.
As morbid as it may seem, it is important that the manager has quietly
planned for the eventual death of the terminally ill employee so that
paperwork posting the job announcement or redefining the position is
ready and can be expedited.

The death related ceremonies of some cultures are very private and
usually only involve family members. If open services, such as a visita-
tion, funeral, or memorial service, are held, the manager is expected to
attend as a representative of the library and in recognition of the contributions that the person made to the unit. Enabling other employees
to attend these is also important. If a service desk is involved, it may be
necessary to solicit volunteers from parallel departments and implement a skeleton-staffing model during the events. Depending on cultural issues, it may be appropriate for the manager to coordinate
contributions for a plant at the services or a donation to a preferred
charity in the employee's name. A preference will usually be defined
by the deceased employee's family. Another appropriate step is to provide sympathy cards for staff in the unit to sign. These cards should be
generic and secular in nature and not reflect a particular religion's perspective toward death, something especially important in publicly

funded institutions. Once the details have been resolved, it is important for managers to allow themselves to let out their emotions and grieve in a safe and supportive environment with family or a professional counselor.

External Crises

The majority of this chapter has focused on responding to crises events that take place within the library environment. However, middle managers may also be called upon to respond in a leadership role to external crises as well. These crises can occur at the university or community level, such as a tragedy involving students getting killed in a dorm fire, church group bus crash, or the Aggie Bonfire collapse. They can also occur at a national level, such as the September 11, 2001, terrorist attacks on the World Trade Center. In these cases, the library middle managers do not have a role in responding to the crisis itself. However, they have a leadership role to assume in response to the emotional distress and confusion experienced by their staff. This is not the time to adopt a brusque "back to work" approach. Rather, managers should assist the staff in having as much knowledge of what is happening as possible and try to provide a stable foundation for staff. To provide information, it may be appropriate to set up a radio in the office or set up a computer to point to a news service Web page. If the library has a facility, such as a media room, that allows televised broadcast, the managers may set up a rotating desk schedule to allow staff to be updated. It can also be important to help staff maintain perspective. This can mean engaging them in conversation, telling them to go get a breath of fresh air or a glass of water, or providing a reassuring pat on the shoulder or (depending on the gender issues involved) a comforting arm. In some cases, a staff member or student worker exhibiting signs of serious depression may need to be encouraged to call home and speak to family or to contact the employee assistance/student counseling services. Middle managers should be careful not to use their own political or religious views on an issue to provide an answer to why something happened or encourage divisive debate. The biggest challenge to managers is putting their own emotions at bay in order to support their staff first, but not to suppress their emotions to such a degree that they will be haunted by them later on. Rather, as discussed in Chapter 12, they will need to turn to their support systems for their own venting and recovery.

Chapter Summary

In conclusion, crisis management is difficult. It requires you to be adaptable and be able to adjust to the demands of the situation. It requires the ability to think clearly through an emotionally intense situation. Most people do now know how they will respond in a crisis situation until actual faced with one. Consequently, it can be hard to prepare from emotional and behavioral perspectives. The key is to learn from events and build the skills necessary to deal more effectively with the next crisis. As a minimum, one needs to have a working familiarity with procedures, resources, and experts associated with the possible crises a library can face.

To Learn More

There are many books and book chapters in library-related texts that deal with developing an emergency or disaster plan. However few of these explore actual managerial behaviors during the crisis event. One book that does introduce this concept is *Blindsided* by Bruce T. Blythe. Though directed toward the corporate and industrial sector, it offers insights into leadership and action team roles during a crisis.[1] A book by Jack Gottschalk is less relevant to the library environment but offers good insights into the media elements of dealing with a crisis. It uses case studies to look at how profit and nonprofit organizations have addressed crisis situations. His focus is on the importance of effective public relations and having a rapid, authoritative, and credible response in the event of a crisis.[2]

Case Study: Middle-Manager Crisis

> **Note:** This case study is specifically tailored to an academic setting because of the unique and complex expectation that academic administrators will assume a more parental role toward students in residence. For a public library setting, the crisis would be addressed more simply by contacting appropriate emergency medical or law enforcement personnel and then notifying the institution's public relations and legal representation. It is also written narrative style to convey that true crises are seldom resolved with simple conversation and will be an ongoing sequence of events over a period of time.
>
> **Sam** – Kate's supervisor, associate director

Kate – internal middle-manager promotion (eight months ago), access services head

Molly – a freshman

Setting: midway through the fall semester

Background: The library is on the migration path for the Mexican Free-Tailed bat. This is a small, nonaggressive bat that eats bugs and fruit. It is customary for a few to try and temporarily roost in the ceiling space, but they have not been a serious problem in the past. Unfortunately, after last summer's drought they seem to be finding more cracks in the building facade and there have been more sightings than normal. Just last week, the health inspector had been contacted and indicated that even though they can carry rabies like any wild mammal they are not a health hazard . . . unless of course they bite someone, which never happens.

Kate is just walking into the building Wednesday afternoon when she is flagged down by the staff member at the front desk. The staff member has a young student, Molly, sitting at the desk and informs Kate that the student said a bat had just bitten her on the foot. Apparently Molly had taken off her athletic shoes while studying. When she went to put her shoes back on, her foot hit something soft in the toe of one of them and she felt a small pinch. When she pulled her foot back out and looked in the shoe, she saw the bat move. At that point she screamed and threw the shoe hard against a wall and then came downstairs to tell the staff member. Kate could see a small red mark on her middle toe.

At this point, Kate realizes the library has a major crisis situation. She knows that there might be rabies exposure and treatment issues. She turns to the library security staff member on the scene and queries them on whether they knew where in the building this happened. Receiving an affirmative response, she instructs them to see if the bat is still there and put an upside-down trashcan over it in order to contain it. They should then contact the facilities officer and await further information. She told Molly that the foot needs to be looked at and offers to call an ambulance. Molly protests that it really does not hurt and she does not want an ambulance. She would rather go to the Student Health Center (SHC) than an emergency room. Kate calls on her assistant to start the walk over to the SHC with Molly and gives him an injury report form to take with him and for Molly to complete. Then she heads to the administrative offices. Fortunately, Sam is available and she is able to brief him on the situation. Sam agrees this is a very delicate situation and the library is going to need to act carefully through this matter, especially since the director is currently out of the country. He tells Kate to go after Molly and stay with her, but also to stay in touch with him as the details of her treatment unfold. He will notify the university administration of the event and brief the library's public relations officer.

Kate hurries over to the SHC and catches up with her assistant and Molly just as they sit down to fill out the patient information and injury report forms. As they fill out the forms, Kate is relieved to learn that Molly is 18 years old and not a minor. The SHC staff call Molly fairly quickly and Kate hovers in the background as the library's representative. She has talked to the library and verified that they have captured the bat but are not certain of the procedure for getting it tested for rabies. The SHC staff are glad to hear that the bat has been captured and provide information on how to arrange for emergency rabies testing. Kate relates this back to the library, and campus police are contacted to transport the bat from the library to the testing site. In the meantime, the SHC doctor recommends that Molly start treatment for rabies, just in case. Unfortunately, they do not keep this medicine in stock and inform Kate and Molly that they will have to go buy it from the local hospital and then bring it back for SHC staff to administer. The cost is going to be several hundred dollars. Not having this much ready cash and her car still being at her apartment off campus, Molly is unsure what to do. Kate calls back to the library to apprise them of the situation and asks whether the library wants to pick up the cost for the drug. She also volunteers to transport Molly to and from the hospital and then home to her apartment. Sam agrees and arranges for a purchase order to be ready for them to pick up in a few minutes. Though a vast improvement over the old style of administering rabies vaccine, the first round of shots in her legs and arm are not pleasant for Molly. If the test results on the bat come back negative, then no more shots will be needed. If they come back positive, Molly has to continue the series and get another shot in the arm in two days.

Exacting a promise from Molly that she will eat some supper, Kate promises to keep in touch, drops her off at her apartment, and heads home. It is about 7 P.M. Once home, she calls and leaves a message for Sam on how the situation currently sits. She realizes that it is important to keep e-mail traffic relating to the event at a minimum for potential liability and litigation issues, but does send one to Sam that summarizes the events of the afternoon in a factual manner.

The next morning Kate checks in with Sam regarding follow-up activities. She discovers that Molly's mother has been in touch with the library. She was on vacation several states away and had spoken to Molly the night before about the incident. She is currently on her way to the university but will have a lengthy drive. She is concerned because Molly indicated she was not feeling well, could not sleep last night, and may not be taking care of herself. Because Molly uses the campus dining hall for her meals, her mother does not think she has much food in her apartment. Molly's mother asks if someone from the library can check on her. After calling the SHC, Sam has discovered that slight fever, muscle aches, and nausea are common side effects to the vaccine and Molly needs to consume light, hydrating foods, such as soups and juices. The doctor also advised an over-the-counter treatment to reduce the fever and muscle aches.

Kate points out that Molly already knows her from their interactions the previous day and volunteers to go get some groceries and look after her. Sam agrees that this is a good plan because he has been called into meetings with university administrators and university building maintenance staff about the bat situation. He advises Kate to keep him updated on Molly's condition and make it her highest priority. Kate checks in briefly with her staff as she heads out and lets them know that she is going to be only minimally available for the next few hours. Then she gets some groceries from a nearby store and goes to Molly's apartment. When she gets there, she discovers that Molly had ordered-in pizza for supper the previous night (not the best thing to have eaten with the pending drug side effects) and has not been getting any fluids. Kate fixes Molly some soup and juice and tells her what the doctor said about reducing the fever. Molly has some of the recommended over-the-counter drug and takes it herself. Before too long, she starts feeling better and is able to doze off.

Taking into account their conversation as Molly ate, Kate comes to the conclusion that Molly will not do very well at looking after herself while she is sick and is going to need someone to look in on her periodically until her mother arrives. She calls Sam, who tells her they have heard from Molly's mother and she is going to be delayed due to car trouble. Realizing that she is going to be spending more time out of the office, Kate leaves to get some lunch of her own and pick up some things to work on. Molly calls Kate and says that the local newspaper has called and wants to interview her about what happened. Kate checks in with the library public relations officer, who has been answering calls and issuing press releases about the incident, and reassures Molly that she is totally free to talk to the press. Now that she is eating and resting better, Molly's youthful resilience has returned and this is all "one big adventure." As Kate returns to Molly's apartment, Molly is wrapping up the interview with the reporter and photographer. Kate hears Molly telling the reporter how well the library has been taking care of her and breathes a sigh of relief. The reporter informs Molly that he just heard, as he came to her apartment, that the bat tested negative. About 5 minutes later, Molly gets her official call about the results and is quite relieved that she will not have to have any more shots. Later that evening, as Molly is eating the supper Kate fixed for her, Molly's mother arrives. Rather than the fearful images she has been traveling with, she learns that the bat tested negative and sees that someone has carefully looked after her daughter.

The next day, the newspaper coverage of the event reflected positively on the library's response to the situation. Realizing that the worst-case scenario could happen, university administration authorized appropriate resources to evict the bats from the library and reseal all of the cracks in the building facade. Molly continued to study in the library and occasionally drops by to visit with Kate, but does not take off her shoes. Eventually Kate and Sam can laugh about the event.

Case Study Observations

- Communication is critical: Especially during a crisis, it is critical that the team members stay in touch so that priorities and logistics can be coordinated.
- Be flexible: Nurturing a sick student was not in Kate's job description. But when the need was identified, she stepped in to help.
- Do not forget they are students: As much as 18-year-old freshmen may think they are now adults, their parents do not agree and a little extra care will go a long way when they are in pain.

Thought and Discussion Exercises

What Do You Do Now?

1. There has been a major power failure in the facility that houses the integrated catalog. No work can be done in the system for at least two

days. Define how this would affect your operational area. What do you do now?

2. It is 8 P.M. on a Saturday, you answer the phone at home and it is the staff member currently on duty at your public service desk. The person is mildly distraught and has just taken a bomb threat against the library. You verify that the university police have been contacted and have just arrived. What do you do now?

3. It is 2 A.M. and a ringing phone awakens you. Your administrative supervisor has been notified that a water pipe has burst near the section of the collection that is your responsibility. This person is already on the scene but is unfamiliar with the detailed procedures for protecting the books (where the plastic supplies are, etc.). What do you do now?

4. You walk through the office area and an obviously upset student worker is on the phone trying to use a phone card. You look to the student's supervisor, who explains that the student just said she needed to call her mother. The student becomes increasing distraught as no one answers. As you try to calm her down you discover that she stumbled while shelving some books and hit the edge of a column in such a way that she has broken her front tooth. What do you do now?

Notes

1. Bruce T. Blythe, *Blindsided* (New York: Portfolio, 2002).

2. Jack Gottschalk, *Crisis Management* (Oxford: Capstone Publishing, 2002). Also available through NetLibrary at http://www.netlibrary.com/

CHAPTER 10

Evaluating Employee Performance

Another challenge faced by all managers is the formal performance appraisal process. For new managers, this can be especially difficult and one's initial experiences can significantly impact one's perception about the effectiveness and value of this process. As with many of the issues covered in this book, different institutions will have different procedures and cultures associated with employee evaluation. However, even as institutions have specific procedures, there are some common elements to any evaluation process. New managers are usually chosen from high-achieving and successful frontline librarians. As such, they may have very little experience writing or receiving an average or unsatisfactory evaluation. Similarly, they have invested in librarianship as their careers and may find that administering an evaluation to an entry-level support staff member making slightly above minimum wage introduces a new and foreign perspective. This chapter will offer resources to better introduce managers to the appraisal process and will focus on the hands-on aspects to conducting performance appraisals in the managerial role.

Adapting to the Culture

Whether one is new to the managerial ranks or just new to a particular institution, it is critical to assess and learn about the appraisal culture in the organization. As a manager, one will have several direct reports, even unit supervisors, who must be appraised. One may also be acting in the capacity of reviewing and signing off on other subordinate appraisals for consistency within the unit. Becoming acclimated to the performance evaluation culture can be accomplished in several ways. The first and frequently most informative is to talk to people. The difficult part is recognizing who should be consulted and assimilating the different perspectives into a cohesive whole. New managers should not be afraid to talk about the appraisal process. They should discuss the institutional culture with their administrative supervisors, human resources representatives, peer managers, and the support staff being appraised. Another way to gain a sense of the organizational culture is to review the previous year's appraisals in an employee's personnel file. New managers may be in for a surprise if they expect a consistent understanding of the role of the performance appraisal and expect that an employee's past appraisals will be consistent with their own observations. The institution may have a history of always giving critical evaluations or may only give lip service to the practice and be comfortable with over-inflated scores. Even if a senior manager's signature is required, new managers will likely see a disconnect between what human resources or administrators wish would happen, what has been the practice, and what the staff members being appraised expect to see and hear. It is also important to understand the role of the performance appraisal. Is it meant to serve primarily as a development tool or does it have ties to variance in pay or benefits? If the appraisal is tied to merit raises, are they distributed with a philosophy that any good performance is rewarded and everyone gets a marginal increase with small differences between a satisfactory and excellent performer? Or is it that only the true excellence of a small group of employees is rewarded and the rewards are significant? All of this plays a role in how the appraisals are perceived and valued. Even if a culture is defined, appraisals are still an individual and subjective process and will be influenced by a manager's perspective and comfort with employee conflict.

The appraisal situation may also be complicated if the library is using a new assessment and appraisal tool or is going through an organizational change with new performance expectations. In this case, there may be significant gaps in what human resources representatives say should be happening and what is actually being done. Even as new managers want to give fair and informative evaluations, they should also work to be consistent with their peers and not represent radical and immediate change from their predecessor, unless overly critical appraisals and unrealistic expectations contributed to the managerial change. The trust between staff and their new manager can be severely damaged if the first evaluation process is handled too strongly. It is best to proceed carefully and actually use the first cycle to clarify expectations on the part of the new manager rather than to try and critically assess the employee's performance during the adjustment period. For an employee to go from excellent to marginal in the space of one evaluation period under the new manager will significantly damage the new manager's credibility within the unit and create a very difficult environment for future change. Reviewing Chapter 8 on managing change can offer insights into guiding employees in the new directions they will be expected to address. Eventually, new mangers will have built an environment that allows them to effectively evaluate employees on their current job expectations without having to worry about the grievance issues covered in Chapter 11.

Appraisal Tools

Most annual evaluation forms for library support staff will consist of four parts: employee information, quantitative or categorized ratings for sections, areas for qualitative comments supporting the quantitative rating, and future goals or objectives. The employee information will often include the employee's name, ID number, title, rank, and a brief description of regular responsibilities in the unit or organization. Quantitative or categorized ratings can be numerical scores, a verbal scale, or both. The verbal scale will use a range of terms such as excellent, above average, exceeds expectations, good, satisfactory, meets expectations, fair, needs improvement, marginal, poor, unacceptable, or unsatisfactory. Often if a manager gives the highest or lowest possible ratings, they must justify the rating with comments. The amount of justification can vary from a sentence or two to several paragraphs, given the area, managerial expectations, and supervisor's writing skill. The goals or objectives section sets the stage for employees to understand what will be expected of them during the coming year if they wish to get a good evaluation next year.

It is actually quite difficult to write an evaluation that truly reflects the employee's performance. The many pitfalls a new manager can make in this process are described in the references in the To Learn More section at the end of the chapter. They include a tendency to focus on more recent events than looking at performance throughout the full year, and not treating each category independently. It is the very rare employees who are either excellent in every single category or are deficient in every category. This is an immediate tip-off that the evaluation is flawed. Sometimes employees and managers forget that an annual evaluation is supposed to be just that, an evaluation of the performance during the past 12 months. Employees may have the perception that as they continue to grow and develop and basically do their job well from year to year, the quantitative part of their evaluations should reflect that and always go up in all categories. If they do not see obvious verification of their growth, it can contribute to them feeling they are in a dead-end job or unappreciated for their efforts. As budget crises have forced institutions to cut back on being able to actually give significant monetary-based merit increases, some managers have responded by giving an overinflated rating of the employee. This is based on a philosophy that "I cannot do anything else for them so I will at least praise them." Additionally, some supervisors or managers might be tempted to put minimal information on the formal written evaluation but make a lot of recommendations for improvement verbally. This is not a good practice because it does not document the agreed upon need for improvement and is more subject to perceived hearing filters or interpretations on the part of the employee.

In addition to each institution using its own form, different employee groups at the same institution may have different forms or timetables for being appraised. This is especially common in academic institutions where librarians have faculty status. Classified or technical support staff may have a uniform and structured appraisal. However, as faculty or professional positions, librarians may have a more open format appraisal that employs a freestyle paragraph approach and qualitative assessment. The latter can vary in expectations of length and level of detail depending on the individual unit or manager. Managers may also want to consider if past evaluations are opened to others during the tenure/promotion process and gauge their comments to allow for cross-disciplinary understanding.

Preparing the Evaluation Documents

In the past dark ages of management, the annual evaluation was the only form of appraisal interaction between an employee and a manager and could be very subjective based on vague generalities. The current management philosophy in most organizations is quite different. Rather than being a stand-alone document handed down from above with the manager's opinion of the employee's performance, the annual evaluation is seen as one of several tools for communicating expectations with the intent of improving performance. Contemporary management philosophy is that nothing on the evaluation should come as a surprise to the employee, but instead should have been discussed previously. Additionally, the comments should be based on specific, detailed events rather than vague areas. This does not mean the manager should become nitpicky and try to describe every event. Instead, it is important to look for repeated performance behaviors and offer examples that support the presence of a pattern. It is also critical that the problem behavior be tied back to the overall performance of the unit. This will go a long way to avoid the classic complaint by an underachieving employee that "You are just picking on me."

As an example, suppose an employee who is responsible for taking outside calls and routing them in the unit is spending a lot of time on the phone for personal calls. In the evaluation, you would want to call attention to a sampling of observed behaviors, such as several days when you documented that the employee was observed engrossed in personal calls for more than 30 minutes at a time. You would also need to point out that by not being able to take unit calls, others had to answer the phone and could not do their assigned tasks. It is also good practice if you can relate the behavior back to a direct service impact on library users, such as being put on hold longer. When completing an appraisal for average employees it is important to provide both examples of areas where the employees have done well or shown improvement, as well as referencing areas where they may have made mistakes they need to learn from or work on overall improvements. Depending on whether employees have glass-half-full or glass-half-empty perspectives or perfectionist tendencies, they will likely see the evaluation as good or bad based more on their own bias than what the manager has written.

One thing that managers should watch for when preparing or reviewing employee evaluations is that the evaluation should address specific performance behavior issues and avoid being an evaluation of the employee's attitude. Generally, managers cannot tell employees that they should be happier, less paranoid, or even less depressing. Instead, new managers need to address the behavior that results from the attitude. One example would be to suggest to an employee with a sour disposition and persistently unhappy expression that you have noticed patrons hesitate to approach her and she might want to attend a workshop on customer service or communications and work on being more approachable. This is more difficult when dealing with deeper personality conflicts within the unit. You may have two student supervisors, one extremely mothering and the other a severe disciplinarian. It is probable that their style differences are rooted in personal values. In truth, a better supervisor will be somewhere in the middle with characteristics of both. If simply told to work together without explaining what should be accomplished, they are likely to become very polarized and not be successful. Whereas, by clarifying your expectation that you want the mothering supervisor to hold the students more accountable and the severe disciplinarian to be more empathic to student immaturity, they may be able to set aside the personal aspect and learn from each other. Similar problems can be encountered between the "happiness and light" and "doom and gloom" personalities. By encouraging them to respect and learn from each other in the context of unit needs, managers may be able to soften and mainstream extremely idiosyncratic personalities. However, when faced with an employee whose performance is a clear disturbance to others in the unit, other disciplinary processes may be called for. Chapter 11 addresses what managers need to do in this situation.

Another important issue in preparing employee appraisal, applicable to both the formal evaluation and informal coaching session, is to try and avoid using secondhand information when addressing performance issues. As discussed in previous chapters, there may be a complex web of interpersonal dynamics between different employees and this can become more apparent when addressing performance issues. Suppose a direct report staff member, Joe, tells you that he has noticed that Sue, an employee who also reports directly to you, is always being confrontational with others in the unit and blaming them for things she herself does wrong. It is important that you verify this before actually addressing it as a performance issue with Sue. You must go through a data-gathering phase of paying close attention to employee interactions. If you do observe conduct problems on the part of an employee, it can be addressed as a personal observation from a position of authority. Otherwise, the employee can become defensive and claim that the colleague who reported the problem misunderstood or is being vindictive for past issues. When faced with a conflict between two employees in a unit, it is important to address it with both employees in the context of their own conduct. It is also extremely important to emphasize that you expect everyone to work together, even those with past personal differences. For many people, it is much easier to respond defensively and engage in conflict than to back off from the person initiating conflict and deny them a target. Having the responsibility to disengage rather than go on the defensive and attack back is something that a manager should emphasize as a conduct expectation. This then allows the manager to better address the original aggressor's conduct more specifically.

Privacy

The previous section ends by discussing the issue of third-party roles in the performance appraisal process. This is a natural lead-in to remind managers that appraisals are formal personnel documents and are subject to a high level of confidentiality. In most organizations it is acceptable to discuss specific performance problems with other managers or administrators. For a new manager, this is desirable and useful because peer senior managers may be able to offer experience-based advice on how to best address a difficult issue. However, the performance of an employee should never be discussed with a peer or subordinate of that employee. This is especially important when it comes to performance problems where the employee may be going through intense coaching or some other disciplinary process. If an employee is reporting a perceived performance problem with another employee, such as the earlier example with Joe and Sue, you should thank Joe for bringing it to your attention and reassure him that the problem will be investigated and addressed appropriately. The manager should also explain to Joe that when there is a follow-up with Sue it will be done privately and he will not be informed of any disciplinary action taken. Frequently, the manager may already be aware of the problem before it is reported and know of extenuating circumstances related to the problem. In these cases, it may be appropriate to again thank Joe for bringing it to your attention and acknowledge that you are aware of the situation, but explain that you cannot discuss it with him. This is especially the case when dealing with health-related attendance or conduct issues.

Given the effort a new manager may employ to keep an evaluation private, it can come as a surprise to learn that many employees share and compare their evaluations with that of their peers, much like schoolchildren compare report cards. Unfortunately, when employees perceive a difference between their own and peer evaluations, without a corresponding perception of a performance difference, interpersonal conflict can increase and morale suffer. Sometimes employees will complain that the supervisor is always reprimanding them but does not reprimand a peer. In this situation, the appropriate response is to explicitly point out to employees that in the same way their own peers are not allowed to be observers during their counseling or disciplinary procedures, they are not allowed to observe the counseling of others and should not be making assumptions.

Discussing the Evaluation

Discussing employee responses to the evaluation is an appropriate transition into the second phase of most formal evaluation processes, the follow-up meeting. Most evaluation processes will include a requirement that supervisors or managers meet with their direct reports to discuss the evaluation and answer any questions the employee may have. For some managers this is the hardest part of the evaluation process because of its unpredictability. One is never quite sure how the employee is going to react to the evaluation document. Some employee evaluation meetings go very smoothly. These employees accept the evaluation as accurate, acknowledge the areas they need to work on more, and agree with the established goals or objectives for the coming year. There will be a few unpleasant meetings where the employee claims the evaluation is an inaccurate reflection of actual performance, resents the manager having pointed out areas for improvement, and does not want to accept the goals or objectives set by the manager. This latter type of session can be extremely difficult for new managers to accept without losing their self-confidence or personalizing the conflict.

Regardless of whether the employee reacts well to the evaluation, new managers should be prepared to answer a very difficult question that is frequently asked: "What do I specifically have to do to get a better rating?" For some evaluation categories, such as attendance, reliability, or quantity of work, the answer will be fairly straightforward. The manager can assign a quantitative expectation, such as copy catalog a specific number of records per day or process recalls the same day that they are received. The manager can refer to documentation, such as time sheets for tardiness, to explain the expectation. However, evaluations often include categories that are difficult to tie to specific work tasks. Answering this question in the context of leadership, diversity in the workplace, collegiality, or customer service can be much more difficult. One often has to rely on anecdotal observations, which can be subject to interpretation, and behavioral examples to explain managerial expectations. For many staff members, accustomed to thinking in absolute terms of right or wrong, understanding the concept of shades of gray and applying judgment skills will be a very difficult learning process. New managers might want to have information at-hand on workshops or reading materials to help employees develop in these areas.

Each time an employee reacts negatively to an evaluation, it will be a slightly different experience. Some employees will claim that the manager is the one in the wrong by suggesting that the manager does not understand what they do or that the manager failed to communicate accurate expectations. Some employees focus on their past history with the library, trying to blur recent performance problems or suggesting that their seniority makes them exempt from performance expectations. Others may claim they are being singled out in some manner by the new manager and discriminated against because the manager does not like them. This situation is most likely to occur when the unit or the individual employee is going through a period of change in either job responsibilities or personal life. The employee can become emotional, reactionary, and even try to beg or bully the manager into changing the evaluation. The first time one experiences this type of behavior from an employee can be very difficult for a new and conscientious manager. The main thing to remember, as the manager, is that even though you may not be perfect, you have made a good faith effort to be fair and are the managerial authority figure. Do not let the employee use the emotion of the moment or your dislike for conflict convince you to revise the evaluation more in the employee's favor. It is important that you stand firmly behind the evaluation as you have prepared it based on the employee's self-evaluation and your own supervisory notes, although you may invite an employee to attach a rebuttal or follow due process to protest an evaluation. If an employee brings something to light that actually would have led you to give a better evaluation, it is important to note this in your supervisory log as reference for the next year's review and explain that it is the employee's responsibility to tell you about his accomplishments and represent himself effectively to you through meetings, memos, and self-evaluation.

Even when new managers are certain they have mentioned performance deficiencies in the past through coaching or counseling, they may be surprised by the employee's reaction to actually seeing the deficiency referenced in an official written document. Employees can hear verbal coaching through a personal filter that is invisible to the manager. What the manager sees as an expectation can be heard as an optional suggestion. Similarly, all employees carry experiential baggage that can cause them to rationalize circumstances to fit their mental model. Employees who do not want to be moved out of their comfort zone will tell themselves a change is temporary and they do not really need to change the way they do things. They can try to defer the change by always contending that they need additional information or support. They can stay busy on other "more important" tasks so that they do not have time to address the new initiatives. These avoidance techniques are more difficult to rationalize when an employee sees a comment about the performance written in black-and-white, thereby leading to the reactionary response. Chapter 11 addresses what a manager faced with a hostile response to a performance evaluation should do to reaffirm that she has acted in an ethical and professional manner and to be prepared for the inevitable grievance that all proactive managers will encounter at some point in their career.

The Manager's Self-Evaluation

Up to now, the focus of this chapter has been on the role of the manager as the evaluator. It is also important for new managers to remember they will be evaluated by their administration and to recognize what is important in preparing their own self-evaluation. In the past as a frontline librarian, one's annual evaluation probably described quantitative tasks that one had accomplished. This might include the number of

instructional classes taught, books cataloged, or vendor contracts negotiated. One could usually point to an organizational outcome based on
one's job, such as helping students get the resources they needed by
working the reference desk. Committee or team responsibilities were
task-focused with specific and accomplishable objectives. As a manager, one no longer has such specific accomplishments to recount.
Instead one's accomplishments come secondhand in the form of the
accomplishments of the individuals in one's unit. Getting two employees with a history of difficulty to work together and collaborate is a
managerial accomplishment. Charging and enabling staff to revise a
procedure in order to provide better service to users is a managerial
accomplishment. Sharing information and collaborating across the
organization, even without a resulting end-product, is a managerial
accomplishment. All of these examples represent how a manager's self-
evaluation will be less populated with independent "I taught," "I
implemented," or "I [insert active verb]" comments and more pep-
pered with "I coordinated," "I planned," "I encouraged," or "I initi-
ated." In some cases, there may not be a visible outcome. Suppose you
were asked to prepare a plan for moving some materials into a remote
storage facility. Depending on the complexity, this might have been a
significant undertaking requiring many hours of work. Then you turn
in the proposal and nothing happens. Later on you discover that
another academic unit got the space. It is still important to represent
the effort in a self-evaluation, even if there is not an actual successful
outcome that was executed and can be seen by all. Referring back to
Chapter 1 on the roles of a middle manager, this is what a manager
does and reflecting it in an evaluation is both challenging and necessary.

Chapter Summary

As a new manager, preparing supervisory and managerial evaluations
of your staff, as well as your own self-evaluation, can be difficult. Much
of the evaluation process is heavily dependent on the culture of the
library and how the assessment of employee performance is implemented. Current trends are toward balanced evaluations that recognize
good performance and identify areas where an employee needs to
improve, with an emphasis on employee growth. The annual evaluation
itself is a summary tool that is only part of the feedback and development provided to employees. When preparing an evaluation, it is important to focus on facts and behaviors, rather than attitudes, and maintain
confidentiality about an individual's evaluation. When doing the follow-
up meetings with individuals, it is important to be adaptable. Many
meetings will go quite smoothly. Managers should also be prepared for

the situation to become unpleasant based on perceptual disconnects between what the employee expected to see on an evaluation and what was actually written. In these situations, it is critical that the manager not get swept up in the emotions of the unhappy employee, instead maintaining a calm but firm demeanor and direct dialogue to the factual aspects of the evaluation. Annually appraising an employee does not have to be a negative experience for new managers. Most new managers find it to be an experience that allows one to reward good performance and help employees recognize areas where they need to improve their performance—not necessarily fun but quite effective.

To Learn More

Most library management and business administration texts will have information about preparing performance evaluations. Additionally, there are entire works focusing on different assessment tools and methods. As with any imperfect process, researchers are constantly looking for better ways to assess and communicate employee performance expectations. As the intellectual property of the researchers, they often have catchy names such as 360° feedback, the balanced scorecard, positive discipline, or positive performance management. The current trend for the past decade has been to emphasize the evaluation and feedback process in a positive light that supports ongoing development and improvement. Euphemisms, such as notices, discipline memos, and unsatisfactory performance, are used to reflect unacceptable or inadequate performance. Because higher education in general, and libraries specifically, are less focused on profit-based performance models, they are often a step behind corporate performance assessment techniques. Total Quality Management (TQM) had already come and gone in the American corporate environment, as many academic libraries were only beginning to incorporate some of the elements into their environments.

Chapter 9 of *Library and Information Center Management* gives an excellent overview of the typical performance appraisal process found in libraries. It goes over the basic purpose behind the evaluation, as well as introducing typical appraisal tools and some of the common inadvertent tendencies that can lead to inaccurate appraisals.[1] Two books by Dick Grote give a more thorough but readable overview of the performance appraisal process. The older 1996 text, *The Complete Guide to Performance Appraisal,* is divided into four sections. The first two sections introduce the context of performance appraisal, address what is supposed to be measured in the process, and offer guidance on preparing and delivering an effective appraisal. For those who are in smaller institutions, the third section offers insights on designing an appraisal instrument. The final section addresses legal issues and emerging trends in the performance appraisal process.[2] Grote's newer book, *The Performance Appraisal Question and Answer Book: A Survival Guide for Managers*, is more of a hands-on reading style with examples, tips, and "Red Flag" sections. Although the actual content is quite readable with minimal jargon, the arrangement may seem less intuitive to the beginning reader. It is structured around a frequently-asked-questions format, with a short answer initially provided and a "Tell Me More" section for additional reading.[3] Another good reference, despite its title, is *Abolishing Performance Appraisals: Why They Backfire and What to Do Instead*. This book addresses the importance that a performance appraisal should not exist in a vacuum and must be an ongoing process between an employee and a manager. It dispels traditional myths about evaluating performance and emphasizes the importance of using positive motivators and coaching as part of the overall process to encourage self-motivation and employee development. Several of the resources on improving communication skills that are cited in Chapter 3 are also relevant in the appraisal context.

Case Study: Evaluating a Static Senior Staff Member

> **Kate** – internal middle-manager promotion (two years ago), access services head
> **Ellen** – senior circulation staff member (15 years in library)
> **Patricia** – Kate's predecessor, retired shortly before Kate's promotion
> **Setting:** Kate's office

Kate is preparing for her follow-up evaluation meeting with Ellen. She knows that Ellen has been with the library for a long time and has been a reliable employee. However, this past year Kate has noticed that Ellen has been noticeably unenthusiastic about some of the changes that Kate has encouraged. Additionally, Kate knows that within the past two years, three employees who reported to Ellen have resigned and as part of their exit interview complained about some aspects of Ellen's supervisory style being overly rigid with unrealistic expectations. Even though she has been trying to coach Ellen to become more results-focused with an emphasis on unit operational tasks rather than strict adherence to historic rules, she is not sure how Ellen is going to respond to seeing this in writing on her evaluation.

Kate rises as Ellen comes into the office and moves toward the small meeting table to the side as she says, "Come on in and have a seat, Ellen. You've had a chance to review your evaluation and my proposed goals for this next year. Do you have any specific questions, comments, or things you'd like to go over in more depth?"

Ellen's lips tighten briefly in a frown before she begins speaking in a biting tone. "Well, I'd like to tell you that I think this is the worst evaluation I have ever received. I've always gotten an excellent rating in the past on every category. I was shocked as I read it and I don't appreciate the things you have put on it. I couldn't believe you said my performance is only satisfactory. You just don't understand what it is to do my job and how difficult it is."

Kate mentally flinches and sighs as she realizes that what she had half-suspected was true. Ellen had perceived the coaching sessions during the past months as mild suggestions, not real expectations. "I'm sorry that you feel that way. I did rate you very highly on several categories, such as reliability and attention to detail. Why don't we go through the sections and goals, specifically identify those that are bothering you, and maybe I can clarify why I have put in the ratings and comments that I did. "

"Well, I mostly resent what you have said about my supervisory style. I have been supervising employees for 10 years and have never been questioned about how I kept people in line. Patricia never had any problem with my rules. She understood the importance I placed on maintaining discipline in the unit. Suggesting that I need to update and refresh my approach by attending the HR Supervisory Skills workshops is an insult." Ellen glares at Kate as she says this.

Kate knows she has to stay calm as she answers Ellen. "One of the issues I was encouraged to address in this unit was the high turnover rate among the frontline staff. No one was staying in the unit long enough to move up the career ladder. You are right in that your management style was considered the correct one several years ago, but things have changed. These days, employees expect to be treated like thinking adults and part of a collaborative team. They like to feel free to offer suggestions for improvements to the workflow. The university is trying to adapt to this model, which is why they have ramped-up the supervisory training opportunities. We are also being told to take into consideration that employees have lives outside of work and where reasonable, make accommodations to support their family-related needs. We discussed this several times during the past year at our monthly unit supervisors meetings. Plus, you and I discussed it in February when we were hiring Gretchen and Marilee, and then again in June when Marilee came to me to ask permission to adjust her schedule one morning a month because of her mother's chemotherapy treatments. I was told by personnel that Gretchen resigned because you would not let her shift her work schedule by 15 minutes each day so she could drop her son off at school."

"I'm not surprised she whined about that to them. She wanted special treatment and I don't go along with that. I told her that I treat everyone the same and rules are rules. She should have made other arrangements. If you start making exceptions for one person, then everyone wants to shift their schedules and the next thing you know, no one comes in on time anymore. As far as offering suggestions, I've worked here for 15 years; what possible good suggestions could someone who has been here for four months possibly make? They just don't understand the traditional way of doing things."

Kate realizes she has a lot further to go than she had thought in getting Ellen to adjust her supervisory style. "It is precisely the fact that they can think past the 'traditional' way of operating that they can offer suggestions from a valuable perspective. As far as Gretchen goes, the point is that she was a single mom and you refused to adjust her schedule because of personal bias and overall rigidity, not because of a sound operational reason associated with serving our library patrons. In doing so, you totally ignored the Balanced Life university initiative announced last year. This is no longer acceptable supervisory performance in this library." Ellen bristles as Kate's tone becomes firmer. "I expect you to adjust your supervisory style to take these issues into consideration. You should be thinking in terms of what it takes for unit operational objectives to be successful, not based on traditional practices of who has to do what. You need to focus more on providing variation and rotate the tasks the staff at the front desk do, so that they have a chance to develop more understanding for all aspects of the unit's operation."

Ellen comments, "This is just some kind of fad that will mess things up. I've been here 15 years and the unit has operated very well the last 10 years while I have been in charge of the front desk. You cannot make me change my mind or my so-called supervisory style."

Kate takes on a very serious and intense expression as she replies, "You are right, I cannot change your mind. However, I am the access services manager and I can define my expectations of your performance. If you do not show sincere effort at working to meet my expectations, I can give you a truly unsatisfactory evaluation and recommend against your getting a merit increase. Additionally, I can decide that it is not in the best operational interest of the unit for you to continue in your current role and reassign you to other responsibilities in the unit that do not include supervision. The fact is that you do not work in an unchanging, static environment and in order to continue to be successful, you *must* adapt to this change."

Ellen is clearly taken aback by this. "You are really serious about this aren't you?" Kate nods meeting Ellen's gaze. Ellen sighs as she says, "I may not like it but if this is how it has to be I will try to be more lenient. Just don't blame me when everything falls apart or blows up."

"First, I don't think everything will fall apart or blow up. If there are mistakes in judgment, I won't blame you for them but I will expect you to learn from them. Also, I will hold you responsible for developing an understanding of where we can be operationally flexible and where we cannot. That sort of judgment is part of your position as the senior staff member in the unit. I have confidence in your ability to meet my expectations, and I still value you as a senior member of the staff. I think that since this is an area that is going to require a lot of adjustment for you, let's set up an every-other-week status meeting. This will give us an opportunity to discuss the issues and go over situations, so that you can better understand where the middle ground is between your past practice and what you seem to perceive I am suggesting."

The meeting continues with focus toward specific objectives for the next year, including Ellen's attendance of HR workshops and having follow-up discussions with Kate.

Case Study Observations

- Many performance problems are the result of changing expectations, with the employee finding the adjustment to be difficult.
- It is important to stay calm but firm during the evaluation review process.
- It is important to set future actions that will monitor the employee's progress toward goals, especially if the employee is reluctant to embrace the goals.
- Maintain a sense of professionalism at all times and base all feedback on facts.

- Do not let an employee's dissatisfaction with an evaluation diminish your confidence as a manager.

Thought and Discussion Exercises

What Do You Do Now?

1. In reviewing past evaluations, you notice that the previous manager gave everyone in the unit excellent ratings with only infrequent vague comments on areas for improvement. You have discussed this with the associate director who supervises you and learned that although past appraisals were lumped together in the two highest ratings, the library is trying to move to a culture that gives more useful feedback and recognizes that although a few performers truly are excellent, most are not. Staff members' self-evaluations offer little insight into plans for growth or development and reflect an overall expectation of another excellent rating. You can definitely identify areas of improvement for each employee but must determine the best way to communicate and document it as part of the evaluation process. What do you do now?

2. Suppose an employee named Bryan comes to you with a complaint that another employee, Chris, is always coming in late and leaving early but is not reflecting this on time sheets. How do you respond to this and what do you do as a follow-up? You subsequently discover through personal observation (hint) that Chris really is not working as much as he shows on the time sheet. What do you do now?

3. You have an employee, Phil, who seems to constantly be getting into conflicts with other employees in the unit. His side of the issue is that the other staff members pick on him and the conflict is always started by the other person. By observing a few of these conflicts, you observe that they seem to start with Phil offering a very critical, unsolicited opinion of the other employee's performance on a task or project. Phil has said he is just trying to help. What do you do now?

4. You have an employee whose attitude really seems to brighten the office. She brings in cookies and donuts every Friday. Anytime someone needs help, she is willing to pitch in. Additionally, she is easygoing with everyone and always in the middle of planning office baby showers, student worker graduation parties, and so forth. As far as you know, everyone really likes her. Unfortunately, she is not keeping up with her assigned work of processing the remote storage and interlibrary services requests. It is evaluation time. What do you do now?

Notes

1. Robert D. Stueart and Barbara B. Moran, *Library and Information Center Management*, 6th ed. (Greenwood Village, CO: Libraries Unlimited, 2002).

2. Dick Grote, *The Complete Guide to Performance Appraisal* (New York: AMACOM, 1996).

3. Dick Grote, *The Performance Appraisal Question and Answer Book: A Survival Guide for Managers* (New York: AMACOM, 2002).

4. Tom Coens and Mary Jenkins, *Abolishing Performance Appraisals: Why They Backfire and What to Do Instead* (San Francisco: Berrett-Koehler Publishers, Inc., 2000).

CHAPTER 11

Dealing with Performance Problems

The previous chapters have dealt with many issues involving building a developmental relationship with employees, encouraging them to change, and assessing their performance. However, no matter how much a manager coaches and counsels, there comes a point that employees have to accept responsibility for their performance. Most employees will respond favorably to coaching and adjust to the new manager's expectations. Some will decide to take advantage of openings in other departments and will leave vacancies that can be filled by people chosen by the new manager. Inevitably, there may be a few employees who will not be successful under the new manager. No matter how much counseling is provided, they refuse to accept the changes and take advantage of the growth opportunities before them. In time, a manager has to accept that an employee is consistently underperforming at an unacceptable level. This is the point where an institutional disciplinary and review process comes into play. Even as one deals with an employee with performance problems, managers must take care to protect themselves in the event the employee carries through with a formal grievance process and a subsequent investigation ensues.

Understanding the Situation

Employees who have chosen to resist change often do so without realizing the potential impact of their actions. They see themselves as the victims, being forced to change when they know they have been doing their jobs the correct and only way they should be done. Sometimes, their own self-doubts hold them back from seeing the changes as opportunities and they find it much easier to want to blame someone else for their own inadequacies. The new manager, serving as the change representative, is the villain of their world. In responding to them, the manager must try to give them a way to move toward meeting expectations at a slower pace without a loss of dignity or opening them up to being embarrassed in front of their peers. Long-time staff members are especially difficult to address in this context because they have established peer dynamics with a defined role that they have developed over time. The manager who decides to take disciplinary action against this employee should be prepared for some peripheral backlash as people begin choosing sides. It is extremely important in this situation to have given the employee sufficient opportunity to reveal his true performance to his peers as well as other administrators. Even as the manager may recognize early on during the change process which employees are going to be resistant to adjusting, it is much more effective to wait until most of the unit has embraced changes and seen positive outcomes before addressing the holdouts within the performance expectations framework. In some situations peer pressure can actually serve to bring the employee around to accept change, where direct coaching would have failed.

Though organizational change often serves as a catalyst that exposes employee performance problems, it is not the only situation where managers may be required to employ disciplinary measures. It is possible for any manager to make a bad hire. An employee that interviewed well and seems to understand the expectations of the position may not be as effective as anticipated. Effective decision making, judgment, and learning ability are difficult concepts to assess during an interview that lasts a couple of hours at most. Even an employee with a good employment history can prove to have difficulty dealing with the cyclical pace, proprietary computer tools, and interpersonal dynamics found in the contemporary library environment. Another common source of performance problems can come about through employees' inability to compartmentalize stressors from their personal lives away from the work environment. An example of this could be an employee who is going through a difficult divorce may become difficult to interact with, especially for colleagues who are the same gender as the conflicting spouse.

Unfortunately, there is not a one-size-fits-all solution or simple handbook that managers can employ in addressing employee performance problems. Each situation will be different depending on the specific circumstances, the nature of the performance problem, the personality of the individual employee, and the relationship with the manager. Many employees are comfortable receiving constructive feedback and want to improve even though they do not understand how to do so. For these employees, the role of the manager is to help them develop a better understanding of the situation and their responses to it. An example of this might be a staff member who is going through her first experience as a student worker supervisor and is having difficulty finding balance between wanting to be in a friend or parent role with the student worker and actually being the employer. In this case, the manager should coach the new supervisor on the importance of recognizing the conflicting roles and assist in defining how the roles should be integrated to better meet the needs of the unit and the manager's expectations. In another case, an employee may be experiencing performance problems associated with lacking a particular skill. This employee will have less need for extended coaching but a greater need for the manager to identify and provide structured training. An example of this might be a new employee with previous sales experience who was hired but is now having difficulty performing a cash register closing transaction. As the manager investigates the performance problem, several different issues could be at the source of the deficient performance. The employee may have learned to enter the transaction on a different style of cash register that operated in an opposite manner from the one the department uses. Similarly, preparing a deposit may require the employee to use a computerized spreadsheet program, again an unfamiliar tool. Finally, the employee may have difficulty multitasking and may be making mistakes because of getting distracted during the transaction. These are all very specific things that a manager can address. Given a basic level of competency, structured repetitive training and written procedures can usually address equipment or computer usage difficulties. Similarly, a manager can help an employee adjust the environment or workflow to address problems caused by distractions or confused priorities. These types of performance challenges are constructive and rewarding for both the employee and the manager because they result in personal growth and create a bond between the employee and manager.

Finding a Solution

In many cases, the first step toward finding a solution involves raising an employee's awareness of a problem. As an example, suppose an employee, Wyatt, is having attendance issues. It seems that he is perpetually late arriving at the start of the day and coming back from lunch. If this has reached the point of being habitual, Wyatt may not even be aware he is doing it. In this case, use of a monitoring or documentation tool, such as a time sheet or time clock can be employed to make the employee more aware of the problem aspects of the behavior.

Similarly, it is important that managers differentiate between a performance problem and an employee idiosyncrasy. A performance problem is something that an employee does where the end result does not meet the manager's expectations *and* has an impact on the actual functioning and operation of the unit. An idiosyncrasy is simply a unique approach that an employee may take to accomplish a task within the context of the manager's expectations. It may seem to be a bizarre approach that makes no sense to the employee's manager or peers but meets the overall performance expectations. In some cases, it is easier to ignore a small, real performance problem than a blatant, everyday idiosyncrasy. A good example of an idiosyncrasy is the clean desk versus stacks of papers organization styles. Unless one is working in a top-secret engineering or biosciences lab, leaving stacks of paper on one's desk is not a crime. However, the decision about whether the organization style has an impact on unit operation is something a manager has to decide before addressing it with the employee. For employees who manage their own workflow and are usually at their desks to provide information as needed, the stacks of paper are an idiosyncrasy and should not be an issue for coaching or disciplinary action. However, for employees responsible for maintaining files in such an order that others can access them for information on whether a particular invoice has been paid or a fine cleared, having papers strewn in disarray on the desk will have an impact on others in the unit and their ability to have relevant knowledge at hand to effectively interact with vendors or users. Then, what otherwise would have been an idiosyncrasy has become a performance problem that should be addressed by the manager. This test is critical anytime one is trying to determine if a performance problem even exists. Even if a performance problem exists, the manager must be able to tie it to a noticeable operational impact on the unit. Without this connection, the manager comes across as nitpicky, and even though morale may be impacted, formal disciplinary processes, especially termination, are not a viable option.

The purpose of the examples in the previous section was to emphasize that many performance problems can be resolved without resorting to a formal disciplinary process. A key thing for new managers to realize as they address a performance problem is that they cannot assume they know anything about understanding the problem and assign a solution based solely on observation. It is critical that a performance problem be approached as an investigation. This means observing and asking questions in such a way as to get to the real problem and its sources, which are usually *not* what the manager initially perceives as the problem. In all likelihood, the problem that the manager initially identified is the result or consequence of the problem not being addressed, but is not the problem itself. Once the problem is identified, the manager must next identify possible solutions to aid the employee in addressing the problem. Just as every situation is slightly different, there is rarely a single perfect solution that fits everyone. Problem solving is not a quick or a hands-off activity. During this entire process, the manager should be investing the time and energy to get to the root of the problem and engaging the employee so that the final solution is a mutually acceptable and achievable one. During this process there are several things managers should avoid saying or implying. Never tell employees who are having difficulties to just work harder, faster, friendlier, and so forth. They would be if they could understand how to get around the invisible barriers contributing to the performance problem. Similarly, avoid making negative comparisons to the employee's predecessor, "Bill could do this job fine, I don't understand why you are having problems." These types of remarks damage both the individual employee's sense of self and the relationship with the manager. On a related issue, most managers are very bright people, which is why they were promoted. When dealing with performance problems, it can be very difficult to keep expectations realistic and geared to the intelligence and learning ability of the employee. Finally, the employee will need to invest in the solution and take responsibility for improving. Without this realization, efforts at coaching and counseling will eventually fail. It is also important to realize that managers may find themselves having to coach some employees more than others. Some employees may be quite needy and will require ongoing coaching on a wide range of issues to perform in a satisfactory manner.

Preparing for Failure

Even as the past several sections have focused on resolving performance problems in a positive manner, inevitably anyone who stays in a managerial role will encounter an unsolvable problem. The problem is an employee who will not or cannot meet the manager's performance expectations. Even as managers accept the realization that an employee is not going to meet their expectations, there are several questions that they must consider before pursuing formal disciplinary measures, especially if the measures might lead to an employee's termination. Will library administration and human resources representatives support the manager in the use of the formal disciplinary process? Will pursuing the formal disciplinary process improve the situation or worsen it? Has the manager exhausted all informal avenues to engage the employee and appropriately documented the employee's performance problems? Has the manager planned for the possible backlash of taking action against the employee? To a new manager going through this for the first time, these questions may seem to be simplistic with obvious answers. However, pursuing formal disciplinary measures without having thought through the representative issues will leave an manager open to being blindsided by a charge of unfair supervisory practices or unprepared to face the considerable stress that results.

Answering the Questions

Even as one begins the disciplinary process, it opens the door for the employee to approach library administrators, human resources personnel, or employee-relations representatives. This is especially likely to occur if the employee resents or refuses to acknowledge the validity of the manager's performance expectations. In this situation, it is critical to have built an administrative relationship that has kept your own administrative managers aware of the situation and your intent and methods used in addressing it. Because of the nature of their responsibilities, most middle managers tend to have a more short-term and operational perspective. In contrast, administrators tend to take the big picture and long-term approach that addressed the broader impact of decisions. In most cases, the administrator will have had more experience with formal disciplinary procedures and will be able to serve as a guide through the process. Because of this experience, the administrator may also be the one to suggest alternate options. These options might include more and different coaching approaches, reassigning unit responsibilities to actually change the performance expectations for the individual employee, wait out the problem, or actually reduce the performance expectations for the employee. The latter situations are most likely to occur if the employee is near retirement or where upholding performance expectations makes the library look like the guy in the black hat, unsympathetic with a cold-blooded bottom line approach. Some administrators might also advise alternate options if there is the likelihood that the employee could have recourse to legally contest the discipline as discrimination against a legally protected group. If they do agree with your pursuing the formal disciplinary process, it is critical to be thoroughly honest and keep them updated as the process unfolds so they will not be taken by surprise if the employee challenges the corrective action.

Many new managers will look at the question about whether the process will improve or worsen the situation, and question how pursuing the formal disciplinary process could do anything but help the situation. After all, it puts the employee on notice to the seriousness of the performance problem, and if the employee still does not improve ultimately will serve to remove the employee permanently through termination. However, if the ripple effect is such that other employees in the unit no longer trust the manager or the employee improves just enough to avoid the next or final step of the disciplinary process but now harbors significant hostility toward the manager, the situation has worsened. Now the manager is stuck with an employee who is performing in a satisfactory manner on the surface but is also probably trying to backstab and undermine support for the manager. Even those employees who brought frustrations about the problem performer to the manager may react poorly to pursuing formal disciplinary procedures, especially termination. Even as they know the person was not doing well, they still experience a "could have been me" realization and often respond by pulling back from the manager. Another way in which the situation can be worsened is if the disciplined employee files an appeal, grievance, or even a lawsuit. This is the purpose behind asking the last two questions on whether all informal avenues have been explored and if one is prepared for the backlash. In this case, a manager will have to justify actions and decisions, may be unable to refill the position immediately, and will need to develop personal coping mechanisms for the emotional stress of the process. The manager may have to go through interviews that question his entire performance, open up unit operations for scrutiny, and prepare to defend actions and decisions. Similarly, because the entire issue is one of employee performance and privacy must be maintained, the situation can leave one feeling very isolated and even rejected. This can be very demoralizing to a new manager, whose self-confidence may be fragile and who has not yet established a peer support system.

Protecting Yourself

If a manager has thought a situation through thoroughly and still feels that pursuing formal disciplinary procedures is the correct action and has administrative support, there are several things one should do to protect oneself in the event of an active hostile response by the employee. Many larger institutions will have a human resources or legal representative who can advise a manager of what is and is not appropriate performance documentation. In the event of a lawsuit, manager's files can be subpoenaed. Because of this, any notes or e-mails should be factual, relevant, balanced, and consistent for all employees at the same level with similar expectations.

In the same way that a manager should guard against an evaluation that is totally negative, so should managerial notes reflect a balance of identifying what an employee does do well. These notes should also document the occurrence of the problem performance, significant coaching episodes, and interactions that relate expectations or instructions. If there is supporting documentation, such as time sheets, incorrectly cataloged records, or patron complaints, they should be included as part of the file. It is usually not appropriate to have a dialogue-style transcript but to capture the topics of discussion and any action items that come out of the conversation. Similarly, e-mails are valuable documentation, especially if they lay out why a particular expectation is being established or a change implemented. It is important to never put anything in writing or in an e-mail that expresses an emotion-based opinion of an employee, such as "I just don't like Julie" or "Joe's personality drives me up the wall." This type of comment can be used to establish a precedent that the person was not given an opportunity to do well because of the manager's personal bias and can undermine the manager's reputation. If a situation has become actively hostile with an employee and there are possible issues of blatant insubordination, it may be appropriate to bring in a neutral manager from another area as a witness during the disciplinary meetings. Alternately, managers or employees can request the intervention of a trained mediator to reestablish more effective communications.

It may also be important to keep notes on the logic behind a particular managerial decision. These can be working notes on an organizational chart or workflow diagram, an executive summary to administration, notes from meetings with the manager's administrative supervisor, or a series of e-mails. Sometimes employees will protest a decision you make as a manager, especially if it impacts their assigned responsibilities. During the investigation into a grievance, these complaints become more significant. Even as it may not be appropriate to explain every single operational decision to staff, prepared managers should make sure that they can justify any decision from an operational or good-business-practices perspective. One does not make changes because of employees, but because of the needs of the users, other interdepartmental customers, or the unit internal workflow as a whole. This can be important because managers frequently find themselves in the peculiar position of having developed a creative solution to a problem brought to their attention, only to find that it was not the solution staff members expected and consequently receives an unenthusiastic reception.

If one has to undergo investigative meetings with an attorney or human resources representative, one may want to have a library administrative representative present. Similarly, it is important to take time before the meeting to get one's thoughts and notes in order. As discussed with the managerial notes, it is important to direct all comments toward specific performance issues. This is not the time to be modest and reticent. Rather, one should explain clearly and firmly what one has done to provide opportunity for employees to improve and find more satisfaction in their work life. Interpersonal problems with an employee should be addressed as challenging. If one is uncertain how to answer a question, ask if one can think about the question and get back with a more complete answer after referring to notes or other memory aids. Keep in mind that if you have tried to do the things outlined earlier in this chapter, then the lawyers and human resources representatives are actually your support system in dealing with the employee with the performance problem. The only manager who has anything to fear is the one that has acted in a vacuum without communicating with administrators or peer managers and who has made decisions in an arbitrary, illogical, and unjustifiable manner.

During the course of going through formal discipline of an employee, especially if one has to deal with subsequent institutional appeals or legal challenges, there may be periods when one battles feeling of failure and self-doubt, becomes frustrated over what seems to be an interminable process, or is shocked at the harsh vitriol expressed by the employee. During this, it is critical to maintain a professional demeanor within one's managerial responsibilities and not neglect the needs of the unit as a whole and other employees as individuals. However, managers need to maintain personal support systems as well, and compartmentalize the problems. This means having balance in your life that allows you to focus on other things away from the library and maintain a sense of personal success and happiness. This concept of balance is addressed in more detail in Chapter 12. If a manager feels overwhelmed, she may want to consult with other more senior managers or administrators who can advise her and put the experience in perspective. Depending on the circumstances of the specific situation, it may be appropriate to contact the institution's human resources training unit or employee counseling program for career management guidance and professional assistance in keeping the situation from becoming unmanageable. Even though each situation will be different, any experienced manager will tell you that the first time you go through the hostile termination/challenge process is the worst. It requires significant growth and learning to accept the situation as an isolated incident without losing one's trust in one's staff as a whole.

Chapter Summary

Managers will encounter employees with performance problems. In addition to recognizing the problem, it is important to work with employees to identify the underlying reasons behind the problem. Many employees will respond well to coaching and counseling that establishes actions they can take to reverse the slippage into poor performance. Unfortunately, there may be a few employees who do not assume the responsibility to meet the manager's performance expectations and instead respond with hostility and continued performance deterioration. For these employees, it may be appropriate to invoke the formal performance disciplinary process, which could include terminating the employee. In making the decision on whether or not to pursue this path, it is important to verify that one has administrative support and recognition for the problem situation, that one has appropriately documented both the performance problem and efforts to resolve it through informal methods, and that any actions or decisions that served to define the employee's performance expectations were supported by operational or patron needs. Finally, even as one becomes embroiled in the disciplinary process with an employee, it is important to do an emotional self-check and establish a personal support system and balance in one's life to help get through the associated stressors of the situation.

To Learn More

Many of the same resources referenced in Chapter 10 and Chapter 6 address motivational options and the disciplinary process for underperforming employees. It is also valuable for new managers to develop an awareness of some political strategies, less from a perspective of using them directly but more as a means to better recognize when one is being manipulated. Organizational politics are often perceived as a negative but persistently present reality. However, *when used in an ethical manner*, the tools and techniques can be effective to help build positive relationships, keep one from becoming a victim, and allow one to counter politically manipulative efforts by others. One recent publication that supports and offers insights into this perspective is *Enlightened Office Politics: Understanding, Coping with, and Winning the Game–Without Losing Your Soul.*[1] Another book that goes into significant detail about the different political strategies related to territorialism and how to counter them is *Territorial Games: Understanding and Ending Turf Wars at Work.* Many of the items presented in the context of peer conflict can also be especially useful when dealing with employees who are trying to guard their turf by resisting managerial-led change.[2] Written as an academic text, *Power,*

Politics, and Organizational Change: Winning the Turf Game focuses on the importance of political survival skills during the process of organizational change and counters traditional theorists who saw change events and internal politics as unrelated.[3]

Case Study: Addressing Attendance Problems

Sam – Kate's supervisor, associate director
Kate – internal middle-manager promotion (three years ago), access services head
Dave – Staff member in circulation (six years in library, four years in circulation)
Setting: Kate has asked Dave to meet with her in her office. In scheduling the meeting she titled it "Performance Update."

After offering Dave a soda, Kate sits down behind her desk and begins speaking. "Dave, I don't know what you were anticipating this meeting to be about, but the reason I set it up is that we need to talk about some recent attendance problems that have come to my attention. I was reviewing your time sheets and realized that during the past six weeks, you've been coming in late every two to three days." Kate passes Dave a photocopy of a list of the dates and times he has come in late. "Some days it is only about five minutes, other days it is closer to half an hour. Plus, every Monday and Thursday for the past month, you've been coming back from lunch about 30 minutes late. Unfortunately, this really came to a head last week when several of the other circulation staff members were out with the flu, and I was at the department heads retreat. According to Sam, a patron reported to administration that the circulation desk opened almost 30-minutes late. I also understand that the student workers were left in charge of the unit when Hailey had to leave make a dentist appointment before you returned from lunch, as she had expected. So my question is, what's up?"

Through Kate's summarization, Dave has become dejected-looking and is sitting leaning forward in the chair, staring down at the floor. He finally raises his head to look at Kate. Given the despair in his expression, Kate realizes this isn't going to be a case of a broken alarm clock or finding a different driving route around construction. Something is significantly wrong. Dave begins to quietly speak.

"I'm really sorry. I didn't realize I wasn't doing my job. I had hoped no one was noticing the absences. To be totally honest, I didn't realize I was running as late as frequently as this. Seeing it laid out with each time listed out . . . well, I'm just really sorry. I guess I should have told you about something a few weeks ago." He takes a deep breath, obviously trying to pull his thoughts together. "Almost two months ago, my wife walked out on me and my 10-year-old daughter, Rebecca. She said she had decided she didn't want to be tied down anymore and wanted a divorce. Well, I'm now responsible for getting Rebecca up, fed, dressed, and dropped off at school. Unfortunately, I'm still trying to figure out how to do that and be on time in the morning. The extended lunch hours are little more complicated. Back when I was in college, I developed a drinking problem. I managed to get it under control before Rebecca was born and had been dry for 11 years. However, right after Chrissy left, I made the mistake of reaching for the bottle. Fortunately, having to be responsible for Rebecca made me realize I had to pull myself together. I am now in a Twelve Step Program. My Thursday lunch hour for the past month has been spent at the support meetings for that and Monday lunches have been at a support group for single fathers. Unfortunately, both meetings are at the community center across town and it is almost impossible for me to arrive, participate in the meeting, and then drive back within an hour."

Kate sits stunned for a minute pulling her thoughts together before she begins to speak. "Dave, I am really sorry for how your life has been turned upside down and can't believe you didn't tell anyone here at work about this."

Dave sort of gives a half-hearted smile as he says, "I didn't know how to bring it up to anyone. The timing never seemed quite right. I couldn't really blurt out the news at one of the office potluck lunches. Just sort of standing up and announcing in a department meeting that my wife walked out and I am now the only active parent of a 10-year-old girl who seems like an alien creature to me seemed a little inappropriate."

Kate nods. "OK, I can understand that. Especially since I'm sure it was difficult for you to talk about it when it first happened. Well, the library and the university do not expect the staff to be emotionless robots that turn on at 8 A.M. and turn off at 5 P.M. We do recognize that sometimes it is necessary to be a little more flexible to support family issues, especially during a crisis or adjustment period. Unfortunately, we don't have enough staffing depth to just allow you to freestyle your schedule. Formally adjusting your work schedule to allow for the longer lunches on Monday and Thursday is not a problem. We can work around that. However, I really need you to commit to coming in on time in the morning and being responsible for opening the unit. As we learned last week, you cannot always expect that someone else will be in to pick up what is one of the primary responsibilities of your position. It puts the other staff members behind in doing their assigned tasks as well. Have you studied your morning situation to determine what the primary problems are that cause you to be late so often?"

"I've thought about it a little bit but am still somewhat overwhelmed by the whole experience. One big part of the problem is that Rebecca's current school is in the opposite direction from the library. By the time I get her dropped off, I'm stuck in rush hour traffic trying to get back in this direction. That should not be as much of a problem next year when she changes schools. Then dropping her off will actually be on the way, and the school building will be open earlier. I think another part of the problem is that I just don't understand young girls. She will try on 4 different outfits trying to decide which she wants to wear, and then there are the 'bad hair days,' which are really beyond me. These are the days when I really run late. Do you have any suggestions?"

Kate looks bemused as she tries to help Dave formulate solutions to his dilemma. "Well despite having been a pre-teen female and recalling my own experience with the accursed 'bad hair days,' I don't have any firsthand experience as a parent. Since we are already at the end of March and only have about two months left with the current school, you really just need a temporary solution. Does Rebecca have any school friends or acquaintances who live nearby. Maybe you could make arrangements for Rebecca to ride to school with them? You might also talk to Renee in ILS about your situation and ask her advice. She was widowed about two years ago and manages to get her four children, ages 8 to 15, up and out the door to school and still makes it in by 8 A.M. to open the ILS desk services. I know I once heard her mention that she has the kids set out their clothes and prepare their lunch bags the night before."

Dave looks thoughtful and seems relieved that Kate is willing to work with him. "You know, I hadn't thought about it but Rebecca's best friend, Susie, lives just two streets over. Susie's mother had called shortly after Chrissy left, asked if we were doing OK, and asked if there was anything she could do to help. I was still pretty shell-shocked at the time and simply used the cliché that we were 'fine.' I could give her a call today and see if she would mind dropping Rebecca off in the morning. I'll also go look up Renee and see if she can give me any pointers. You know, just talking it out and having defined a course of action helps."

Kate smiles at Dave and agrees. "Recognizing and exploring options is always better than just floundering. I want you to keep me updated if the transportation situation with Susie's mother doesn't work out. Worst case, I could approach one of the other staff about doing a schedule exchange and taking the opening shift until school is out. Also, I think you might want to casually mention to the others in the unit that you are now a single dad, just so that if Rebecca does need to reach you, they will appreciate the importance of the call. I don't think they will be too nosy."

"Thanks, that would be a good way to introduce the topic. I will definitely keep you updated on my progress and recovery, and I appreciate your help."

Setting: shift to Kate's routine status meeting with Sam

Kate has just finished explaining the results of her investigation of why the desk opened late and Dave's situation. "So that is what was going on with Dave, what an awful mess. Fortunately his daughter's friend's mother was glad to give Rebecca a ride and has even offered to keep an eye on her on the days that Dave works a little later to make up for his long lunch hours. Also, I think Renee may have given him some organizational tips as well. He hasn't been late a single day since the meeting last week. He has told the others in the unit what has been going on, and Ellen was really sympathetic when I approached her about adjusting lunch hour coverage on the days Dave is out the extra half hour. She has worked out a solution that actually pleases everyone. It looks like we have weathered another performance crisis, for which I am very grateful. I really didn't want to have to write up a formal reprimand given everything else he is dealing with."

Sam nods in agreement as he comments, "It is always better when a situation can be resolved like this rather than sending someone into a real depression by jumping to a formal reprimand without taking the time to really find out what is going on. You may want to keep an eye on Dave for future coaching, though. Being a male single parent as his daughter is going through puberty is not going to be easy on him. You may need to periodically encourage him to step back, reach out to others, and put things in perspective."

Kate laughs. "Yeah, I remember enough of my own teenage years to know he still has a lot of adjusting to do. But knowing the situation, I can watch a little better for warning signs that he is getting overwhelmed and do more active preventative coaching."

Case Study Observations

- Never assume you know why an employee is having a performance problem. There are always unseen issues that need to be explored and taken into account.

- Recognize that as a manager you can make suggestions on how to address the problem issues, but it is the employee's responsibility to follow through.

- Even as the specific performance problem has been resolved, be aware that the employee may still have future performance concerns. Be prepared to use heightened awareness and preventative coaching to help the employee.

- If an employee does not follow-through with improved performance, one must be willing to follow-through with an appropriate formal disciplinary process to address the deficiency.

Thought and Discussion Exercises

What Do You Do Now?

1. You learn that a staff member has gone to human resources with a complaint that you are treating her unfairly by always assigning her a particularly undesirable and monotonous task. You feel that the employee has misrepresented the situation in a way that hides her own performance deficiencies. You have assigned this task to the employee because her performance on more detail-oriented tasks has been inadequate. You have a record of having coached and arranged training for the employee to become more proficient with the detail-oriented tasks. What do you do now? Bonus: How do you interact with the employee now that this has happened?

2. A male employee comes to you with the complaint that he feels discriminated against in the open architecture office because a female employee with a desk near his is always telling jokes that put men down. Some of the jokes are rather crude, with sexual innuendos. You more closely observe the female employee in question and agree that her conduct and the environment she promotes is somewhat male-hostile. What do you do now?

3. After repeated coaching and retraining, a fairly new employee (but past probation) is still making frequent errors in her assigned tasks and not performing in a satisfactory manner. She always promises to work harder and try to do better, but without visible improvement.

This has been going on for eight months. You have decided that you must begin the formal disciplinary process to possibly terminate the employee if she still does not improve. What do you do now?

Notes

1. Michael Singer Dobson and Deborah Singer Dobson, *Enlightened Office Politics: Understanding, Coping with, and Winning the Game—Without Losing Your Soul* (Kansas City: AMACOM, 2001).

2. Annette Simmons, *Territorial Games: Understanding and Ending Turf Wars at Work* (New York: American Management Association, 1998). Also available through NetLibrary, Inc. at http://www.netlibrary.com

3. Dave Buchanan and Richard Badham, *Power, Politics, and Organizational Change: Winning the Turf Game* (Thousand Oaks, CA: Sage Publications, 1999).

CHAPTER 12

Motivation and Balance

Until now, this book has focused on providing insight into the types of workplace situations encountered by library middle managers. Coverage has included resources to allow professional growth and skill development. The exercises have been outward-focused toward managing staff and circumstances. This chapter takes a more inward focus. It explores appropriate reasons that librarians have for going into the management track and encourages managers to look to their own care and support. In addition to its precautionary guidance for new managers, it can also serve to remind experienced managers, caught up in constant problem solving, that their own health and mental attitudes are just as important as that of their staff. The chapter offers ideas for self-initiated techniques to avoid becoming a disaffected, disillusioned, or cynical manager. Burnout is a special concern for new managers as they take on new types of responsibilities. Left unaddressed, it can cause those with excellent managerial potential to lose faith and confidence in themselves, their staff, and upper administration. This chapter offers some insights and reminders to avoid this.

The stress levels and potential for burnout do not have a formulaic definition. Rather they are a function of the individual librarian or manager, the culture of the organization, and the role of the individual in that organization. Some stressed librarians do not burnout per the classical definition, but instead become cynical or apathetic to their environment. The key to overcoming any of these negative situations and continuing to develop as an effective manager is to engage in introspective recognition, preventative measures, and coping techniques.

Why Become a Manager?

Having read through all the challenges and difficulties that can come with being a conscientious manager, some librarians may be wondering where the benefits are that make it worthwhile. It cannot be for the praise heaped on them by the staff or the easy demands of their work routine. Just the reverse is often true. In some ways, blaming or ridiculing management is a cultural tendency, as illustrated by the boss characters in comic strips Dilbert or Sally Forth. The truth is that there are significant rewards to becoming a manager. Some, such as a higher salary, are obviously quantifiable and may be part of the initial attraction. However, the salary seldom fully compensates for the burden of responsibility that comes with it. The real reasons that lead one to explore a management track and work to become a good manager are more personal and will vary from one individual to another. When discussing their careers, an observer will hear managers tend to come back to several central concepts on why they have taken the managerial path. These often include growing personally, enjoying challenges, responding to a broader understanding of organizational issues, and making a difference. It is not because of self-promotion but more for the good of the whole that motivates good leaders.

The managerial career path in libraries is one that forces individuals to continue growing and developing skills to address ever-changing expectations and initiatives. Even as one set of skills related to managerial practice is mastered, a new methodology and practice may be just over the horizon. During the past several decades, management has moved from a top-down, Theory X, micromanagement style where the manager is the one making and dictating all operational decisions, to an environment of staff self-management with open door policies and consensus-building. Organizations have moved from being extremely hierarchical and bureaucratic to incorporating matrix management or becoming team environments or learning organizations. Many of these represent idealistic theories that may not be applicable to all aspects of the public or academic library environment. But most contemporary library administrators are more open to new management concepts and will try to integrate specific elements where appropriate. The overall organizations are multi-faceted ones, with some teams and some hierarchical structure, some top-down decisions and some consensus-based decision making, and with some areas of strict management (time and leave sheets) and some areas with a more casual approach (discussion meetings). In some organizations the changes in management styles over the past decades have led to significant managerial turnover. In other environments, managers have continued to learn, adapt, and experience growth as the organization's perspective changes. New managers should recognize that becoming a manager is truly the start of a new lifelong learning opportunity and not an end step that will be static, even if one stays in a middle manager's role

Along with changing styles of management, organizations continue to undergo dramatic shifts in operational and service initiatives to meet the changing expectations of users. These may include the introduction of totally new services or modifications of existing practices. Either way, the introduction of change and continuing engagement of staff through new initiatives and implementations is a challenge. Many successful managers are problem-solvers or pioneers who enjoy leading others to explore new areas and ideas. They get bored with the day-in and day-out drudgery of the status quo. Their managerial roles engage this aspect of their personalities and offer a guided outlet for inquiring minds in a way that is mutually beneficial to both the individual and the organization.

As librarians spend time in the profession, some may find ongoing comfort and satisfaction within their specific area of responsibility. Others may find a natural tendency to develop a broader understanding of the interplay of issues in the organization. Eventually, the latter may feel that they have accomplished everything they can within their specific area of responsibility. The need to continue accomplishing something, combined with the broadened understanding of issues is a natural lead-in to exploring the management career path.

Last, but not least, a common reason librarians may want to become managers is because management offers more opportunities for making a difference in their world and for providing service to the institution. As managers, they will have a say in refining the direction of new initiatives and strategies. They will be charged with how-to decision-making authority. Through the opportunity of leading and developing staff, they make a difference in other people's lives and provide them with growth opportunities. This is an extension of the public good, educational roles traditionally associated with modern librarians, and focuses toward making a greater impact that will have a successful ripple effect at a broader and deeper level.

Maintaining Balance

The role of a manager is not a light one. Depending on one's unit staffing and functional responsibilities, the load can actually be quite demanding. Chapter 2 discussed the importance of balancing one's meetings and other workload commitments. Implicit in this was the importance of having well-developed time management skills. But there are other ways a new manager can get overwhelmed by the job.

Setting Reasonable Expectations

One important element in staying healthy as a manager is to base one's performance on reasonable self-expectations. As with any new job or responsibility, a desire to do well is normal. Often it is the librarian with a history of excellent performance who is encouraged to look into management opportunities. Unfortunately, this can lead a librarian to set unrealistic expectations of immediate results and highly visible success. As discussed in Chapters 7 and 8, upper administrators usually do not expect overnight miracles. They are experienced enough to understand organizational momentum and the hurdles one will encounter. Similarly, they are aware that some success is measured more often in the small, continuous improvements than in the launch of a grand plan. It is critical for new managers to engage in dialogue with their supervisors about what is expected of them.

Additionally, new managers must recognize that they are now part of a management team and there will be times that despite their best efforts they cannot change a distasteful outcome. Accepting this concept of having a limited sphere of control and not being in the position to make everyone happy and solve all of the library's problems upfront can help a manager move past disappointment or frustration to areas where she can be more effective and experience professional satisfaction.

Nurturing Outside Interests

Along with setting reasonable personal goals and objectives, it is critical that new middle managers guard against letting the job consume them. Initially this can occur because the new manager is in an intense learning mode. Regardless of whether one is new to the particular institution or just learning a new operational area, there will be a lot of information for new managers to assimilate rapidly. Even a manager who has been promoted from within the department will have a learning curve, though it may be based more on shifting interactions with staff than learning the base operation. As managers mature and are increasingly integrated into the full scope of their responsibilities, they are expected to take on additional participatory roles in organizational level initiatives, such as strategic planning. In either situation, there is a temptation to stay a little later at the office or take a little more work home. Unchecked, this pattern can escalate until the manager either burns out or wakes up to the realization that no matter how much time one spends on the job, there is always still more that could be accomplished. In the meantime, these managers have exhausted themselves, neglected their families and friends, and invested their entire identity into their jobs. As a manager experiences this, he can have a sense of exhaustion, feel overwhelmed or inadequate, be physically ill, and experience subsequent difficulty coping with even the small issues of daily life. In order to avoid this trap, new managers should acknowledge from their first week, and periodically remind themselves, that the job will never be "done" and establish effective preventive habits. This includes developing skills to manage multiple priorities, prioritize initiatives, delegate to others, accept leaving some things undone, and, especially, maintain the importance of outside interests.

In the same way that today's employers seek well-rounded graduates with evidence of extracurricular activities, good managers will be engaged in areas outside of work. This may take the form of involvement with family or friends, getting involved in community volunteer opportunities, or more independent activities such as sewing, gardening, or playing golf. Wherever the focus lies, it should be something that takes one away from the work environment and job-similar concerns. For example, even as your family may be part of your personal support system, when you spend several hours each evening relating the details of the workday, you are not giving yourself the mental break you need. The same would apply to volunteering at the local public library or offering to organize a library at your place of worship.

Along with developing mental and emotional separation from work issues, it is also important to be aware of the physical impact of taking a managerial job, and maintain balance in this area as well. The majority of managerial work is done at a desk, behind a computer, or in meetings. Most managers spend less time leading tours, walking in the stacks, lifting books, or pushing book trucks than their frontline colleagues. Their schedules may also now include less-nutritious working lunches, either solitary, hurried ones over the computer or high-calorie restaurant meals with working agendas. Combined with the previously mentioned tendency to stay a little later or take work home, new managers may find themselves experiencing their own version of the "Freshman 15" weight gain. Add in new job stressors and one introduces the potential for additional fatigue and hypertension/high blood pressure issues. One resolution all new managers should make at the same time they accept their managerial appointments is a commitment to an appropriate exercise program.

Addressing Collegial Relationships

Another element of maintaining balance outside of work is to recognize that by becoming a manager, one's colleague-based peer group has changed. This was mentioned briefly in Chapter 2 but is relevant here as well. The familiar cliché about "being lonely at the top" can be appropriate even when one has just begun to take the first steps on the ladder. Even as a manager stays friends with pre-management colleagues, there will be occasions when there will be a wall between them, and the manager will feel somewhat isolated. One contributor to this is that the manager will be privy to information before the nonmanager friends. Additionally, there may be administrative positions that the manager must support that the nonmanager friends find unpleasant. In essence, there is now an imbalance in the relationship. Even as they may remain friends and come to terms with their different roles, the friendship will have changed. Generally, friendships that sustain across the manager/ nonmanager boundary will have been based on considerably more depth and common interests than simply the colleague relationship.

To a nonmanager, the managerial ranks may be perceived as something of an exclusive club. Unfortunately, new managers should not expect to find replacement friendships among their new peer group. It is a much smaller subset of the work community and often the only common area of interest is the managerial role. There may be significant differences in age and personal interests among the group. Additionally, the peer managers may choose not to develop a friendship within the managerial cadre because of their own need to get away from reminders of work. It is important for new managers to differentiate between actual friendships and collegial relationships based on professional roles. The former relationships, actual friendships, may form between peer managers but are less common.

Even as the peer managers within a single institution may not be large enough to form the basis for a new peer group, new managers may find it useful to look to professional peers at other institutions. Often this can be accomplished through state or national library associations. Many library associations, such as ALA, PLA, ACRL, and ARL offer management-skills workshops and conference programs addressing management issues. By attending them, middle managers from different institutions can meet, network, and develop supportive collegial relationships. These relationships allow managers to realize that their experiences are not unique, but often encountered by other managers as well. Exchanging war stories can tend to put a particular problem into perspective and offer ideas for new approaches that were effective somewhere else. Overall, it reinforces to the middle managers that they are not alone and provides a sense of reassurance and revitalization.

Within the library environment, marriage or an intimate partnership between two librarians, or a librarian and a support staff member sometimes occurs. When one of them becomes a manager, the couple must address the situation very carefully. There might be times that the nonmanager may feel caught between spousal loyalty and his or her own feelings about an issue. Most organizations prohibit a manager from being in the spouse's direct supervisory chain. However, there are secondary relationships, such as the managerial peer relationship with the spouse's manager, that must be carefully and neutrally developed. There should be a clear understanding that managers in this scenario should not be held responsible, by themselves or by their spouses, for addressing administrative issues in the spouse's work environment. There are times when the relationship will require additional careful handling and open communication between themselves, as well as extra degrees of discretion on the part of the couple in the work environment.

Sectioning Off Problems

A key of maintaining balance is to be able to compartmentalize specific issues. Inevitably there will be times when things do not go well. These distractions can be caused by job issues, such as staffing problems, technology failures, and budget cuts, or caused by personal issues, such as marital problems, aging parent health concerns, and raising children. Whatever the source, it is critically important to compartmentalize the problem and make an active effort to keep the emotions associated with the stressor from overflowing into other areas. This does not mean to suppress it in a mentally unhealthy manner but to express it at the right time and the right place. In some cases, this may require seeking help from a neutral party. The same way managers might advise an employee who is going through a personal crisis to seek professional counseling through an employee assistance program or health benefits plan, they should be willing to do this themselves when appropriate. A good counselor can assist a manager to restore perspective to the problem and move past residual emotional responses that may be poisoning other areas. For example, a new manager who has experienced a perceived betrayal by someone may find it difficult to trust others and may become distant or defensive. A professional counselor can help the manager move past the sense of betrayal to see the other peer managers and employees as individuals and focus on sustaining a more effective attitude by compartmentalizing the problem as an isolated incident, one to be learned from but not agonized or obsessed over.

Chapter Summary

The transition from frontline librarian to middle manager is not an easy one. If you are not careful, it can rip you to shreds emotionally and physically. However, several techniques can help prevent managers from burning out. One technique to reground yourself is to remind yourself why you have become or think you wish to become a manager. Reconnecting with the positive reasons behind your career choice is important in putting things in perspective. Even though the detailed reasons relating to why you choose to be a manager are often very specific and personal, there are some common elements among all successful managers. They include an ongoing need for personal growth and self-improvement through new skills, an appreciation for and enthusiasm toward tackling challenges, and a desire to understand and make a difference on issues at an organizational level. The second technique is to establish reasonable expectations and celebrate small successes. A third technique is to compartmentalize problems. In the same way any professional will try to avoid bringing problems at home into the work environment, work problems should be left at work and not allowed to intrude into your home life. One action that helps with compartmentalization is to sustain areas of interest and activities that have nothing to do with work responsibilities or who you are in the library. In addition to activities that support emotional and intellectual balance, it is important to maintain a physical activity routine to counteract the physical effects that can be caused by taking on the rather sedentary and often stressful managerial role.

To Learn More

The concept of burnout is not generally associated with librarianship by those outside the profession. However, the business world has studied burnout among middle managers and identified it as a very real problem to guard against. A search for the term *burnout* in EBSCO's Business Source Premier in October 2003 resulted in 865 hits. Combining it with *manager* still returned 80 articles. A search of library professional literature gives fewer results but there has been some study of burnout within the profession. The burnout issues presented by Anne Wordsworth are in the context of library directors. However, even as she explains, they parallel many of the frustrations experienced by library middle managers.[1] Janette S. Caputo's book, *Stress and Burnout in Library Service* provides a very good overview of the stressors related to the library environment. It offers several tips on recognizing early burnout indicators and several coping mechanisms to reduce stress levels. The references section offers a number of additional resources.[2] The importance of a balanced approach to work is reiterated in a brief piece found in a fairly recent issue of *Library Personnel News.*[3] Though there have been empirical studies done about burnout in librarianship, David P. Fisher suggests that many of the results are inconclusive.[4]

Case Study: Finding Balance

Beth – hired as new manager 18 months ago (six years prior experience at another institution with increasing responsibilities) head, general reference

Bob – experienced middle manager in library, head of acquisitions

Sam – Beth's supervisor, associate director

Setting: Bob enters a small conference room to retrieve a notepad portfolio he had left there earlier in the day and finds Beth sitting with her back to the door. Her shoulders are slumped, her hands are covering her face, and her whole body is hunkered into itself as if to hide from the world.

Bob grabs a box of tissues sitting next to the demo computer as he comes up beside Beth and sits down next to her. Beth visibly starts and tries to curl in upon herself even more. Bob sticks the tissues in front of her and quietly starts talking.

"I won't ask how you are doing as it is fairly obvious that 'fine' might be the polite but grossly inappropriate answer. I've noticed that you have seemed on edge lately but you look pretty miserable right now. Is there anything I can do to help? My staff tell me I am a pretty good listener."

Beth replies as she visibly tries to regain her composure, pausing periodically to swallow hard. "I'm not sure what is wrong. Maybe I wasn't as ready to be a manager as I thought. I just feel really battered and I'm not sure what is the right thing to do anymore. I seem to be constantly overreacting to situations instead of responding to them in a thoughtful or rational manner. Just a little while ago I snapped at Vickie because she got the numbers transposed and ordered the wrong size of hanging file folders. She just stood there looking stunned and stuttered that she would try to get to the store to rush an exchange. Why did I do that? It was only a $15 order. But it doesn't seem like any of my staff can do the smallest task without screwing it up. And I am just so tired of picking up after them and holding the unit together."

Bob looks thoughtful. "I remember about a year ago we had talked about you simplifying your schedule a bit because you were feeling overwhelmed. How did that go?"

"I don't know." Beth moans. "In some ways I was able to catch up but then people started making mistakes and I'd have to backtrack and walk them through it. Plus it seemed like for every committee or team I got off of, there was another waiting in the wings to take its place."

Bob looks thoughtful as he says, "I think this may be a classic case of the straw that broke the camels back sort of analogy. The straw itself, Vickie's supply order, was not that big but it was the latest of a huge pile of straws. How long have you feeling like this?"

Beth sighs as she says, "I think this may have started a couple of months ago when a staff member took a complaint about a decision I made to human resources. Even though it was resolved in my favor, I just feel like I am constantly waiting for something else to blow up in my face. I'm second guessing myself all the time."

Bob slowly replies, "I think I know a little bit about the incident, and you are probably not supposed to talk about it because of employee confidentiality rules. However, I haven't noticed Sam or any of the other managers in the library thinking less of you. I know a few of us have been worried because you've seemed a little stressed in some of the meetings. But from what I've seen, you really have been doing a good job. This is your first actual management position isn't it?"

"Yeah. I was really surprised when I was offered the position. I figured there would have been others in the pool that had more experience as a manager. I honestly thought becoming a department head would still be a few more years out. I've been trying really hard to be a good manager, throwing myself into learning all this new stuff that is done differently here. Even though I came from a reference background, the place I worked before was considerably smaller with less focus on looking to the future and reaching out to the users. This place has been a big change, but I really do like it and I really wanted to live up to everyone's expectations." Beth's voice cracks on this last sentence.

"OK, first of all, I think you are expecting a lot more of yourself than 'everyone' else in this organization expects. All of us who have been in the trenches for a few years or more know how much momentum staff can have and how complex individual units ops can be. Take my unit for example. A lot of people think we just order and unbox books. They don't see all the other stuff we do to keep orders going smoothly. You've been through two evaluations as the department head. How did Sam think you'd done?"

"Actually, even with the staffing complaint issue, I got a really great evaluation both times. I just feel that I've set a really high bar and I've got to keep topping it. I'm already staying up here until about 8 P.M. every night and taking my laptop home on weekends. It's just getting to where I can't do everything. I don't even remember why I wanted to go into management. I sure didn't expect it to be like this." This last ends on a forlorn sounding note as Beth starts to tear up and reaches for a tissue.

"Beth, with that attitude and unreasonable self-expectation, you will burnout within another year," Bob says bluntly. "You have got to establish some balance and outside interests and compartmentalize so you are not always obsessing about work. Have you ever referred any of your staff to the Employee Assistance Program?" Bob continues as Beth nods hesitantly. "Well, I don't supervise you. But as a colleague and friend, I think you ought to consider making a self-referral. You've been bottling up a lot of emotions, including some unresolved stuff over the staff complaint. As much as I like you I'm not a trained counselor. The EAP staff are and they will be much more able to help you find perspective on your doubts and regain a sense of personal control. They may also be able to refer you to some workshops on managing time and multiple priorities.

"I will tell you, though, that what you are experiencing is not that uncommon among new managers. Most go through a period of self-doubt and 'how in the world did I get here and what do I do now' at some point or another during their careers. However, you cannot let it stop you. You need to come to terms with the situation in order to move forward and continue to grow. Just think about it." Bob starts to get to his feet to leave.

Beth looks up at him. "Thanks a lot for the mentoring. You've given me a lot to think about. The fact that you found me in the situation you did indicates that I'm not handling things as well as I thought I was. I'm not sure how comfortable I am with the idea of counseling, but if they can at least route me to something that will help me get a handle on the stuff on my desk, that would help. But first I am going to go wash my face, and then I am going to apologize to Vickie."

   Setting: Six weeks later. Bob enters a small conference room prior to a meeting and finds Beth sitting back in her chair, also an early arrival. She looks relaxed but sits up straighter in the chair as she sees him come in the room.

Beth smiles as she says, "Hi Bob. Did you get drafted for this project too?"

Bob sits down and says, "Yeah. Sam promised it would only take a meeting or two to revise the relevant procedures. I figure five at least, but that is still pretty manageable. As long as I don't get tapped for any more permanent committees, I'm happy. How are you doing these days?"

"I've been meaning to look you up and tell you 'thanks' and let you know that I'm doing really well these days. I took your advice and contacted EAP. It only took a couple of sessions for me to better understand why I was reacting the way I was. I remember now why I wanted to be a manager. They also taught me some really good reminder techniques for managing the stress, regaining some balance my life, understanding that everything is not a number one priority that I am solely responsible for, and compartmentalizing the problems. For example, I actually have a few things on my desk that are just going to sit there until the other people involved in the project also think they are important. I've realized that it isn't my responsibility to make sure the employment application gets revised. I'm just assigned to the team to provide feedback. I've also talked to Sam about making my annual evaluation goals much more specific and accomplishable so I can actually say I've finished something. Last but definitely not least, I've gotten back into my furniture refinishing hobby, joined the local gym, and only get hung up here one to two nights a week until about 6:30 P.M. I'm taking things much more in stride . . . even with my staff sniping at each other on the chat reference implementation and getting put on another ad hoc committee." Beth rolls her eyes as she makes the last comment.

Bob smiles broadly as he enthusiastically responds, "Wow, it sounds like you are back to the Beth we hired. That's really great!"

"Yeah, it feels great too. I know I will have to watch against letting my perfectionist tendencies get the upper hand, but I am dealing with the little daily crises so much better these days," Beth finishes as two more committee members come in the door.

Case Study Observations

- Becoming overwhelmed by one's job is a gradual, insidious thing that starts with just a little problem, like too many meetings, but left unchecked will continue to grow and consume the new manager.
- Don't be afraid to admit you are not perfect . . . no manager is.
- It is very important to set reasonable goals that can be addressed in a manner that reminds one of having been successful and to allow oneself to recognize the successes.
- Balance, prioritization, and compartmentalization are key elements to having a sustaining and rewarding career as a manager.

Thought and Discussion Exercises

What Do You Do Now?

1. Your library administration has asked you to change into a middle manager's position in a unit you have only worked with occasionally. You recognize this may be your big break into management but you do not know any of the staff or the operational details. What do you do now?

2. After reading this book, you think you want to become part of the management team. You know that a manager in a sister unit to yours will be retiring in about three years. At that time, the position will be posted internally prior to an external posting. You want to position yourself to apply for it by working to develop a managerial skill set. What do you do now?

3. You see a position posted at another institution for a department head in your area of specialization. The location is good and you decide to apply for the position. What do you do now? (Hint: A manager's cover letter, vita, and interview presentation topic needs to focus on different things than an entry-level librarian's.)

Notes

1. Anne Woodsworth, "Getting Off the Library Merry-Go-Round: McNally and Downs Revisited; the Best and the Brightest Directors Are Burned Out," *Library Journal* 114 (May 1, 1989): 35–38.

2. Janette S. Caputo, *Stress and Burnout in Library Service* (Phoenix, AZ: Oryx Press, 1991).

3. "Employers Urge Workers to Chill Out Before Burning Out: Moves Aimed at Cutting Turnover," *Library Personnel News* 13, no. 1/2 (spring/summer 2000): 12–13.

4. David P. Fisher, "Are Librarians Burning Out?" *Journal of Librarianship* 22, no. 4 (October 1990): 216–235.

Annotated Bibliography

Alessandra, Tony, and Phil Hunsaker. *Communicating at Work.* New York: Simon & Schuster, 1993.

Written for the popular market, this book offers a thorough yet easily readable introduction to workplace communication issues. A 250-page paperback, it addresses a variety of communication issues, including nonverbal communications, seating impact, and conflict resolution.

Alexander, David C., and Randall A. Rabourn, eds. *Applied Ergonomics.* New York: Taylor & Francis, 2001.

This book is a good example of a recently published, fairly readable text on the topic. Directed toward a generic workplace, the editors go into considerable detail on various activities that might lead to ergonomic concerns in libraries.

Bishop, Sue. *The Complete Guide to People Skills.* Brookfield, VT: Gower, 1997.

At 220 pages of text, this book introduces issues related to understanding and developing people skills. Focusing on the managerial role, it offers different communication techniques that are effective for different situations. Depending on the individual, the style of communication to use when empowering or motivating an employee may be different from the style used to correct poor performance.

Bissel, Ben, and W. R. Shirah. *Facing the Challenge of Change.* TAMCO—Training and Management Consultants, 2002. Videotape.

This is one example of the self-help videos available that are related to change. This fast-paced 36-minute video uses humor and a straightforward approach in a motivational speaker style to both validate the concerns that individuals may have with change and offer coping methods for improving performance in a changing environment.

Bradford, Lawrence J., and Claire Raines with Jo Leda Martin. *Twenty Something: Managing and Motivating Today's New Workforce.* New York: Master-Media, Ltd, 1992.

At 200 pages, this book is a good introduction to managing Generation X employees. Written as the group was entering the commercial business environment, it offers numerous tips and applied techniques for successfully integrating Generation X professionals into traditional work environments.

Brammer, Lawrence M. *How to Cope with Life Transitions: The Challenge of Personal Change.* New York: Hemisphere Publishing Corp, 1991.

One way to learn more about dealing with change as it impacts frontline staff is to explore the behavioral aspects of change from a psychological perspective. This brief 120-page text provides a readable and thorough introduction to the study of change as it impacts the individual.

Bridger, R. S. *Introduction to Ergonomics.* 2nd ed. New York: Taylor & Francis, 2003.

This title is a good example of a recently published, fairly readable text on the topic of ergonomic issues. Directed toward a generic workplace, the book goes into considerable detail on various activities that might be applicable to ergonomic concerns in libraries.

Buchanan, Dave, and Richard Badham. *Power, Politics, and Organizational Change: Winning the Turf Game.* Thousand Oaks, CA: Sage Publications, 1999.

With 248 pages of small type, this academic text focuses on the importance of political survival skills during the process of organizational change and counters traditional theorists who saw change events and internal politics as unrelated. Though not a light read, it offers some different insights for the manager interested in exploring the dynamics of organizational politics and power.

Caputo, Janette S. *Stress and Burnout in Library Service.* Phoenix, AZ: Oryx Press, 1991.

At only 160 pages, this book provides very good overview of the stressors related to the library environment. Even though it is not specifically focused on managers, it provides accurate insights into understanding why a librarian or manager can become disillusioned. It offers several tips on recognizing early burnout indicators and recommended coping mechanisms to reduce stress levels. The references section offers a number of additional resources.

Chan, Janis Fisher. *Academic Administrator's Guide to Meetings.* San Francisco: Jossey-Bass, 2003.

This 90-page handbook offers a good introductory text that is short, readable, and focused toward the academic sector. It takes into account the tendencies of faculty to think independently and bring differing perspectives into a meeting.

Coens, Tom, and Mary Jenkins. *Abolishing Performance Appraisals: Why They Backfire and What to Do Instead.* San Francisco: Berrett-Koehler Publishers, Inc, 2000.

Despite its misleading title, this book is a good reference text, covering 338 densely worded pages. It addresses the importance that a performance appraisal should not exist in a vacuum and must be an ongoing process between an employee and a manager. The authors dispel traditional myths about evaluating performance and emphasize the importance of using positive motivators and coaching as part of the overall process to encourage self-motivation and employee development. With emphasis on job satisfaction factors other than salary, some of the ideas are especially relevant to the library environment.

Dickey, Terry. *The Basics of Budgeting.* Menlo Park, CA: Crisp Publications, 1992.

At 130 pages, this Fifty Minute Series book is a quick way to bring yourself up to speed on basic organizational budgets. It includes terminology and applied tips for understanding budget issues.

Dobson, Michael Singer, and Deborah Singer Dobson. *Enlightened Office Politics: Understanding, Coping with, and Winning the Game—Without Losing Your Soul.* Kansas City: AMACOM, 2001.

Though not a quick read at 305 pages, this book is an excellent introduction to understanding organizational politics and using political techniques in an ethical manner. The examples are easy to relate to and the bibliography extensive.

"Employers Urge Workers to Chill Out Before Burning Out: Moves Aimed at Cutting Turnover." *Library Personnel News* 13, no. 1/2 (spring/summer 2000):12–13.

This brief, recent article reiterates the importance of maintaining balance in one's work and personal life.

Farmer, Lesley S. J. *When Your Library Budget Is Almost Zero.* Englewood, CO: Libraries Unlimited, 1993.

With 115 pages of text and an extensive bibliography, this book offers a wide range of ideas for stretching one's budget and seeking additional funds. Light-hearted yet practical, the book encourages the reader to develop a positive and creative attitude about managing within a limited budget. Ideas range from inexpensive desk signage to seeking grants for start-up services.

Fisher, David P. "Are Librarians Burning Out?" *Journal of Librarianship* 22, no. 4 (October 1990): 216–235.

This article delves into past studies done on librarian burnout and suggests that the research methodology of using small study groups or leading questions makes previous results inconclusive.

Furnham, Adrian. *The Psychology of Behaviour at Work: The Individual in the Organization.* Hove East Sussex, UK: Psychology Press, 1997.

This book explores communication within the context of organizational structure and workplace dynamics. Though not for casual, light reading, the 700-page book provides extensive depth in understanding the subtleties of employee and managerial communications in complex hierarchical and team-based environments.

Gilbert, Richard L. *How We Change: Psychotherapy and the Process of Human Development.* Boston: Allyn and Bacon, 2002.

At 230 densely worded pages, this text offers a scholarly and in-depth understanding of the emotions and reactions associated with change, both as an individual and a social group. Although going into more depth on individual and social psychology, it is still readable by someone with minimal psychology background and is a good self-education tool.

Greer, Michael. *The Project Manager's Partner: A Step-by-Step Guide to Project Management.* 2nd ed. New York: AMACOM, 2002.

At 167 pages, this book is very readable, with significant sections focused on project definition and planning. The examples tend to be familiar activities such as home improvement projects. This allows the novice reader to focus on the technique rather than trying to decipher the project being presented.

Grote, Dick. *The Complete Guide to Performance Appraisal.* New York: AMA-COM, 2002.

At 378 pages divided into four separate sections, this book lives up to its title and provides a thorough overview of the performance appraisal process. The first two sections introduce the context of performance appraisal, address what is supposed to be measured in the process, and offers guidance on preparing and delivering an effective appraisal. For those who are in smaller institutions, the third section offers insights on designing an appraisal instrument. The final section addresses legal issues and emerging trends in the performance appraisal process. Despite its length and breadth, it is not difficult to read, incorporating checklists and scripts.

——. *The Performance Appraisal Question and Answer Book: A Survival Guide for Managers.* New York: AMACOM, 2002.

Despite having 236 pages, this book is actually a quick read. Directed toward an introductory, hands-on reader, it is organized similar to a frequently asked questions concept, with the broad questions grouped into nine separate sections. Many questions have a short paragraph answer followed by a "Tell Me More" section that goes into more detail. It offers numerous "Red Flag" and "Hot Tip" asides that are quite relevant to the performance appraisal newcomer.

Gudykunst, William, et al. *Building Bridges: Interpersonal Skills for a Changing World.* Boston: Houghton Mifflin, 1995.

A 450-page academic textbook, this book provides a good understanding of all aspects of communication and interpersonal skills. It addresses contemporary issues that can cause conflict.

Guirdham, Maureen. *Interactive Behaviour at Work.* 3rd ed. New York: Prentice-Hall, 2002.
This book explores communication within the context of organizational structure and workplace dynamics. Though not for casual, light reading, the 575-page book provides considerable depth in understanding the subtleties of employee and managerial communications in complex hierarchical and team-based environments.

Harvey, Thomas R. *Checklist for Change: A Pragmatic Approach to Creating and Controlling Change.* Edited by Lillian B. Wehmeyer. 2nd ed. Lancaster, PA: Technomic Publishing Co., 1995.
At 170 pages, this book addresses some of the specific challenges faced in a change environment and includes many process checklists for managers to use in communicating issues related to change. The third section of the book explores some of the unique aspects of managing a committee, as opposed to individual employees, through a period of change.

Henderson, George. *Human Relations Issues in Management.* Westport, CT: Quorum Books, 1996.
This 260-page book goes into considerable depth and builds a better understanding of the background behind human relations and why it has such a significant impact on the organization. The book addresses selected issues, such as alcoholic workers or burned-out workers, in significant detail and offers strategies for understanding and addressing difficult staffing situations.

Kliem, Ralph L. *The Project Manager's Emergency Kit.* New York: St. Lucie Press, 2003.
An excellent, brief reference book for those who want to gain a better understanding of the concepts behind the jargon of project management. Each technique is presented in terms of what it is, how it is used, what steps to follow for implementation, and the inherent goals and obstacles.

Kossen, Stan. *The Human Side of Organizations.* 6th ed. New York: Harper Collins College Publishers, 1994.
At 650 pages of traditional textbook styling, this book is truly introductory in nature and designed for traditional learning. It addresses issues in a contemporary manner with attention to social issues and diversity initiatives. Thorough in coverage, it presents terminology and concepts with less detailed case studies and exercises.

Kotter, John P. *Leading Change.* Boston: Harvard Business School Press, 1996. Also available through NetLibrary, Inc. at http://www.netlibrary.com

This book offers some practical advice for leading change within an organization. At 200 pages it is a fast read that looks at why change stalls and fails and offers an eight-step process to sustain organizational change.

Kotter, John P., and Dan S. Cohen. *The Heart of Change: Real-Life Stories of How People Change Their Organizations.* Boston: Harvard Business School Press, 2002. Also available through NetLibrary, Inc. at http://www.netlibrary.com

This book offers practical advice for leading change within an organization. It expands upon the ideas in *Leading Change* (also by Kotter) and offers many case studies and anecdotes to address more effectively the challenges associate with change.

Lamberton, Lowell H., and Leslie Minor. *Human Relations: Strategies for Success.* Chicago: Irwin: Mirror Press, 1995.

This 410-page softbound book differs from traditional textbook styling by focusing more on an applied perspective with extensive case studies and numerous lists of tips and techniques. It is more readable in context for the person who has the basics but wants to develop a stronger skill set in understanding the human relations issues in a unit. Although written in 1995, it addresses issues in a contemporary manner with attention to social issues and diversity initiatives.

Martin, Lowell A. *Library Personnel Administration.* Metuchen, NJ: Scarecrow Press, Inc, 1994.

Though quite readable at less than 200 pages and focused on libraries, this book is almost outdated from a legal perspective. It should only be used for background knowledge of library-specific issues, such as the professional versus paraprofessional debates.

Mayo, Diane and Jeanne Goodrich for the Public Library Association. *Staffing for Results: A Guide to Working Smarter.* Chicago: American Library Association, 2002.

Part of the PLA Results Series, this book gives sound hands-on guidance for changing staffing models. It addresses the importance of communication and addresses aspects of managing the changes effectively. Though tailored to a public library reader, many of the issues are relevant to academic libraries as well.

Mech, Terrence F., and Gerard B. McCabe. *Leadership and Academic Librarians.* Westport, CT: Greenwood Press, 1998.

A book that goes beyond the typical chapter in a management text, the essays explore the nature of leadership opportunities in the academic library environment, both as an administrator and as a nonmanager. The book offers a good introduction and food for thought on the concept of leadership for those who are still struggling to define it.

Nelson, Sandra S. for the Public Library Association. *The New Planning for Results: A Streamlined Approach.* Chicago: American Library Association, 2001.

Written for public librarians, this book offers an excellent overview of organizational planning with relevant and familiar examples. It focuses on the qualitative thinking aspects of planning and assessing the impact aspects of implementation specific to a medium or large public library environment.

Nelson, Sandra S., and June Garcia for the Public Library Association. *Creating Policies for Results: From Chaos to Clarity.* Chicago: American Library Association, 2003.

Part of the PLA Results Series, this book gives sound hands-on guidance for developing effective policies. It addresses the importance of having clear policies and addresses aspects of change management in creating support from staff, patrons, and administrators. Although tailored to a public library reader, many of the issues are relevant to academic libraries as well.

O'Neil, Sharon Lund, and Elwood N. Chapman. *Your Attitude Is Showing: A Primer of Human Relations.* 10th ed. Upper Saddle River, NJ: Prentice Hall/ Pearson Education, 2002.

At 230 pages, this book is surprisingly easy to read and is an excellent resource for developing an initial understanding of some of the interpersonal dynamics and human relations situations in the workplace. It introduces issues relative to understanding motivational factors, informal communication networks, bonding between employees, and the importance of developing the supervisory relationship as well.

Pinto, Jeffrey K., ed. *The Project Management Institute: Project Management Handbook.* With a foreword by Lewis R. Ireland. San Francisco: Jossey-Bass Publishers, 1998.

At 460 pages, this book is for the librarian who wants to seriously delve into project management methodology. It offers a thorough development of project management methodologies and techniques for the most complex of projects.

Raines, Claire. *Beyond Generation X: A Practical Guide for Managers.* Menlo Park, CA: Crisp Publications, 1997.

For the manager needing tips and tools in a hurry to address intergenerational conflict, this 120-page book is a fast and informative read. Focusing less on the background of the generational issues, it goes directly into recognizing and diffusing misunderstandings based on generational assumptions and ambitions.

Richman, Larry. *Project Management Step-by-Step.* New York: AMACOM, 2002.

At 280 pages, this is a good text for interdisciplinary readers. The book presents similar concepts to the Greer book but with more depth and details. In addition to a thorough section on planning, this book goes into project team management strategies. Each chapter includes case studies and some application exercises.

Rounds, Richard S. *Basic Budgeting Practices for Librarians.* 2nd ed. Chicago: American Library Association, 1994.

Published by the American Library Association, this book was revised in the mid-1990s and provides a good overview to general types of budgets and working with revenues and expenditures. The author has packed a lot of content into 150 pages and written it toward the perspective of the practicing librarian, as opposed to a novice. Although many of the examples and practice experiences are directed toward the public library environment, most are general enough that the process is transferable to academic libraries.

Rosse, Joseph G., and Robert A. Levin. *Jossey-Bass Academic Administrator's Guide to Hiring.* San Francisco: Jossey-Bass, 2003.

At 140 pages, this book is quite readable and goes into significant detail over some of the unique challenges of hiring, recruitment, interviewing and retention within the academic setting. Though some specifics of the interview process are less applicable to libraries, many of the issues of recruitment and retention are quite relevant.

Shim, Jae K., and Joel G. Siegel. *Complete Budgeting Workbook and Guide.* New York: New York Institute of Finance, 1994.

For those with a personal fascination for more study into the budgeting process, this book is quite detailed and extensive. With more than 600 pages of text and examples, it allows the reader an opportunity to develop specialized skills in this managerial area. It includes coverage of such issues as budgeting for capital expenditures and using financial forecasting models.

Silberman, Mel, assisted by Kathy Clark. *101 Ways to Make Meetings Active: Surefire Ideas to Engage Your Group.* San Francisco: Jossey-Bass, 1999.

For managers trying to lead participatory meetings with a comatose group, this book offers some excellent tips and strategies. Unlike many books on meeting engagement techniques, almost all of these suggestions treat meeting attendees as adults. Additionally, each strategy shows a graphical meter rating on whether it is a "serious" or "fun" technique. This can be a critical factor when dealing with meetings including academic faculty or administration. The techniques are divided into categories based on the type of meeting and purpose of the activity, from engaging participants to managing controversy or conflict.

Simmons, Annette. *Territorial Games: Understanding and Ending Turf Wars at Work.* New York: American Management Association, 1998. Also available through NetLibrary, Inc. at http://www.netlibrary.com

At 218 pages of text, this book delves into the importance of recognizing and defusing political games that focus on territorialism or defense of one's turf. The book is divided into three sections, with the second and third sections going into details of the territory-based political games. In the first section, the author explores why territorialism is so prevalent in organizations and what is the underlying psychology and cultural history of this behavior.

Smith, G. Stevenson. *Accounting for Libraries and Other Not-for-Profit Organizations.* 2nd ed. Chicago: American Library Association, 1999.

At 314 densely worded pages, this book goes into significantly more detail on accounting practices and introduces some of the special concerns libraries face as not-for-profit organizations. Less relevant to the immediate needs of the middle manager, it is a good informational source for understanding the issues faced by business operations staff and upper administrators. The text includes chapters that explain accounting practices for capitol campaigns and large projects, such as a major renovation or construction of a new facility.

Steele, Victoria, and Stephen D. Elder. *Becoming a Fundraiser: The Principles and Practice of Library Development.* 2nd ed. Chicago: American Library Association, 2000.

At 125 pages of text, this book is an excellent and straightforward introduction to being part of a fundraising team in a library. It addresses feasibility issues, developing fund raising plans, the role of a Friends of the Library group, and dealing with major gifts and grants.

Steward, John, ed. *Bridges Not Walls.* 8th ed. New York: McGraw-Hill, 2001.

Recently revised, this textbook provides a good understanding of all aspects of communication and interpersonal skills. It addresses contemporary issues that can cause conflict and includes coverage of gender-based communication issues and the importance of the perceptions in relationships.

Strauss, William, and Neil Howe. *Generations: The History of America's Future 1584 to 2069.* New York: William Morrow & Co., 1991.

The definitive work on defining generational issues, it introduces the theory behind characterizing behaviors and attitudes as part of generational identities and provides brief overviews of the past and predictions on future generational groupings. At 430 pages, without including appendices, it goes into significant detail on each major generational group in America since the 17th century. However, it is well organized so that managers can go directly to those sections that represent their current workforce.

———. *Millennials Rising: The Next Great Generation.* New York: Vintage Books, 2000.

As a follow-up to their earlier book, *Generations: The History of America's Future 1584 to 2069*, this 375-page work takes an in-depth look at the generation that was born after 1981 and has started to enter the workforce at the turn of the century. Combining scholarly analysis with anecdotal comments and case studies, the book provides considerable insight into this population group.

Stueart, Robert D., and Barbara B. Moran. *Library and Information Center Management.* 6th ed. Greenwood Village, CO: Libraries Unlimited, 2002.

Recently updated to the contemporary library management environment, this book is often used as the primary text for MLIS management courses. At 494 pages, it is not a light or quick read but is an excellent reference text for factual detail. It gives a thorough review of the library as a complex organization and focuses on operational practice and process, such as strategic planning and organizational structure.

Toma, J. Douglas, and Richard L. Palm. *The Academic Administrator and the Law: What Every Dean and Department Chair Needs to Know.* ASHE-ERIC Higher Education Report, volume 26, no. 5. Washington, DC: The George Washington University, Graduate School of Education and Human Development, 1999.

Written for the educated academic administrator, this 150-page book requires the reader to concentrate. It provides a complete perspective of some of the legal issues encountered in the academic environment and includes issues that might impact student privacy issues as well.

Tracy, William R. *The Human Resources Glossary: A Complete Desk Reference for HR Professionals.* Boca Raton, FL: St. Lucie Press, 1997.

At 416 pages, this is an excellent reference tool that will provide general definitions of terminology and overviews of legal milestones and key concepts. Entries are arranged alphabetically and run the gamut from simple terms, such as the official definition of "keyboarding," to more specific ones, such as the "Hazard Communication Standard of 1988" that defined how employees were to be notified if exposed to chemicals in the work environment.

Tropman, John E. *Making Meetings Work: Achieving High Quality Group Decisions.* 2nd ed. Thousand Oaks, CA: Sage Publications, 2003.

This is the book for the manager who wants to become a meetings guru and is involved in group decision making on operational- and business-style issues. Deceptively short at 230 pages, the book includes a wide breadth of material on making meetings effective at an organizational level. This book goes specifically into Total Quality Management (TQM) style meetings and detailed group dynamics.

Tulgan, Bruce. *Managing Generation X.* Revised and updated. New York: W.W. Norton & Co., 2000

Written for the trade market by an author credited with doing breakthrough work in defense of Generation X, this book offers valuable insights into understanding the motivational issues associated with this generation.

Its 270 pages are an entertaining read with numerous case studies in a variety of work situations.

Wilson, Lucille. *People Skills for Library Managers: A Common Sense Guide for Beginners.* Englewood, CO: Libraries Unlimited, 1996. Also available electronically through NetLibrary, Inc. at http://www.netlibrary.com
At 120 pages, this introductory book focuses on communication in the library environment. It includes coverage of some of the issues of communicating with peer managers and administrators.

Woodsworth, Anne. "Getting Off the Library Merry-Go-Round: McNally and Downs Revisited; the Best and the Brightest Directors Are Burned Out." *Library Journal* 114 (1989):35–38.
Though presented from the context of library director burnout, this article links it to the same sources of frustration experienced by middle managers and gives insights to those issues that can be problematic.

Zemke, Ron, Claire Raines, and Bob Filipczak. *Generations at Work: Managing the Clash of Veterans, Boomers, Xers, and Nexters in Your Workplace.* Chicago: AMACOM, 2000.
At 250 pages of readable text, this is an excellent follow-up book to *Twenty Something: Managing and Motivating Today's New Workforce* and addresses the challenges faced by managers in the multi-generational workplace. In addition to providing updated information on the maturing characteristics of the generations, it offers numerous case studies with applied techniques for positive cooperation between the generation representatives.

Index

About the Author

PIXEY ANNE MOSLEY is a graduate of the University of Texas School of Library and Information Science and is a professional library manager. She has published many articles on the problems of library management.